Universities for Sale

Neil Tudiver

Universities for Sale:
Resisting Corporate Control over Canadian Higher Education

A CAUT Series Title
James Lorimer and Company Ltd., Publishers
Toronto, 1999

James Lorimer & Company Ltd. acknowledges the support of the Ontario Arts Council. We acknowledge the financial support of the Government of Canada through the Book Publishing Industry Development Program (BPIDP) for our publishing activities. We acknowledge the support of the Canada Council for the Arts for our publishing program.

Canadä

Canadian Cataloguing in Publication Data

Tudiver, Neil
    Universities for sale: resisting corporate control over Canadian higher education

Copublished by the Canadian Association of University Teachers
ISBN 1-55028-691-9 (bound) ISBN 1-55028-690-0 (pbk.)

1. Universities and colleges — Canada. 2. Industry and education — Canada. I. Canadian Association of University Teachers. II. Title.

LC1085.4.C3T82 1999   378.71   C99-932580-9

A CAUT Series Title
James Lorimer & Company Ltd., Publishers
35 Britain Street
Toronto, Ontario
M5A 1R7

Printed and bound in Canada

For Simon
who makes it all worthwhile
the future is in your good hands

Contents

Acknowledgments

The solitary task of writing is also social and collective. Family, friends and colleagues keep you going, with support of every conceivable kind—emotional, conceptual, technical, editorial and strategic. I want to thank the following people who helped me start this work and stay with it over these many years.

Sari, as always, stands out—a full partner-in-life of the highest order. I turn to her for my greatest support and receive from her my severest criticism. At times, she seems to know me and my work better than I do. Her wisdom helped me grapple with ideas and issues. Her professional perfectionism has made this book far better organized and written than it might have been. Simon enriches both our lives beyond measure. His questions challenge my thinking and his music feeds my soul. He makes my work stronger and truer.

Working for the University of Manitoba Faculty Association drew me into university and union politics. Thanks to Ian Kerr for recruiting me, and Sylvia Jansen for helping to make the presidency an exceptional job. My bargaining teammates—Bryan Schwartz, Tom Booth, and Monica Cook—were outstanding negotiators and a joy to join at the table. I have benefited enormously through UMFA, from the sage advice of so many people, especially Dennis Felbel, president when I was chief negotiator, Ken Osborne, vice-president when I was president, Trevor Dandy, who initiated me to bargaining, and Mel Myers, the association's legal counsel.

Three long-time friends—Mark Gabbert, Robert Chernomas, and John Loxley—have deeply influenced my thinking on virtually every matter in this book. They are truly comrades in every good sense of the word.

Joe Connor, Walter Isaac, Joe Kaufert, Joe Kuypers, Paul Toolan, Neal Rose, and Joe Ryant—our men's group—have shared my joys and helped me cope with anxious moments through the life of this project. Thank you for your caring and encouragement.

Colleagues at the University of Manitoba Faculty of Social Work have always lent a receptive ear to my meanderings on faculty unions and the state of the university. Joe Kuypers, the first person outside my household to read early drafts of chapters, made me confront the core messages of the study. Ranjan Roy has given me constant support and good advice.

Directors Addie Penner and Pete Hudson, and Dean Don Fuchs have maintained an enviable workplace and been personally helpful throughout this project.

I want to thank people who shared their reflections in discussions and interviews: David Bates, Brett Cemer, Guy Chauvin, David Clipsham, John D'Orsay, Bill Graham, John Griffith, Ken Hartviksen, Maureen Kilgour, Pat Kerans, Ian Macdonald, Robert Moore, Jan Newson, Marion Perrin, Ester Reiter, Bob Rosehart, Harriet Rosenberg, Briggite Schotch, David Williams, Daniel Woolf, and Ernest Zimmerman.

I have been privileged with an outstanding group of reviewers and editors who made considerable efforts on my behalf. Jim Silver, Errol Black, and Bill Bruneau provided invaluable critiques of the entire manuscript, as did Jan Newson, Don Savage, Mike Bradfield, and Bill Graham for selected portions. Two anonymous reviewers provided very helpful critical comments. Russell Wodell's copy editing brought me fresh understanding of how to write.

Thanks to the Executive of the CAUT for risking this first publication in a new series, and to CAUT staff for statistical and historical information and general reflections on this work. Robert Léger and Louise Desjardins provided specific material on very short notice.

Jim Turk moved the manuscript from draft to published work with characteristic efficiency and infectious enthusiasm. He is an author's dream manager. Thanks also to James Lorimer for the fine job of publishing the book.

Finally, my appreciation to the University of Manitoba/SSHRC Fund Committee for a research grant that supported literature review for this study, and to Barbara Crutchley for her assistance in preparing the application.

Preface

WHEN I ARRIVED AT the University of Manitoba in 1977, I joined a thriving institution full of debate and critical inquiry. Academic and administrative staff shared a commitment to quality education, and everyone was part of the broader research and teaching enterprise. Faculties were mostly in charge of their own destinies. Funding was certainly tighter than a decade earlier, but not yet a serious problem. Progressive growth—broadening the university's curriculum and making higher education more accessible—still seemed eminently possible.

Just over 20 years later the same campus landscape has acquired a distinctly commercial feel. Prominent public space has been taken up by "donut", sandwich, pizza, and taco franchises. Pepsi logos are everywhere: the corporation obtained exclusive distribution rights in exchange for undisclosed sums paid to the university. (Coca Cola has made similar deals with other universities.) Corporate culture has infiltrated the everyday language and practice of the university, now a lean and mean system paying more attention to cost and management control than to quality and independent thought.

This is not mere generational grumbling. Even the undergraduate mood on campus is pessimistic. Higher tuition and residence fees exclude those who cannot afford to pay up front for their education. The university has ever more students yet fewer staff. My own faculty of social work has lost about a third of its full-time teaching personnel and such core services as faculty supervision of students' professional field placements. Budget cuts perpetually undermine working conditions. Everyone is expected to do more with less. In many departments professors now must pay for long distance calls, voice mail, photocopying, and classroom presentation supplies.

In 1982 I joined the bargaining team for the University of Manitoba Faculty Association. Over the past 17 years, while working to protect faculty interests as, variously, president, chief negotiator, member of the association's executive, and picket captain, I have seen conditions deteriorate steadily. I have witnessed extensive conflicts between faculty and administration throughout the university. Grievances and arbitrations have consumed an enormous amount of the association's human and financial resources. Union activists on other campuses report similar experiences. Where is the collegial community we once knew? Why is there so much tension in the system?

This book examines labour-management struggles in Canadian universities over the past 50 years, showing how and why these conflicts developed. Even though most professors were unionized by the early 1980s, routine collective bargaining failed to resolve widening differences with their employers. Canadian campuses have become sites of bitter labour disputes.

In 1951 the Massey Royal Commission on the Arts, Letters and Sciences issued an early warning that the fundamental intellectual and moral purpose of Canadian universities was endangered by low funding and commercial influences. Commission chair Vincent Massey called on the federal government to make up for decades of inadequate support. Unless far more money was allocated to higher education, he argued, universities would be taken over by materialistic values. (A half century later this has a chillingly contemporary feel.)

Massey's plea was heeded in an optimistic post-war era. Ottawa gave new money for unprecedented improvements. There were more and much larger universities. Additional spaces and lower tuition allowed far more people to obtain university degrees, choosing from more diverse programs than ever before.

Universities were taken aback by the acute funding shortfalls they faced by the mid-1970s, just 25 years after federal money started pouring in. By the 1980s financial difficulties had mounted to crisis level.

Universities now turn to the private sector with appeals to wealthy individuals and corporations, aggressive marketing of academic programs, and attempts to earn profit from faculty research. Government meanwhile encourages corporate partnerships that steer university research to bow to the demands of business.

Private, commercial concerns are on the brink of replacing core academic values. Universities are being run more like businesses than institutions devoted to teaching, research, and community service. Administrators promote a conception of intellectual property which turns free ideas into marketable commodities. Entrepreneurship is becoming valued over scholarship.

Commercialization threatens the university's mission to engage in the broadest and deepest levels of research and to freely share knowledge with the wider community. Professors have been able to slow the corporatization of the university through unionized collective bargaining; but their stance has been mainly defensive. Gaining public support will require broader vision. Universities must develop models of demonstrable relevance to our social and economic needs in the 21st century.

A NOTE ON ABBREVIATIONS

No contemporary history of education can avoid discussing a multiplicity of government agencies, professional association, unions, commissions, and non-profit groups, most with complicated names which convenience demands be presented in acronym form. Every effort has been made to avoid constructions of the dreaded "the AMD began the AGM with an IMHO tribute to the CAUT" type. But readers may still find the following table of the most frequently used abbreviations useful.

AAUP	American Association of University Professors
AIB	Anti Inflation Board
AUCC	Association of Universities and Colleges of Canada
AUT	Association of University Teachers
BILD	Board of Industrial Leadership and Development
BUFA	Brandon University Faculty Association
CAAT	Colleges of Applied Arts and Technology
CAUT	Canadian Association of University Teachers
CCF	Cooperative Commonwealth Federation
CMEC	Council of Ministers of Education of Canada
CPUO	Committee of Presidents of the Provincially Assisted Universities of Ontario
CUA	Committee on University Affairs
CUPE	Canadian Union of Public Employees
CUS	Canadian Union of Students
FAUST	Faculty Association of the University of St. Thomas
LUFA	Lakehead University Faculty Association
MAFA	Mount Allison Faculty Association
MPHEC	Maritime Provinces Higher Education Commission
NCE	Networks of Centres of Excellence
NFCUS	National Federation of Canadian University Students
NCCU	National Conference of Canadian Universities
NRC	National Research Council
NSERC	Natural Sciences and Engineering Research Council
OLRB	Ontario Labour Relations Board
SMUFU	Saint Mary's University Faculty Union
SPUL	Syndicat des Professeurs d'Université Laval
SPUQ	Le Syndicat des Professeurs et Professeures de l'Université du Québec à Montréal
SSHRC	Social Sciences and Humanities Research Council
UCBC	Universities Council of British Columbia
UGEQ	Union Générale des Étudiants de Québec
UMFA	University of Manitoba Faculty Association
YUFA	York University Faculty Association

Chapter 1

Introduction

The impression that universities can be bought and sold, held by businessmen and fostered by university administrators trained in playing for the highest bid, is a reflection of the deterioration of western civilization. To buy universities is to destroy them and with them the civilization for which they stand (Harold Innis 1946, 75).

Privatization of Research and Teaching

AS THE WINTER OF 1997 set in, there was heated debate at the University of Manitoba over president Emöke Szathmáry's Task Force on Strategic Planning and its plans to transform the university for the 21ˢᵗ century. The major aims were clear: to forge a combined Arts and Science faculty, eliminating smaller units through mergers and acquisitions, and to centralize control with the Board of Governors and the President. There was to be more detailed and more frequent administrative monitoring of professors' performance, with financial rewards tied to the results of these evaluations. Last came a popular theme for the 1990s, stated by the task force in the language of the day:

Technology transfer and commercialization of research and intellectual innovation should become a natural extension of the scholarly activity that led to the discovery in the first place.

After a round of consultations, the university's senate approved the amended plans in principle and turned them over to senior officers for implementation. Except for the suggestions opposed most strenuously by faculty and students—merging Arts and Science, joining Social Work with Education, and closing down the Faculty of Human Ecology—the initial proposals remained intact. The University of Manitoba Faculty Association brought several issues arising from the review to the bargaining table. These concerned the use of performance indicators for faculties, compensation tied to regular evaluation of faculty members, technological change, and researchers' rights to patents and copyrights of their work.

These plans hark back to a warning issued 25 years before by Kingman Brewster, Jr., President of Yale University, in his 1971–72 annual report: that academic freedom was threatened as much by administrators and colleagues *within* the university as from clients, customers or absentee bureaucrats (Brewster 1972). Brewster spoke eloquently against what he called "periodic score keeping." Subjecting academics to constant evaluation inhibited scholarship. It encouraged professors to prepare for annual quantitative reports instead of engaging in longer term exploration and discovery. "Curiosity-driven" research, the heart of the academic enterprise, would give way to projects designed to make the investigator look good on evaluations. Keeping score of faculty members' output would draw them away from risky paths of research to follow safe, accepted routes to promotion and financial reward.

Brewster's far-reaching statement resonates even more today. Manitoba's initiative was designed for the commercial age in academia. Streamlined organization would give the administration greater control over faculties. Performance indicators would reward units meeting requirements set by the administration and penalize those following different goals. Annual performance reviews would force academics into the work that promised the greatest returns to their salaries. More effort would go into president Szathmáry's priorities for research with potential for commercialization.

Harold Innis, one of Canada's most prominent economists, cautioned in 1946 that universities would be destroyed if turned over to business. Since then alarm bells have rung more frequently. In 1971 Robert Nisbet wrote about *academic capitalism* transforming professors in the United States into entrepreneurs constantly seeking capital, revenue and profit (Nisbet 1971). Nisbet wrote about a significant turning point in the United States: commercial forces began to transform universities after centuries of marginal impact on them. By the late 1980s, Janice Newson and Howard Buchbinder (1988) described the *corporate agenda* in Canada, and how higher education was harnessing itself to the priorities of corporate development.

In their book *Academic Capitalism* (1997) Sheila Slaughter and Larry Leslie argue that universities in the late 20th century have simply *become* businesses. Employees of public universities "are academics who act as capitalists from within the public sector; they are state-subsidized entrepreneurs." Public policies have advanced academic capitalism in all four countries studied: the United States, Australia, the United Kingdom, and Canada.

It is noteworthy that Canadian universities succumbed to market pressures later than in the other three countries. Canadian academics have been able to resist pressures by business and the federal government more successfully than their counterparts. Slaughter and Leslie argue this is because higher education policy remains less centralized in Canada, but there are other reasons as well. Pressures to commercialize came later, partly because fewer opportunities existed in Canada for serious corporate involvement. Compared to the United States, state support for Canadian universities insulated them from market pressures. Core revenue from government enabled universities to maintain their independence and sustain their traditions. Finally, Canadian universities have not been able to commercialize as rapidly as in the United States because of faculty's strong, decentralized unionization.

Fully developed commercialism is the most recent, but by no means either the first or the only, way in which universities have served business. Providing trained graduates to meet corporate demand for employees has been a major service. Post-secondary education was expanded in the 1950s and 1960s specifically to increase the supply of technicians, professionals, and managers. Universities used government money to create programs in business, engineering, computer science, and other fields. Businesses hired graduates without underwriting the cost of their training, in effect a public subsidy that its recipients understood and appreciated, as noted in the following excerpt from a 1960 editorial in a business journal:

> Supporting higher education, business is to a certain extent just buttering its own bread.... Graduates of engineering and science faculties are being channelled directly into the service of business so that universities actually are saving the businessman considerable expenses that might be encountered in on the job training ("What Does Business Owe to Education?" *Trade and Commerce*, August 1960).

After absorbing the full impact of government cutbacks, universities became ripe for deepening liaisons with corporations (Beverley 1978). Companies had traditionally contributed a minor portion of university income in the form of charitable donations to support students, construct buildings, or purchase equipment. Companies usually did not try to make profits from these donations. When universities appealed for money to replace what they were losing from government, business people seized the opportunity to capture immediate and direct material returns. As formidable research institutions, universities had much to offer industry —if properly directed. With Ottawa's support, business began to use university research to serve its own interests. Corporations shifted the focus for money they paid to universities, and charitable donations gave way to investments and commercial partnerships.

Corporations now have a strong presence on virtually every campus across the country. Entrepreneurial terms have become an integral part of campus language: students are termed *customers*, corporations *partners*, and research *investment*. Teaching now requires marketing plans, because students are needed to pay for core services formerly covered by government. Research projects now have revenue targets to cover the cost of overhead, and profit objectives from royalties and commercial spin-offs. Venture financing promises even more substantial proceeds from discoveries that eventually reach the market. Fields like biotechnology and microelectronics offer considerable profit from product development (Bloom 1990, Minister of Finance & Minister of State for Science and Technology, Canada 1987).

Business penetration of academia constitutes a fundamental shift away from the independence that developed in the 1960s. Government funding allowed universities autonomy from business and the state and the independence necessary for quality research and teaching. The corporate era of the early 21st century entails deepening ties with corporations and consequent dependence on what they choose to offer. Government has encouraged these ties by requiring university researchers who apply for federal grants to form partnerships with industry.

Universities must now also rely on their own business revenue. Competition to sell teaching and research as commodities is fierce. Campuses wage aggressive campaigns appealing to consumers on the basis of product, image, and price. Location, traditionally an important factor in university education, has become less important as electronic classrooms allow universities to offer courses wherever a market can be found.

Not only do public universities operate in the market like private corporations, governance is also transformed. Administration, originally set up to *support* teaching and research, has been recast as *managerial control*, with far greater command over institutional objectives and policies (Newson 1992). Like their corporate counterparts, university managers exercise power to shape and direct the institution. University management is larger and more hierarchical than ever. Managers have broadened their scope by appropriating power from faculty and academic bodies. They pursue extensive ties with the private sector for fund-raising, marketing university services, and locating franchises on campus for exclusive sale of soft drinks, fast foods, and other products and services. Opportunities have even mushroomed for university presidents to obtain perquisites traditionally enjoyed by corporate officers, such as lucrative positions on corporate boards. In November 1997 the *Multinational Monitor* listed close to

$1 million in fees collected by presidents of 20 leading universities in the United States for sitting on a total of 36 corporate boards—this in addition to an estimated average president's salary of $300,000 (Kniffin 1997).

Where universities have traditionally operated from a professional model, the corporate university follows a business model: capitalizing on research as an *investment*, seeking profit from its ventures, and forming partnerships with corporations through equity financing and licensing. Arrangements of this nature are already commonplace, and attract more interest every day (Sadlack 1992). Even the Medical Research Council, the main federal granting agency for medical research in Canada, seriously considers equity financing for research it sponsors.

Licensing and spin-off companies are the main mechanisms for commercializing university technologies. Licensing agreements by which corporations purchase rights to exploit the market potential of discoveries on campus are now commonplace. In 1997 Canadian universities received US $11.3 million in gross income from 750 active licenses and options in life sciences and physical sciences, compared to US $3.3 million in 1991. The amount is still small, but the rate of growth is impressive. New licenses issued in 1997 totalled 227, compared to 49 in 1991 (Gu and Whewell 1999). The prospect is strong for steady increases in the future.

Spin-offs are companies started by universities in order to market new discoveries. About 67 percent of 366 spin-off companies enumerated in 1998 had been created after 1990. Most were in five technology fields: 90 in biotechnology/biology; 66 in health sciences; 58 in engineering and applied sciences; 55 in information technology; and 73 in mathematical and physical sciences (Gu and Whewell 1999).

Until recently business influenced universities at global levels, far above the dynamics of teaching or research. When they needed trainees, business representatives lobbied government to expand the post-secondary system. They gave donations for designated capital campaigns or scholarships, and returns came in the form of plaques, buildings, and scholarships named after the donors, or honorary degrees for especially generous individuals. Recipient universities were rarely expected to return more substantial or concrete benefits. For the most part, corporate benefactors maintained official arms length relations with universities, unless they had seats on boards of governors.

Corporate demands for material returns are now having a profound impact. Few observers depict the trend to privatization better than Garry Trudeau's popular satiric *Doonesbury* cartoon strip. B.D., the new football coach at Walden University, extols the benefits of playing for team Nike at Walden to a new recruit and his mother:

> For openers, our athletes have great uniforms! Eric here will *never* be caught in raggedy or out-of-style colors! Off the field, same deal. Our starters here wear nothing but Tommy Hilfiger, and all our underwear comes to us courtesy of Calvin Klein! Also, as a member of Team Nike at Walden, you'll be lining up against the class of the field—Reebok, Adidas and many other leading brands (Trudeau 1997)!

Eric seriously ponders the offer. He seems interested because, it turns out, he has "always wanted to kick Reebok butt."

Trudeau's symbol for privatization is the ubiquitous, prominent corporate logo that has invaded campuses in the United States, the legendary home of commercialized university sports. The University of Wisconsin-Madison, a prominent player in these arrangements, signed an exclusive 1996 contract that required its athletes to wear only Reebok shoes and apparel in practices, games, and media interviews. Another proposed clause in the contract (removed after a storm of student protest) would have prohibited sports team coaches from any negative comment about Reebok apparel, its labour practices, or the university's association with the company (Multinational Monitor 1997, New York Times 1996).

Universities remain one of the last public holdings to fall to the privatizer's gavel. Governments have justified privatization on grounds that they can no longer afford to pay for the services. This exaggerated position masks a more fundamental reason. Public organizations have value that can be made available to private investors. When public enterprises earn surpluses, business interests want them removed from the public realm to make their profits available for shareholders.

This has certainly been true for crown corporations, with the best of them long gone through a process that transferred immense public wealth to private shareholders. Ottawa and the provinces together privatized some of the nation's most important public assets, including Canadair (an aircraft manufacturer sold to Bombardier) and Air Canada, PetroCanada, Canadian National Railway, the Potash Corporation of Saskatchewan, and Manitoba Telephone System, which remained intact and were transferred through sale of their shares on the Toronto Stock Exchange. Airports and the air traffic control system itself are also being privatized. Provincial hydroelectric systems may very well be on the drawing board in Ontario and Manitoba. Premier Gary Filmon of Manitoba gave a strong clue in Spring 1999 that, if reelected, his government would consider privatizing the provincially-owned hydroelectric corporation by, ironically, announcing that his government would not consider privatizing Manitoba Hydro under any circumstances. This is suspiciously similar to the statement he made just before the 1995 provincial election that he would never sell the provincially-owned Manitoba Telephone System. Once in office, his government promptly privatized the telephone company.

Canada's huge education sector is still under public ownership and control. It offers enormous opportunity for cash-rich corporations seeking new forms of investment. Our vast student population is a valued consumer market. Universities are already changing to accommodate investor concerns.

University privatization proceeds on a piecemeal basis that is less noticeable than the all-or-nothing decisions with crown corporations. Manitoba Telephone System's privatization in 1996 caused a huge outcry across the province. Nobody could miss the fact that ownership of a state-held corporation was being transferred to private shareholders. University privatization is more subtle, and managed without formal changes in ownership. Rather, value is transferred through licensing arrangements and partnerships. Even though Canadian universities remain legally public, their resources are steadily more available for private gain.

Universities are already well down a path towards privatization, in the sense that more revenue comes from private sources, services are geared to corporate supporters, and decision-making follows classic business patterns based on profit centres instead of service units.

Merchandising the Campus

The campus itself has become an exploitable commodity. One summer morning in 1984, during a sabbatical leave at the University of Warwick near Coventry, England, I witnessed traffic held up while hundreds of brand new Volkswagens were driven into campus parking structures. The university rented storage space to Volkswagen while students were not using it.

Large university campuses hold populations of well over 20,000 students, plus thousands more staff—a daytime population equivalent to the size of a small town. Food sellers, bookstores, computer outlets, and clothing boutiques can reach this clientele by just opening their doors, without spending money on advertising or promotion. A resident bank is likely to capture business for student loans and to retain student account holders who will earn above average incomes after graduation.

Until recently, universities operated their own cafeterias and restaurants. The scene changed dramatically after the late 1970s as part of a trend that swept through hospitals, shopping malls, and highway rest stops. Beverage giants and fast food franchises offered to sell their goods on campus in exchange for rental charges and licensing fees. In return for undisclosed amounts of money, universities grant monopolies to fast food franchises. Food choice is narrowed to the handful of chains dealing in hamburgers, submarine sandwiches, pizza, chicken, or tacos, without any consumer input whatsoever.

For a sum of money they will not disclose, in 1995 the student society and Board of Governors of the University of British Columbia granted Coca Cola exclusive rights to sell beverages on campus. Proceeds from this contract were apparently spent on physical access projects to serve people with disabilities—services that should have been funded by government. The student's society was reported to receive about $100,000. Other universities called UBC to learn more about its deal with Coke (AUCC 1996c).

In 1996 the University of Manitoba and the students' union contracted with Pepsi-Cola for a 10-year monopoly to sell its integrated line of soft drinks, juices, bottled tea, and water (Reid 1997). Franchising spread to food services as the university replaced cafeterias with Robin's Donuts, Domino's Pizza, Taco Bell, and Mr. Submarine. These corporate contracts have also been kept under wraps.

Coke's exclusive contract at Memorial University in the same year drew particular criticism because it was chosen over a bid by the local Pepsi distributor, even though the Coke bottler was based in Montréal. The Pepsi distributor contributed more than $20,000 a year to Memorial in scholarships, athletic sponsorships and general donations (Cochrane 1997). This controversy is interesting because it was limited to *which* commercial enterprise should benefit from exclusive access to students and staff at the university. Whether a campus monopoly should be granted to agents of a global corporation was never at issue.

These contracts are a new form of privatizing and commercializing the campus. Franchises replace broader-choice cafeterias with limited selections of factory-produced food. Universities are attracted to the fees they receive for rental and licencing; food companies earn profits that end up in the accounts of their transnational corporate owners. But these operations amount only to another method of exploiting students. The money they must pay for dubious food subsidizes the university and adds to profits of absentee corporations.

Franchises are the highly visible manifestations of turning the campus over to industry, since students, staff, and visitors must face a daily barrage of company logos and products. Yet the significance of franchises pales compared to the consequences of turning research over to industry. Intellectual property agreements are transforming knowledge that should be freely available into a commodity for the benefit of investors. They pose a serious threat to the university's viability.

Labour versus Management

Professors have traditionally set their own agendas for research and teaching as a labour of love, commensurate with low salaries and the tenuous state of tenure and academic freedom. An implicit contract exchanged lower lifetime earnings for the promise of job security and the right to teach and do research without interference. In the 1960s they gained greater say in university affairs and improved compensation. By the mid-1970s professors were forming unions in reaction to employers' attempts to roll back their pay and job security.

The current fiscal scene on campus is a far cry from the latter 1950s and 1960s, when money flowed from governments riding the crest of an economic wave. Funds were readily available to construct facilities, recruit faculty, and create new programs for the postwar baby boomers as they reached university age. Between 1957 and 1965, Ontario alone established eight new universities: Waterloo, York, Laurentian, Trent, Brock, Guelph, the Ontario Institute for Studies in Education (OISE), and Lakehead. Spending on higher education soared from 1 percent of the provincial budget in 1965 to 11 percent in 1969 (Axelrod 1982).

This flush period lasted for about 20 years. By the mid-1970s, even though the system was still expanding with more students every year and a physical plant ever more costly to maintain, governments reduced the flow of money. Faculty were the natural target for savings. Hiring slowed to a standstill and sowed the seeds of future gender and age disparities. Young Ph.D.s had to settle for part-time appointments, waiting in line to compete for the few full-time positions still available. Women faced the added hurdle of hiring procedures dominated by male bias. Women were hired less frequently than men—making up less than 13 percent of full-time professors in the mid-1960s—and thereafter were promoted at a slower pace (Backhouse, Harris, Michael and Wylie 1989, Caplan 1992, Stalker 1995).

Universities became dominated by money concerns: how to spend less and find new ways to bring in more. Cutbacks resulted in support-staff layoff and reduced maintenance of physical plant. Cost-saving measures were aimed at faculty by freezing salaries, reducing contribution to pension plans, and attempting to eliminate benefits that seemed secure just a few years before. Legislation in some provinces allowed employers to impose days off without pay.

The campus became a battlefield between administrators vying to gain ground and professors holding on to their turf. Professors have held on to their jobs more effectively than other workers, but have not been able to prevent their income from sliding. But saving money is just part of the picture. Faculty are in a struggle with administration for control of their jobs, their work and, ultimately, of the university.

In most industries managers control the labour process by breaking down whole jobs and redistributing the pieces. Academics have so far kept their work intact. Their autonomy stems from control over every stage of their labour process, from the germ of an idea to an end product that could be a research project, a new product, a textbook, a course outline, or a lecture. New administrative initiatives threaten to fragment teaching into packaged courses that can be delivered without an actual professor present in an actual classroom. Major universities have established huge research divisions to manage the direction and content of research once controlled entirely by professors. Administrators scrutinize faculty performance with new evaluation systems and use the results to set salary increases.

Service versus Profit   Universities have been transformed from modest roots to large, complex business organisms over the course of about 60 years. Post-war growth turned them into large, complex, decentralized institutions. By the 1970s, administrators under pressure to trim their budgets vied for more control, adopting centralized business models for budgeting and cost containment. Large administrative bureaucracies became the order of the day. Corporate terminology entered administrators' language, with requirements for greater efficiency and top-down accountability. Elaborate marketing plans were used to sell university programs, and accounting systems to price tuition based on cost and return on investment. Running the campus like a business created a divide between administrators and academics, and faculty unionization was the inevitable outcome of the intense conflicts that ensued.

Until the 1980s, the fruits of university research and teaching stayed largely in the public domain. Academics made their products available to all, through teaching and publication. The notion that they might profit from selling their products was considered contrary to academic ethics and traditions. Success stemmed from the quality and quantity of one's work. Fame was occasionally attainable to scholarly superstars who made important discoveries, but fortune was rarely feasible.

Through the 1980s and 1990s, universities began to commercialize research and teaching. Portions of the system became businesses that favoured programs with the greatest financial returns. Entrepreneurs were placed in high regard, because they seek business opportunities and lucrative markets. Teaching and research became the means to the end of financial gain.

Corporate universities convert a system hitherto inaccessible to business into a source of profitable exploitation. Such opportunities are rare. Canadian precedents of privatizing public enterprises in transportation, defence, telecommunications, aeronautics, and energy, where public investment ultimately supported private gain, were in sectors already accessible to business, where crown corporations competed with private ones. Universities are different. They comprise an entire industry producing considerable value from which business was not able to profit. Now they are on the verge of becoming centres for private gain. Government and industry are co-operating to place this immense public asset into service for business.

Privatizing universities amounts puts a price on knowledge formerly valued both for its own sake and for its broad social and economic contributions. Privatization does not *increase* the value produced by universities; it merely changes who gets the surplus by transferring valuable elements to investors who can capture the value and turn a profit. The public continues to pay for the parts that business does not want.

Chapter 2

Flaws in the Foundation

CANADA'S UNIVERSITIES DESCEND from a system of small secular and ecclesiastical institutions emphasizing classical education in liberal arts and pure science. At the time of Confederation in 1867 only Laval, McGill, Toronto, Victoria, and Trinity had more than 100 students.

These were elite institutions catering to the children of the dominant classes. Students and instructors alike came from acceptable religious backgrounds. Dalhousie University, under the Church of Scotland since 1838, admitted only self-professed Christians, and teaching faculty were exclusively Presbyterian. The Presbyterian University of Kingston, established in 1840 and renamed Queen's University in 1841, required professors to declare adherence to the Westminster confession of faith. The College of New Brunswick granted degrees exclusively to Anglicans. Anglican King's College in Nova Scotia, established in 1789, allowed non-Anglicans to attend but would not grant them degrees. Graduating students were required to take the oath of allegiance to the 39 articles of the Church of England. Even McGill University, chartered as nondenominational in 1852, excluded non-Protestants from its board until as late as 1934.

Sectarian colleges were gradually forced to affiliate with secular universities, sacrificing autonomy for access to degrees, superior facilities, and (most importantly) public funding. The first merger of this kind was the 1877 incorporation of the University of Manitoba which brought four church colleges under a secular umbrella: Catholic Collège Saint Boniface; Anglican St. John's College; Presbyterian Manitoba College; and Methodist Wesley College. Saint Boniface and Wesley have long since become independent as, respectively, Collège Saint Boniface and the University of Winnipeg; St. John's is still a college within the University of Manitoba.

Although formal denominational control was ceded, many colleges maintained religious approaches in administration and teaching. When legislation in 1887 created the federated University of Toronto it retained affiliation with three theological colleges: St. Michaels, Knox, and Wycliffe. A fourth, the Toronto Baptist College, became McMaster University.

Many sectarian institutions chose to remain independent well into the 20th century, foregoing (except for colleges in Québec) access to public funds. Religious control fell away in the 1950s as provinces restricted any promise of more generous funding to secular institutions (Cameron 1991, Masters 1996).

This small, stable system held sway until the first phase of expansion in the 1920s. Between 1920 and 1930, university revenue rose from $9 million to $14.5 million, and enrolment from 23,000 to 33,000. But even by 1930, small sectarian institutions still characterized the system. Universities were under provincial jurisdiction but enjoyed no government commitment for core funding (which the Flavelle Royal Commission on the University of Toronto had called for in 1906). Only Ontario accepted the Commission's recommendation to provide 50 percent of revenue from succession duties, amounting at the time to some $275,000 per year for universities.

Modest provincial funding was supplemented by tuition, contributions from individuals and foundations, and earnings from endowments. The federal government did little to reduce inequities among the provinces, limiting federal support to direct payments to students under a program initiated in 1919 for returned military personnel. The only other federal money consisted of grants from the National Research Council (NRC), founded during World War I to promote scientific research (Cameron 1991).

During the Depression every province cut back funding for universities, sometimes severely enough to threaten their survival. Universities almost invariably laid off faculty and reduced salaries. The University of Saskatchewan's provincial grant fell from $676,727 in 1930–31 to $398,600 in 1933–34, while enrolment in degree courses rose from 1,610 to 1,810. By 1937–38 the operating deficit reached $125,000, while the grant, at $468,600, was still well below the 1930 level. Tuition rose from $30 a year in 1930 to $90 in 1934, at a time when incomes were stagnant and general price levels fell. The first academic staff to be laid off were the young and unmarried. Salary cuts were imposed on others, at between 16 and 30 percent (Thomson 1970). Faced with deep funding cuts in 1932, the University of British Columbia dismissed 11 untenured professors (Horn 1999).

Financial hardship took other forms as well. Scandal surfaced in 1932 at the University of Manitoba. John Machray, chair of the board of governors, the university's honorary bursar, and head of the law firm responsible for the university's investments, had defrauded the university for more than $970,000 through embezzlement going back as far as 1903. Not until

Machray had decimated the endowment fund was he tried, convicted and jailed; the money was never recovered. Manitoba's financial hardship was compounded by reductions in the government grant of almost 50 percent between 1931–32 and 1933–34. Tuition was raised and faculty were laid off to make up the shortfall (Harris 1976, Morton 1957, Horn 1999).

McGill's Depression experience epitomized the contradictions of the period. In the late 19th century McGill was supported by wealthy Montréal industrialists including William Molson, Peter Redpath, Thomas Workman, Sir William Macdonald, and Sir Donald Smith. A 1920 centenary campaign raised more than $6 million. The Carnegie and Rockefeller foundations supported substantial capital projects through the 1920s and well into the 1930s. By December 1929, the university's governors were assured that their investment managers took advantage of the slump by purchasing high-grade equity stocks at low prices, thereby strengthening the portfolio for the long run. Short-term finances did not fare as well. Investment income fell from $700,000 in 1927 to $392,000 in 1934. In 1932, all salaries were cut by three to 10 percent for married men, and four to 10 percent for unmarried persons. The university also reduced funding for several programs, including the McGill School of Graduate Nurses (Harris 1976, Frost 1984).

In the fall of 1933 McGill closed its School of Social Work; thereafter social work training was delivered by volunteers at the independent Montreal School of Social Work. Its only revenue came from modest student fees plus contributions from alumnae, professionals, and business people. Graduates received no certification until 1945, when McGill conferred bachelor's and master's degrees in social work. McGill did not reopen the School of Social Work until 1950 (Frost 1984).

Despite the suspension of social work teaching, McGill housed one of the most important social research projects of the Depression. With an initial 5-year $100,000 grant from the Rockefeller Foundation, and a $50,000 renewal in 1936, Leonard Marsh directed the McGill Social Science Research Council through dozens of influential studies of unemployment and the social needs it created. His pivotal 1943 *Report on Social Security for Canada* was a decisive influence in the founding of the Canadian welfare state (Marsh 1975).

Other Canadian universities, particularly in the Maritime provinces, called on considerable support from private foundations in the United States. Between 1920 and 1940 the Carnegie Foundation granted more than $4 million to 37 colleges and universities (see table A–7), and more than $600,000 to 21 non-degree organizations (Harris 1976). Canadian professors and their widows received more than $2 million through the Carnegie Foundation for the Advancement of Teaching and the Teachers Insurance and Annuity Association. Carnegie supported new academic programs, especially in adult education, fine art, child study, library science, medieval studies, and music. At the request of J.D. Rockefeller, the Rockefeller Foundation set aside $5 million to establish "a Dominion-wide policy" to promote medical education in Canada. McGill and Toronto were major recipients, with approximately $1 million each; Alberta, Dalhousie, and Manitoba each received upwards of $500,000; and Montréal took in $375,000 (Fisher 1978, Corner 1964, Reid 1984, Harris 1976).

Strategically placed foundation grants impacted on university development. Scientific research and medicine were the two highest priorities for Rockefeller and Carnegie. Dalhousie had no operating grants from the province of Nova Scotia between 1920 and 1940, when Carnegie provided about $2.1 million for the medical faculty, endowed chairs in arts and science, and general grants. Rockefeller supported the medical school, public health, and an Institute of Public Affairs. (Dalhousie also raised more than $1.7 million from Canadian private citizens and corporations.) Carnegie helped to create Memorial College in St. John's, Newfoundland with a 5-year grant of $75,000 in 1924. Carnegie was the major funder for the extension department of St. Francis Xavier University during its formative years, 1931–37 (Harris 1976, Reid 1984).

Rockefeller and Carnegie used Canadian programs as pilots for larger efforts in the United States. A Rockefeller official noted in 1936 that Dalhousie's Institute of Public Affairs was "a control experiment against which to measure experiments supported in the United States" (May 1936). Carnegie had a similar rationale for proposing a central Maritime university, a project that failed to garner sufficient interest from universities in the region (Sills 1922).

By the end of the Depression, university funding had not been restored to its modest pre-Depression levels. Foundation money, however instrumental for new and specialized programs, did not sustain core teaching functions. For example, by the late 1920s Rockefeller emphasized research almost exclusively over teaching (Kohler 1978).

World War II: Catalyst for Change

Still reeling from the Depression, universities were especially unprepared for the tumultuous changes brought on by World War II. Government issued unprecedented demands for trained personnel to run the military and conduct advanced research in all aspects of weaponry, transportation, communications, and personnel management.

Canada's 21 universities still did not figure prominently in the economy. Enrolment of 37,200 in 1940 was only moderately higher than 33,000 in 1930 (Harris 1976). Universities offered training mainly in theology, medicine, and law, with scattered programs in agriculture, engineering, and a few new professions. Supply of graduates was chronically short of demand, so employers recruited immigrants to fill the shortfall. This dearth of university graduates continued all the way through the 1960s.

Wartime functions gave universities an unprecedented spot on the public policy stage. Requirements rose dramatically for military scientists and technicians. Ottawa encouraged students in designated fields to remain in school to complete their studies before being called up. Faculty in high priority disciplines were exempted from the draft, as were students with acceptable academic standing. By contrast, in low priority areas—the humanities, social sciences, commerce, law, and theology—only students in the upper half of their classes were permitted to remain in university (Pilkington 1983, Axelrod 1984, Harris 1976, Kiefer & Pierson 1989).

This new attention necessitated deeper intrusion by government to ensure universities complied with federal requirements. Ottawa regulated movement of scientific and technical personnel, and monitored students —who could not proceed to graduate work or even transfer between faculties without approval from the National Selective Service (Frost 1984).

Government interference with university autonomy elicited little concern. University presidents preferred to capitalize on government's new interest and support rather than oppose the increased control that came with it. In fact they endorsed greater intervention, coordinating even closer working relationships with federal agencies through the National Conference of Canadian Universities (NCCU), predecessor of the Association of Universities and Colleges of Canada (AUCC).

University military training was compulsory for males over 18, with at least six hours a week in military drills and lectures. In turn, government accepted university study as essential national service, subject to adequate performance. Eventually the government regulated who was eligible to continue their studies. The 1942 Federal Order-in-Council 8343 required expulsion of failing students. By December 1942, Queen's University had expelled 81 failing students, reporting to the District Officer Commanding that they were no longer entitled to academic exemption from military call-up. Twenty-nine failing students in applied science were also reported to military authorities, even though they were not required to withdraw under the regulations. By February 1943 the Canadian University Press reported that 692 undergraduates had been expelled from 11 campuses across the country (Pilkington 1983, Thomson 1969, Gibson 1983).

In the same year, Principals James of McGill, and Wallace of Queen's, members of the NCCU executive, proposed "to suspend all teaching in the faculties of arts, commerce, law, and education for the duration of hostilities." Although endorsed by other members of the NCCU, and supported by government officials and Prime Minister Mackenzie King, their proposal eventually died in the face of concerted opposition from prominent academics in the Social Science Research Council and the Royal Society of Canada, who sent a national petition to the Prime Minister (Pilkington 1983, Harris 1976, Gibson 1983).

Infringements on autonomy seemed minor compared to benefits for scientific and military research. University laboratories produced significant advances in radar, optical glass, refrigeration of food for long-distance transportation, and technology of war gases and ballistics. Scientists in war-related activities, especially top-secret research, enhanced their prestige. Money flowed in for research, equipment purchase, and hiring of personnel. Direct military application was the immediate aim of this work, but there were also civilian benefits in medical and food-related areas (Axelrod 1984).

This work required altering and suspending time-honoured academic traditions. Military research contracts necessarily bypassed usual procedures for review of proposals and findings. Most of the work was covered by a cloak of secrecy that actively forbade customary practices of disclosure, publication, and external scrutiny. Much of the research was development of offensive weapons, with scant attention paid to any negative aspects, and these patterns survived well past the end of the war. Wilfred Eggleston put it well:

> Universities are ruthlessly raided in wartime: their wisest teachers and most ingenious investigators are conscripted for applied research... "[T]he amount of new fundamental knowledge uncovered anywhere between 1939 and 1945 was almost negligible compared with that of any other six years of this century." (Eggleston 1950, 256, quote from Rivett 1948, 128)

In 1941 investigators at McGill developed a manufacturing process for R.D.X., the "Super Explosive of World War II." McGill scholars also took part in developing the atomic bomb. In late 1942 the British government transferred its nuclear research program to the safer environs of Montréal, where it established a laboratory to produce an atomic reactor. The Montréal Laboratory employed about 70 scientists, conducting heavy water studies and supplying vital raw materials to the project. This laboratory was eventually transferred to Chalk River (Frost 1984, Nicholls 1981).

McMaster University is a salient example of adapting university policies to government priorities. In 1939 McMaster (not chartered as a private university until 1957) was still under the Baptist Convention of Ontario and Québec. To accommodate military research, McMaster had to lift its Baptist restriction against accepting state funding. The impasse was solved by creating Hamilton College, a separate secular college of science affiliated with the denominational McMaster. Harry Thode, a specialist in isotope research, worked on analysis of heavy metals and heavy water, key ingredients for nuclear fission in the atomic reactor project. Chemists Ronald Graham and Laurence Cragg studied synthetic rubber materials for motorized and aerial warfare, and detection and control of poison gases. After the war, all of these projects were incorporated into ongoing research and teaching. By the 1950s the work on isotopes was being used in medical research (Johnston 1981).

By the end of the war university research enjoyed far greater legitimacy than ever before. With the federal government convinced of the practical benefits of research, new money was allocated, especially at larger universities. Even though this money was most welcome on cash-starved campuses, it did not address funding shortages for core teaching. Teaching would remain underfunded for some time to come.

Federal-Provincial Conflict in the 1950s

Canada emerged from the war with a strong and stable economy and a government committed to active fiscal management. Spending rose steadily on social programs and the military, with more money targeted to the Department of Defence for equipment and operations. Unemployment insurance put money back into the economy when it was most needed; family allowance paid monthly benefits to mothers with dependent children.

But universities did not immediately benefit from this post war munificence. If anything, they experienced greater stress, as staff and physical resources were stretched to the limit. Fuelled by 37,000 military veterans, enrolment rose to over 80,000 in 1947–48 (Axelrod 1984, Pilkington 1983). Starting in 1946, the federal government paid operating grants of $150 per veteran student directly to universities under the Veterans' Rehabilitation Act of 1945. Veterans also received personal grants to cover tuition and a living allowance—a significant boost to university income; but except for research grants, it was the only federal money that universities received.

Spending on veterans, the first national program of its kind, demonstrated Ottawa's capacity to move quickly when conditions were right for decisive action. Nonetheless, paying money directly to universities was fraught with difficulties. Even though this was a special case for moving veterans through the system, it overrode provincial authority to establish universities, finance them, and determine their overall missions.

Grants were in fact meagre in light of what they were supposed to cover. When Ian Mackenzie, Minister of Veterans Affairs, approved a request from the NCCU for $150 for each veteran, he required the universities to provide counselling, residence accommodation, assurance that classes would not be excessively large, control over admission of non-veterans, a minimum of two admission periods a year for veterans, and classes to run for 12 months a year. Even though these extensive conditions were a costly burden, and an intrusion on academic autonomy, they were readily accepted (Stager 1973).

Meeting Mackenzie's requirements proved difficult with the modest sum of $150. Funding did not anticipate that enrolment of non-veterans might also grow. There were no allowances for new facilities or equipment to handle an influx of students. Universities were given surplus military supplies and permission to use abandoned facilities. They held classes in old schools, army huts, church basements and vacated military installations. The University of Toronto's Ajax campus occupied a former munitions plant (Sheffield 1970). McGill established a temporary campus, Dawson College, at the former Number 9 Air Observer Training School and an RCAF repair depot. Another RCAF depot in Lachine was converted to a residence (Frost 1984).

Staffing was inadequate for the increased work. Faculty were expected to teach twice the usual number of students, requiring large classes and squeezing two full academic sessions into each 12 month period. Few professors were able to sustain their research under these conditions. Principal Robert Charles Wallace of Queen's University summed up the dilemma in his 1949 report to the trustees:

> The heavy strains of the war years and the postwar influx of students have taken their toll in the health of our staff.... Too many breakdowns have taken place, and several others are at the breaking point. Continuous teaching throughout the year, large classes and other demands on time, have had the effect of wearing down even resistant constitutions (Gibson 1983, 209).

The program ended in1951, when most of the veterans had graduated. By 1952–53 enrolment was down to 63,000, the lowest it would reach in the post-war period, but still more than 50 percent higher than the pre-war figure of around 40,000 (Hanly, Shulman & Swaan 1971).

By 1950, Ottawa paid for just 8,000 veterans who were still in the system. New money was desperately needed to cover increased enrolment by non-veterans. In 1951 the Massey Royal Commission on the Arts, Letters and Sciences concluded that a financial crisis threatened the future of Canadian universities. It recommended that the federal government bypass the provinces with immediate direct payments to universities based on enrolment. The direct route was faster and more certain of approval than working through all the provinces, even though it constituted an infringement on provincial rights (Massey 1951, Pilkington 1983).

Ottawa allocated 50 cents per head of population, distributing provincial totals amongst the universities based on full-time enrolment in degree programs. Over $7 million was spent in the first year of the program. Direct payment to provincial institutions violated the relationship established by the 1867 British North America Act that gave the provinces control of health, education, and social welfare. Because of its greater taxation powers, Ottawa was expected to subsidize provincial spending. Bypassing the provinces was not anticipated. The provinces had not resisted the veterans' program, since it was set to end once they graduated, and support for veterans was appropriately a federal responsibility. Circumnavigating the provinces for regular students was a different matter. The provinces have rarely welcomed federal intrusion, although they have relied since Confederation on Ottawa to fund their increasing responsibilities. Direct payments solved the immediate problem of getting money to universities, and created a new era of federal-provincial conflict (Stager 1973, Axelrod 1984).

By 1955, with the per capita grant still at 50 cents, universities pressed for bigger increases. Enrolment was expected to double in the next decade to 120,000, given the huge number of children born just after the war, and more people seeking degrees to meet employers' training requirements. Enrolment grew faster, reaching 128,000 by 1961–62 (Bissell 1957, Sheffield 1955, Sheffield 1970). Existing staff and facilities could not accommodate them.

NCCU's lobbying over the course of the year was effective. At the 1956 NCCU conference, Prime Minister St. Laurent announced that the per capita grant would be doubled to $1.00. He also committed $100 million to create the Canada Council for the arts, humanities, and social sciences, with half the fund earmarked for capital projects over the next decade. Federal grants rose steadily after this, to $1.50 in 1958–59, $2.00 in 1962–63, and $5.00 in 1966–67, the last year of the program, when the total was $99 million (Stager 1973).

The new money was easily absorbed by a rapidly expanding system. But the formula proved unfair to universities in poorer provinces. Grants were based solely on population, with no allowances for differences in provincial enrolment, costs of running universities, or fiscal capacity of their home province to support them. Provinces with large populations and mostly in-province students had the greatest advantage. They received higher payments per student than smaller provinces whose universities served several province regions.

The formula was insensitive as well to variations in enrolment. Each province received the same per capita amount, regardless of the number of foreign students served. Universities received money only for full-time students, making those with large part-time enrolment even worse off.

Nova Scotia's small population and large number of out-of-province students gave the province the lowest percentage of federal money. In 1952, the first year of per-capita grants, the national average of $120 per student ranged from $93 in Nova Scotia to $483 in Newfoundland. Memorial University in St. John's received more than twice the amount per student than Dalhousie in Halifax. By 1957, when the national average was $221, Nova Scotia stood at $155 and Newfoundland at $561. Dalhousie drew students from the entire region and other countries, but its grant was limited to a portion of Nova Scotia's allocation, based solely on population within the province (Pilkington 1983, Stager 1973, Cameron 1991).

The provinces opposed direct federal grants, with Québec the most forceful opponent. In the second year of the program (1952–53) Premier Duplessis threatened sanctions against any Québec university that accepted federal money. By 1953-54, the province compensated Québec universities with grants to replace the foregone federal money. In 1957, when the federal government again offered money directly to Québec universities, Duplessis forced them to return the cheques. From 1956–57 on, Ottawa paid the money to the NCCU in trust for Québec universities (Frost 1984).

The dispute between Québec and Ottawa was resolved in 1960, after the 1959 election of a Liberal government headed by Paul Sauvé. By 1960–61, Ottawa agreed to transfer an extra one percent of corporate income tax in lieu of grants, and to top up this amount if it fell short of what Québec would have received in per capita grants. Québec assumed the full burden of university financing. Infusion of new public funds made possible the system-wide expansion that followed (Carter 1982, AUCC 1965, Frost 1984).

Ottawa's agreement with Québec established no connection between funding and need or expected cost. Using provincial population failed to cover enrolment increases beyond population growth, from the postwar baby boom and an increasing portion of the population attending university. Using one percent of corporate income tax made even less sense: there is no logical connection between corporate taxes and university costs. The formula became more problematic over time, as university budgets rose faster than total provincial spending and corporate income taxes fell as a portion of total revenue.

By the mid-1950s federal transfers were still too small to finance needed expansion. Universities were growing rapidly to meet labour market demand, and their faculty were doing more and more research. As these benefits were recognized, universities gained favour with both government and industry—but favour which took some time to translate into higher grants.

The 1960s: Expansion Without Direction

By the early 1960s Canadian universities were barely equipped to handle the student body of the day, let alone the expected influx over the succeeding decade. Shortages were acute for academic staff. Until more Canadians received higher degrees, universities would continue to hire immigrants. Forty-three percent of new university teachers were hired from outside Canada in the early 1960s. During a hiring surge in 1968, one estimate claimed that 86 percent of new appointments went to non-Canadians (Porter 1970, Mathews and Steele 1969).

The booming economy produced more money for all spheres of government. Ottawa spent more on its own programs and transferred new funds to the provinces through tax points, block grants, cost-sharing agreements, and equalization payments. Social spending grew in health care, education, and income security—programs delivered by the provinces but subsidized by the federal government. By the end of the 1960s free universal health care was in place, and under the Canada Assistance Plan Ottawa covered 50 percent of social assistance costs in every province.

In 1966 Ottawa's payments to universities, at $5.00 per capita, were far below what was needed. The federal government announced a new arrangement at a federal-provincial conference in October 1966, without consulting or warning either the provinces or the universities. The 1967 Federal-Provincial Fiscal Arrangements Act paid money to the provinces for distribution to universities within their jurisdictions. Ottawa increased the annual payments to the greater of $15 per capita or 50 percent of operating costs. This gave the provinces vastly improved flexibility and capacity to spend, and in most cases led to more generous grants. It also reestablished provincial fiscal authority over universities (Stager 1973).

For 1966–67 Ottawa paid out $400 million, compared to $99 million a year earlier. Universities' share of provincial education budgets rose to 24.7 percent in 1967–68 from 16 percent in 1960. By 1970 federal payments reached $628 million, with education receiving 22.2 percent of total government spending, compared to 17.5 percent in 1964. Government covered 75 percent of operating costs, compared to 55 percent in 1955. Governments' share peaked at 81.2 percent in 1975–76 (Hardy 1984, Neatby 1987, Hurtubise & Rowat 1970, Cole 1972).

The provinces quickly took advantage of the incentive to spend cost-shared money. New money supported dramatic expansion. Between 1960 and 1969, Ontario established six new universities, British Columbia two,

Alberta two, one each in New Brunswick, Nova Scotia and Prince Edward Island, and Québec built five campuses of the Université du Québec.

Several new universities incorporated smaller private and sectarian institutions which stood to benefit from converting to public status. Until 1966 their identity was safe because federal grants did not distinguish between church and secular institutions. (Provinces paid less to sectarian than public universities, and Ontario gave no public money to universities with religious affiliations.) Once financing came under full provincial control, the vast majority of church colleges and universities dropped their official religious status. A secular, publicly financed system quickly emerged. Religious studies carried on in small pockets, as church units became semi-autonomous parts of larger universities (Hurtubise & Rowat 1970, Neatby 1987).

By the late 1960s universities were flourishing beyond the most enthusiastic expectations of a decade earlier. In the pervasive optimism of the period, they were seen as contributing to economic growth, supplying educated and trained employees, and fostering significant research. Degrees became more highly valued among an ever-rising portion of the population as tickets to better jobs and more rewarding careers. Within a generation after the Second World War, universities had moved from relative weakness to great strength.

Government's role went from restraining development to stimulating growth. Government money paid for capital expansion and increased operating expenses. Most was given with little direction or strings attached. Planning was rare, either before the spending programs were put in place or to guide the path of the system into the future. The provinces had not studied the extent of current and expected need, or their implications for the fate of the system, and had few plans or policies to guide their actions. Ottawa's approach was no better. It relied on provincial priorities without developing national objectives, policies, or standards. Prime Minister Lester Pearson epitomized this stance when he announced Ottawa's intention to cease paying money directly to universities.

> The arrangements... are designed to take particular account of provincial financial needs for post-secondary education, but in a manner that manifestly exerts no influence on the structure and content of provincial programs for higher education and enables each provincial government to determine its own approach to post-secondary education generally (Carter 1982, 6).

Pearson favoured a decentralized, provincially driven system without federal standards or coordination. By the early 1970s, Ottawa still had no initiatives for a national system, a matter noted by the OECD as a glaring

oversight (Carter 1982). Financing decisions were ad hoc. Ottawa responded to pressure without the guidance of an overall framework. Except for the
occasional federal-provincial gathering on finance, there was no national
forum to discuss post-secondary policy. The only national vehicle was the
Council of Ministers of Education of Canada (CMEC), formed by the provinces in 1967 to share information across provincial boundaries but never
empowered to set policies for participating provinces.

Initiatives for national policies came from the Association of Universities and Colleges of Canada (AUCC) and the Canadian Association of University Teachers (CAUT), who jointly sponsored the Duff-Berdahl Commission on university governance in 1965. In 1970, with a $150,000 grant from
the Ford Foundation, they joined with the Canadian Union of Students
(CUS) and the Union Générale des Étudiants du Québec (UGEC) to launch
the Hurtubise, Rowat Commission on relations between universities and
government. The AUCC sponsored on its own the 1965 Bladen commission
on financing higher education in Canada. Neither the findings nor the
recommendations of these initiatives had much influence on federal policy
(Hurtubise & Rowat 1970, Bladen 1965, Porter 1970).

The provinces responded to local pressure without considering system-
wide priorities. Premier Robarts of Ontario described a classic political pos-
ture in 1960, over whether a new university would be established in Peter-
borough. He said the government would wait, and base its decision on
where there was strong enough support from local communities. A similar
position was taken by Ontario's Minister of Education in the 1950s over
creating Lakehead University in Thunder Bay (Skolnick 1987, Axelrod
1982).

Patterns of growth remained institution-specific without national or
provincial character. More campuses dotted the landscape across the
country, in response to greater demand for higher education. Larger universities became the order of the day in every major urban centre, but there
was no overall design to the system. The provinces were unprepared for
planning. Except for a brief period between 1964 and 1971 in Ontario, none
had a separate department for university affairs. After 1971 Ontario
expanded the university portfolio to include colleges of applied arts and
technology. Everywhere else, responsibility for post-secondary education
was lodged within departments of education or colleges and universities.
Few of these departments engaged in system-wide or institution-specific
planning. They appeared to have little control over the accelerating expansion of universities and no overall vision. To address the ever-increasing

portion of their budgets going to universities, the provinces took two types of initiatives.

Between 1960 and 1974 every province sponsored a major inquiry into higher education. Some had an influence on expansion plans, such as royal commissions in Québec and New Brunswick in 1961, Prince Edward Island in 1964, and Newfoundland in 1968, and a 1962 inquiry in British Columbia. Québec's CEGEP system was based on recommendations of the 1964 Parent Royal Commission of Inquiry on Education. The multi-campus Université du Québec resulted from another recommendation of the commission. Other inquiries began long after expansion had begun, with royal commissions in Nova Scotia (1971) and Saskatchewan (1974), commissions of inquiry in Alberta and Ontario (1972), and a 1973 task force in Manitoba. These focussed on reorganizing and monitoring systems already in place.

The provinces set up conduits between government and universities, modelled on the British University Grants Committee, an intermediary body with an established record of managing university finances (Carswell 1985). Provincial bodies reviewed university plans and advised government on global budgets and allocations to each institution. A few (New Brunswick, Manitoba, and Alberta) possessed executive power to distribute money to universities and even to approve new programs (Manitoba, British Columbia, and Québec). They were established between 1963 and 1967 in Nova Scotia, Prince Edward Island, New Brunswick, Québec, Ontario, Manitoba, and Alberta and by 1974 in Saskatchewan and British Columbia, usually without any consultation with the universities themselves. Newfoundland joined an umbrella commission formed in 1974 for the four maritime provinces (Cameron 1991, Campbell 1982).

Intermediate bodies had a brief and ineffective life. Universities rarely supported them, since they were perceived more as arms of government than advocates for education. They remained secretive, refusing even to publish their proceedings. When provinces imposed budget cutbacks, intermediate bodies tended to pass them on without defending or supporting the interests of the universities. They served as filter between government and university, focussing on global budgets and leaving universities in charge of the details (Hurtubise & Rowat 1970, Cameron 1991).

Several provinces began to question their value. Alberta eventually terminated its Universities Commission and Universities Coordinating Council. A review of their short-lived existence concluded they did not carry out their respective mandates, rarely had contact with each other, and were so preoccupied with mundane matters that they failed to address issues of substance or concerns for planning (Campbell 1982). Saskatchewan terminated its Universities Commission in 1983, in response to university accusations that it was a costly and unnecessary bureaucracy. For similar reasons, British Columbia discontinued its Universities Council after pressure from university presidents. With or without these bodies, higher education seemed to move along at its own pace, lacking overall vision or direction for the system as a whole.

Once founded by legislative act, universities took on lives of their own, with wide latitude to proceed as they saw fit. Paul Axelrod has argued that this autonomy was due more to a long legacy of government indifference than to any concerted support for independence. Between 1917 and 1950 in Ontario there was not one recorded vote in the legislature on a university matter. Similar disinterest prevailed in every province. Blair Neatby has suggested provincial politicians devoted such scant attention to universities because it was in fact unnecessary: higher education already served the interests of provincial elites. Autonomy reflected a tacit agreement amongst the elite that universities were to serve the upper echelons of society (Axelrod 1982, Neatby 1987).

By the 1960s Canada's universities had shed much of their secular past and were on the way to being a significant force in the economy. They could create new programs as needed with minimal interference from government. There was little planning or coordination of the system during this crucial period of expansion. The provinces showed scant interest in universities even as they sprouted in haphazard fashion, creating high quality programs, improving accessibility, turning out graduates who prospered in the expanding economy, and consuming ever more public money.

Ottawa and the provinces had set a course that placed them in constant conflict over financing. Each level of government focussed on minimizing what it spent on post-secondary education. They were forced to devote considerable effort to financing, without ever properly planning, a system of higher education. These dynamics would exert heavy tolls when Ottawa and the provinces entered the budget-balancing era.

Chapter 3

Administrative Rule

The Conservative 1950s

ALTHOUGH THE UNIVERSITY ENVIRONMENT changed considerably during and after World War II, few attempted to alter the status quo. Universities remained conservative and stable until market conditions of the 1960s forced them to change.

Universities were in fact squarely in the mainstream of the widespread conservatism of the era. Professors were mostly male and, once hired, maintained gender privileges through higher salaries and senior rank. Few women attained the station of associate or full professor, and by 1960–61 they made up only 11.2 percent of the 6,455 full-time faculty in Canada and held only 58 full professorships, compared to 1,554 held by men (Statistics Canada 1991). This imbalance did not change appreciably during the hiring booms of the 1950s and 1960s.The student body was also predominantly male, and from middle and upper income backgrounds. In 1955–56 women comprised just 25 percent of undergraduates, and there was limited student access for people from disadvantaged groups (Ford 1985, Porter 1970).

Universities possessed an aura of shared governance marked by informal, collegial relations between faculty and administration, an *academic community* where professors enjoyed freedom to carry out their work. Administrative hierarchies were relatively flat. Department heads reported to deans who had only vice-presidents and president above them. Professors were not ruled by any other chains of command, and few officials appeared to exercise much authority over them. They could do pretty much as they saw fit in the classroom, without threat of appeal from students or discipline by officials. Terms such as equity, fair procedure, due process, student rights, affirmative action, and sexual harassment were not yet part of the vocabulary.

Cut from a conservative cloth, management belied this collegial air. Small numbers of people in senior positions made most of the important decisions. A hierarchical command structure gave senior administrators authority over resources. Presidents, who usually had permanent appointments with no fixed term, wielded supreme authority. Boards of governors set budgets and policies, and administrators controlled implementation. Board and administration were authorized to run universities without participation by faculty, students, or anyone else in the system. (Millett 1962).

Professors were rarely consulted, even on the choice of president, vice-president, or senior officers. Deans, who often came from within their own faculties, were typically appointed by presidents without any formal input from members of the faculties over which they presided. Donald Rowat's 1956 analysis of legislation, calendars and bylaws of the 35 member institutions of the NCCU found just four out of 35 universities where faculty had a voice in choosing either presidents or deans (Rowat 1957).

Decision-making used a bicameral system: a lay board of governors for financial matters and an academic senate for educational issues. This structure contributed to the air of shared power, where senate controlled the content of the university and board approved the financial wherewithal to carry it out. In practice, boards were senior to senates and held ultimate authority to manage the entire institution. Subject only to senate's advice on academic policy, they determined overall direction and controlled policies, budgets, programs, hiring, firing, salaries, and benefits.

Senates set admission and graduation standards, approved programs and courses, and awarded degrees. Theoretically in charge of educational policy, they acted chiefly as a rubber stamp for routine approval of minor business. Presidents, senior administrators, and boards of governors ruled over matters of major import. Senates were located between the more senior boards of governors, to which they deferred on university-wide matters, and junior bodies like faculty councils for course and curriculum issues, whose submissions they were expected to approve (Duff & Berdahl 1966).

Senate was supposed to be faculty's voice, to openly debate core policies, and govern programs, curriculum, and courses. But most campus senates held closed meetings dominated by presidents and administrators. Faculty usually comprised a minority on a body made up of alumni, outside persons with special interests in higher education, government appointees, and large contingents of administrators. Rowat's study found only 13 of 35 universities with elected faculty on senate or any other governing body, and at seven of the 13 they held less than one-third of the seats. Even by 1962, just 36 percent of the University of Toronto's 165-member senate was elected by faculty, compared to 59 percent chosen by alumni. Seven of McMaster's 35 senators were selected by faculty, 15 out of 41 at Manitoba, and nine of 38 at McGill. Queen's was an exception, with 12 faculty on a 19-member senate (Duff & Berdahl 1966, Rowat 1956, Cohen 1964).

Typically composed of people from outside universities, boards of governors offered fewer opportunities than senates for faculty or student participation. Provincial governments appointed the majority of board members for public universities, while boards at private institutions perpetuated themselves since outgoing members elected their successors. McGill was a classic example in the early 1960s: its board chose 24 of its 29 members. These undemocratic methods produced homogeneous boards rarely in touch with the constituents they were supposed to govern. Members were recruited mostly from business, selected for their services in fund-raising or expertise in financial management but less well suited to higher education policy-making (Reid 1964, Duff & Berdahl 1966).

Teaching staff were mostly forbidden to join boards of governors, while students were simply excluded. These practices dated to the 1906 University of Toronto Act which stipulated a lay board of governors on the United States model of governance by barring faculty, contrary to the British practice of having faculty represented at all levels of the institution. The pattern of exclusion was emulated across the country. Even by the mid-1950s only one campus allowed faculty on its board: St. Francis Xavier University, with three faculty on its 30-member Board of Governors (Cameron 1991, Abbott 1985).

Presidents wielded power through top-down administrations that set policies and budgets for board approval. Senior administrators and deans ruled on requests for sabbaticals, arranged workload and course assignments, determined salaries, benefits, and merit increases, confirmed promotions, imposed discipline, hired and fired, and established expenditures for faculties and schools. Offices of central administration in the 1950s were smaller and less formal than their descendants two decades later but still run hierarchically, with minimal input from faculty, other employees, or students. This was a period described by W.M. Sibley as the *Age of Authority*, when management was based on custom and convention, with few, if any, written rules of order or codes of conduct (Sibley 1976).

Administrators shaped the teaching environment through setting course section sizes and determining the money available for grading assistants. Large sections virtually demand lecture format and preclude running seminar discussions without a sufficiently large number of teaching assistants. Grading exams and papers in large classes is notoriously time-consuming. If grading becomes too onerous, and there is no money to hire graders, instructors may assign short-answer (or, in the present day, computer-graded) multiple-choice tests which eat up far less time, even though they are less effective instruments for learning.

Their financial decisions determined the teaching environment, but administrators could not control the academic staff whose salaries made up the largest item in the budget. This was because universities maintained a separation between administration and academic work, on the premise that effective teaching and research depend upon independent scholars using their expertise and following their interests. Faculty were obliged to teach courses assigned by deans and department heads, but made their own decisions about content, textbooks, assigned reading, methods and style of teaching, and student evaluation.

Research was even less amenable to administrative rule. Administrators could not influence research to the same degree as teaching because they could not control grants from sources outside the university. Further, research encompassed a wide range of activities: reviewing literature, delving into archives, carrying out surveys, interviews or experiments, analysing data, preparing grant proposals, and writing articles. Faculty determined subject matter and research methodology, deciding whether to work alone, collaborate with local colleagues, or join with researchers in other parts of the world. Given this degree of autonomy, many faculty claimed ownership of their work, even though it was carried out as employees of the university.

During the quieter 1950s, professors seemed content to engage in their work and leave running the university to boards and administrators, rarely confronting people in the administrative hierarchy. Autonomy and the intrinsic satisfaction of engagement with one's work appeared to compensate for exclusion from the university's corridors of power, poor working conditions, and low rates of pay. This status was destined to change. Poor working conditions could not coexist with the market realities of the 1960s. Greater demand for their labour gave professors more bargaining power.

Limits to Academic Freedom

Low professorial compensation pervaded the 1950s. Money was simply not available from universities whose funding could not meet their needs. For more than a decade after the war, the steady growth in enrolment stretched limited physical and human resources to the limit. Professors were underpaid and overworked. Without salary structures, they received ad hoc increases far below the level of other professionals. Senior administrators enjoyed more privileges, better compensation, and superior working conditions, but professors rarely made a fuss over these matters.

In 1951 the Massey Commission pressed for federal money to raise academics' deplorable rates of pay. University presidents lobbied for funds to improve compensation. F. Cyril James, Principal and Vice-Chancellor at McGill, noted in his 1952–53 annual report that unreasonably high faculty workloads coexisted with compensation far behind other fields (Abbott 1985). Sydney Smith, president of the University of Toronto, stated in 1956 that faculty were pressed into "genteel poverty…. Too few Canadian universities can pay salaries that are even close to being commensurate with the value of the services received" (Smith 1956, 195).

A 1956 survey by the National Research Council showed academics' earnings compared poorly to other professions. Ph.D.s in Canada started at $6,520 in industry and $5,520 in government, but only $3,500 for the highest starting salary as lecturer at the University of Toronto (Woodside 1958). From 1940 to 1954, faculty salaries failed to keep up with inflation, as real income declined by 3 percent. Physicians' pretax earnings rose by 80 percent. Earnings across Canada varied beyond amounts justified by differences in cost of living (Buckley 1954 & 1955). By the late 1950s the CAUT pressed for minimum national standards on salaries, pensions, and sabbaticals (Abbott 1985).

Other perquisites were not much better. A 1956 study of conditions at 23 Canadian universities and 25 in the United States found wide variation in regulations and practices for sabbaticals. Only six surveyed universities had formal sabbatical policies; Acadia, Alberta, Dalhousie, Memorial, Queen's, and Saskatchewan. Thirteen with no policies granted leaves at full or partial salary to professors who pursued scholarly research; four had no provision at all for sabbaticals (University of British Columbia Faculty Association 1956).

Even though expected to attend scholarly conferences to present research papers, professors received little money for travel and commonly covered these expenses from their own pockets. Professors were frequently required to share offices and telephones in cramped quarters. Support services were minimal for the typing of manuscripts and articles. Professors could not count on these services unless they raised additional money through research grants.

These matters were not sufficient cause for professors to challenge the status quo. Low compensation and mediocre working conditions were a matter of concern, but they were balanced by the freedom academics enjoyed to carry out satisfying work.

Threats to tenure and academic freedom proved a different matter. Protecting these fundamental aspects of their work eventually drove faculty toward unionization. We will see this theme repeated in the following chapters.

TENURE prevents employers from dismissing professors unless they are shown to be incompetent or display unprofessional conduct. Even layoffs are precluded, except under extraordinary financial circumstances endangering a faculty or an entire university.

ACADEMIC FREEDOM allows tenured professors to speak their mind without repercussion from employers. They cannot be disciplined or dismissed for what they say or believe, no matter how far they may stray from prevailing norms.

Although the principle of tenure has long been established, practice was far from optimal. Before it was strengthened through collective bargaining, tenure was enforced by understandings or unspoken agreements that were easily abrogated. It rarely had formal protection in policies, contracts, or legislation. Practices were guided by moral suasion and ideology rather than written policies. Professors could be dismissed for stating unpopular opinions or criticizing their employers. Presidents and boards were free to remove professors on their own initiative or in response to pressure from politicians or the press. Professors might be safe under supportive presidents, or on precarious ground under presidents or boards who wavered at defending their freedom to voice unacceptable or inappropriate opinions. These employers reprimanded, suspended, and dismissed professors who spoke against the status quo in government, business or the university. Penalties were difficult to overturn, as there was virtually no appeal to third parties (Whalley 1964, Abbott 1984, Horn 1979, 1984, Monahan 1984).

Long before the issue became contentious in Canada, egregious violations of academic freedom prompted formation of the American Association of University Professors. In 1915, Professor Scott Nearing, assistant professor at the Wharton School of Finance and Commerce, was dismissed by the University of Pennsylvania for espousing radical and untested theories to his students. The dismissal and reasons by the Board of Trustees were supported by numerous alumni, despite Prof. Nearing's performance being deemed satisfactory. In the same year, 17 faculty resigned from the University of Utah to protest several dismissals by the Board of Regents. Dr. A. A. Knowlton was fired, according to President Kingsbury, because he "has worked against the administration of the University. Dr. Knowlton has also spoken very disrespectfully of the Chairman of the Board of Regents. My opinion is that respect is due the Regents... and that therefore the author of such remarks should not be retained in the employment of the University." President Kingsbury also dismissed professor George C. Wise because "I am convinced that Professor Wise has spoken in a depreciatory way about the University before his classes, and that he has also spoken in a very uncomplimentary way about the administration" (Metzger 1977).

Academic freedom was usually respected within Canadian universities, but freedom to speak out beyond campus borders was not as widely condoned. Intolerance of views that strayed from a narrow mainstream perspective was widespread. When academics spoke out against political or economic injustice, or voiced unpopular opinions, they risked direct repercussions from employers. Openly disagreeing with university policies, especially within sectarian institutions, could land them in serious trouble. These problems eventually came to a head in prominent cases where faculty were dismissed for what they said rather than over their competence.

Several cases surfaced between the 1930s and 1950s of universities punishing left-wing academics following attacks by politicians and the press for expressing partisan socialist or liberal views. They included prominent academics like Frank H. Underhill at the University of Toronto, E.A. Havelock and W.H. Alexander at Alberta, E.A. Forsey and F.R. Scott at McGill, R.A. MacKay at Dalhousie, and J. King Gordon at United Theological College in Montréal. Carlyle King at the University of Saskatchewan, A.R.M. Lower at United College and G.M.A Grube at Trinity College, Toronto, were pursued for expressing disloyalty to Canada's ties with Britain (Horn 1982).

Tenure offered no protection for Professors Salem Bland and A.J. Irwin of Winnipeg. In June 1917 they were dismissed from Wesley College, an affiliate of the University of Manitoba. Bland, who had a 14-year record of teaching and service in the Theological Department, was also an outspoken advocate of the left-wing Social Gospel, and acknowledged as a friend of labour and a pacifist. Official grounds for the terminations were financial, but the college was openly criticized for political motivation. The case was appealed to the college board and the Methodist Court of Appeal, without success. Since there was no organization to assist or represent them, Bland and Irwin had to undertake the appeals on their own.

Financial justification was also used in the case of King Gordon, fired in 1933 from United Theological College in Montréal. Gordon was a critic of corporate activities who advocated applying Christian ethics to the social system. His views were unpopular with business members of the board, especially A.O. Dawson of Canadian Cottons and Sir Charles Gordon of Dominion Textiles. Speculation that Gordon's dismissal was political rather than financial grew when the college board rejected an offer from an outside source of additional money to cover his salary. Gordon did not obtain another teaching job at a Canadian university until well after World War II (Abbott 1984, Horn 1980, 1981).

More direct attacks did not resort to financial artifices. In 1940, Frank Underhill, a University of Toronto historian, founding member and first national president of the left-wing League for Social Reconstruction and the Cooperative Commonwealth Federation (CCF), was assailed for stating that the United States was more important to Canada's security than the United Kingdom. Enraged empire loyalists demanded his dismissal. Ontario Premier Mitchell Hepburn, supported by Leader of the Opposition George Drew, suggested that grants to the university might be reduced unless people like Underhill were removed from their posts. Members of the board of governors and university President Reverend Henry John Cody urged Underhill to resign. Underhill refused, and managed to retain his job due to strong support from distinguished colleagues like Harold Innis, who presented to Cody letters from prominent faculty members threatening to resign if Underhill was dismissed (Abbott 1984, Francis 1975, Horn 1982b).

This was not the first time Underhill was chastised for his political views. In 1933, he and E.A. Havelock, a classicist at Victoria College, were encouraged by their employers to resign from the provincial executive of the Ontario CCF clubs. Havelock created a stir during the 1937 auto workers' strike in Oshawa by criticizing Premier Hepburn and Colonel Samuel McLaughlin, founder of General Motors in Canada. The provincial government exhorted Victoria College to dismiss Havelock. Underhill and Havelock held their positions, but the attacks had an impact. To avoid censure for his socialist views, Underhill used a pseudonym for 51 of 54 articles and editorials he contributed to the *Canadian Forum* in the late

1930s. After his close brush with dismissal in 1940, he published anonymous public affairs commentaries for several years (Horn 1980, Abbott 1984).

In June 1949, the University of Alberta board of governors dismissed biochemistry professor George Hunter, a pacifist, and known supporter of the Edmonton Peace Council, an affiliate of the Communist Party of Canada. Hunter also attended meetings fostering friendship between Canada and the Soviet Union. In April 1949, 17 of the 257 students in his course signed a petition complaining that Professor Hunter had used the occasion of his last lecture of the term to discuss the negative aspects of war, denounce the decision to use the atomic bomb on Japan, and criticize the formation of NATO. The board did not give Hunter the reasons for his dismissal, nor afford him an opportunity to respond to these accusations. Hunter left Canada for England, where he worked in a laboratory but never taught in a university again (Horn 1999).

The University of Toronto eased Professor Leopold Infeld out of his job for no apparent reason other than bad publicity. A prominent theoretical physicist, Infeld worked with Einstein during the war and coauthored *The Evolution of Physics*. His 1949 application for a year's leave to visit his native Poland gave rise to accusations by *The Ensign*, a small Catholic weekly, that he intended to pass atomic secrets to the Soviet Union. In 1950 George Drew, leader of the opposition, accused Infeld in the House of Commons of being a potential traitor. President Sydney Smith of the University of Toronto refused Professor Infeld's request for leave. Infeld eventually resigned and left Canada for Poland, where he continued a distinguished career until his death in 1968 (Horn 1999, Abbott 1985).

Tenure and academic freedom offered a thin veil of protection easily penetrated by politicians, business executives or members of the press. Professors' full freedom of speech was limited to the confines of their respective institutions, and even then only if they avoided offending members of governing bodies, prominent politicians, or business persons. They could be attacked for what they said in public or the classroom on political or religious matters outside their area of expertise. The small number of prominent cases was a constant reminder of the risks in speaking out of turn. Without backing from a university president or well-placed colleagues, professors could be censured, disciplined, coerced to resign, or flatly dismissed.

Harry Crowe's dismissal, the most prominent academic freedom case in Canada, garnered national attention from the press and aroused active debate by faculty across the country. In 1958 the Board of Regents of Winnipeg's United College, a Presbyterian institution with a teaching staff of 50, dismissed Professor Crowe for a personal letter he wrote to colleague W.A. Packer criticizing the board for pressuring faculty to contribute to the building fund. He also made biting comments about ministers involved in public administration. Packer never received the letter; a month after it was written, the letter appeared on the desk of the college's Principal, Rev. W.C. Lockhart. The board fired Crowe for being dismissive of the college's purposes and showing disrespect and disloyalty to the administration.

Professor Crowe had no hearing, nor was he granted an appeal. On the prompting of the Queen's University faculty association, the CAUT became involved in its first investigation of an academic freedom case. A committee chaired by V.C. Fowke of Saskatchewan recommended Crowe's reinstatement, on the grounds that the dismissal by United College was arbitrary, without cause, and a violation of his academic freedom. Soon after the committee released its report, Crowe's colleagues J.H. Stewart Reid, Kenneth McNaught and R.M. Stingle publicly indicated their intention to resign in protest unless Crowe was reinstated. The board agreed to reinstate Crowe, but refused to reconsider the three resignations. Ultimately Crowe and 13 of his colleagues resigned from the college (Savage & Holmes 1975, Campbell 1991).

Serious confrontations like these were rare. Most academics were not disciplined because their behaviour remained within acceptable bounds. Nonetheless tenure and academic freedom were not secure, especially for those who pushed the frontiers of convention. Threats of sanctions were sufficient to forestall "unsuitable" behaviour or the issuing of "radical" or "unacceptable" statements.

Freedom of expression varied from campus to campus. In the 1930s Queen's and McGill were reasonably tolerant of professors' left-wing political involvement, but the University of Toronto did not take kindly to professors expressing leftist positions. The University of Alberta took a hard line on conventional political involvement. In 1935, the board of governors prohibited all faculty from running in federal elections after William Hardy Alexander, a classicist, was nominated by the CCF in the constituency of Edmonton West (Horn 1980, Underhill 1936).

Academics had few sources of support when disciplined for espousing radical or unpopular positions. Faculty associations had no legal standing to represent them or to negotiate on their behalf and were mainly oriented to academic and professional issues, with no experience in bargaining or grievances. Formal grievance procedures were not yet available on any campus. Professors' only recourse was political pressure upon presidents and boards of governors. These conditions changed as the CAUT began to defend academic freedom and tenure.

Defending Academic Freedom: CAUT Appeals

The CAUT formed later than comparable organizations in the United States and Britain. The American Association of University Professors (AAUP) organized in 1915 to address violations of academic freedom. The Association of University Teachers (AUT) in Britain was established in 1919.

The CAUT was preceded by the NCCU, formed by university presidents and deans in 1911, the National Federation of Canadian University Students (NFCUS) in 1921, and the Canadian Association of University Business Officers in 1938. Canadian academics had not previously faced serious pressures or crises. Overt attacks on academic freedom were limited to a handful of cases.

The CAUT was inaugurated when just eight faculty associations existed across the country, at Alberta, Toronto, Queen's, McGill, Laval, Saskatchewan, British Columbia, and McMaster. Consensus was growing among Canadian academics on the need for a national organization to forestall being absorbed into the AAUP, which already had a few Canadian members. Professors from the University of Alberta and Queen's University convened a meeting during the 1950 Learned Societies meetings at Royal Military College to consider concrete proposals for a national organization. A provisional committee organized the founding meeting of the CAUT in Montréal, in June 1951, during the sessions of the Learned Societies at McGill.

The organization's initial focus was on matters related to compensation and benefits; in light of their dismal levels, salaries were an obvious starting point. Interventions to reform governance, protect academic freedom and support unionization came later. The first CAUT publication was a 1952 national salary survey that showed earnings increases well below inflation. Associate professors' median salaries rose by 25.4 percent between 1940 and 1950, compared to a 57.7 percent increase in the cost of living. Low earnings and major regional differences in pay scales drove the CAUT lobbying effort for a national scale with higher salaries. Its first proposed scale was published in 1957. These positions on compensation were supported by university presidents, who decried the low salaries they were able to pay (Abbott 1985).

Even by the time of the Crowe case at United College in 1958, the CAUT still operated without a national office, staffed entirely by members' volunteer labour. Membership covered 78 percent of Canadian university teachers, with 26 faculty associations and 3,400 full-time faculty. CAUT services were mainly informational: annual salary surveys and the yearly *Income Tax Guide* started in 1953. The *CAUT Bulletin* launched in the same year concentrated on university government, salaries, productivity, and the declining status of the university in Canada.

By 1956, efforts expanded to include lobbying, starting with a brief to the Royal Commission on Canada's Economic Prospects (Gordon Commission). *The University Teacher and the Crisis of Higher Education in Canada* urged the federal government to acknowledge the importance of universities, double its grants for education, and establish the Canada Council for student scholarships. The Commission responded favourably, with a request for an analysis of salaries that the CAUT delivered in November 1956 in its newly approved national salary scale, with proposals for modest minimum salaries for lecturer, assistant, associate, and full professor. A 1958 report on income taxation launched lobbying to allow tax deduction of professional expenses for books, travel and tuition fees (Fowke 1964).

After working on Crowe's dismissal the CAUT began regularly to defend professors against wrongful discipline. Further investigation after the Fowke Committee's report revealed that tenure was poorly protected right across the country. In September 1959, the CAUT established a Standing Committee on Academic Freedom and Tenure, hired an Executive Secretary, and opened a national office. Formal investigation procedures for academic freedom and tenure disputes were established in 1960 (Neatby 1985, Fowke 1964, Monahan 1970).

The very existence of CAUT appeals made a significant difference in relations between faculty and administration. A national organization gave faculty both an extra measure of protection and a greater degree of confidence in asserting themselves with employers. CAUT backing put employers on notice that they could be monitored by a third party with the resources to investigate and publicize the findings. The prospect of national attention was often sufficient impetus to settle a controversy.

Until the late 1950s professors endured conservative governance, low compensation, weak protection of academic freedom, and poor working conditions. They enjoyed freedom of speech in teaching but were constrained in voicing views on controversial issues or challenging the status quo. They were poorly represented on university governing bodies and had no organizations of their own with standing to challenge managerial authority.

Market forces in the strong economy of the 1950s and 1960s eventually created conditions for cracking this traditional conservative mold. Unprecedented expansion left very little of the university system untouched—including the ways it was governed.

Chapter 4
Moderating Conservative Traditions

The university is so many things to so many different people that it must, of necessity, be partially at war with itself (Clark Kerr 1963).

CLARK KERR WROTE THIS REFLECTION on the eve of turmoil upon campuses in Canada and the United States, and across the globe. In the 1960s the campus became a laboratory for radical transformation. Students and faculty challenged corporate and state policies, and questioned conservative traditions in most aspects of university life. Calls for reform were louder and more frequent on university campuses than anywhere else, perhaps because of the pressures to which Kerr alluded.

This was at bottom an optimistic period. The Depression and World War II had marked Canadians with insecurity but had a much smaller impact on the postwar generation. Students of the 1960s matured in a far more secure era, having never directly experienced either war or rampant economic depression. Unemployment remained low and incomes rose throughout the decade. Those practically guaranteed a good job after their university degrees were understandably more secure in challenging the status quo.

Governments increased spending to expand programs and devise new ones. Post-secondary education was one of the major beneficiaries. Throughout the 1960s and early 1970s, universities were flush with new money. The system grew rapidly, with ever more students and new facilities to accommodate them. Financing rose at a pace that seemed almost to meet universities' insatiable appetite for funds. Accessibility improved for women and those requiring financial assistance.

Public sector largesse was bolstered by business, which saw post-secondary education as both a profitable investment for the nation and directly beneficial to the companies that built and serviced the system. Education as an investment was a significant departure from conventional views of public spending as pure cost, and as a result universities began to receive substantial support as a choice investment for the future. The Economic Council of Canada estimated that the return on investment in education of 10 to 15 percent was superior to most other ventures, even when all private and public costs were included (Economic Council of Canada 1965). A year later the Council reiterated its support for increased spending, arguing that education greatly enhanced the productivity of labour (Bertram 1966).

The pace of change on campus accelerated. Universities became larger, with more young faculty and more students from a widening range of backgrounds. Revolt and rebellion were also in the air as the campus became a centre for antiwar protests, especially against United States military involvement in Vietnam. Student political activism spread to include power relations within the university, with demands for more progressive academic content and greater participation in governance. Faculty eagerly joined the press for change. With far better job opportunities than ever before, they could choose among offers from competing employers. This factor alone pushed their salaries upwards. Professors used their new-found security and status to press for governance reforms, arguing that traditional authoritarian means were not suited to large size and rapid change.

Growth in the 1960s

University enrolment grew by nearly 300 percent between 1955 and 1968, compared to a 45 percent increase in the population. Demographic change was only part of the reason: participation for people between 18 and 25 increased from 4.7 to 11.4 percent. Enrolment might have peaked once the baby boom generation worked its way through the system and began to exit in the 1970s. Growth continued because more people at all ages sought university degrees (Porter 1970, Pike 1970, Bladen 1965, Johnson 1984).

Female enrolment rose from less than 26 percent of full-time students in 1960–61 to almost 40 percent in the mid-1970s. (By the late 1980s women would form the majority of full-time students.) Part-time enrolment was another important aspect of the overall enrolment increase. It rose from small numbers (exact data are not available for 1960), to 164,200 in 1974–75, about one-third of all registered students. Women made up almost 55 percent of part-time undergraduates. From 1970 to 1975, the number of people graduating with degrees, diplomas, or certificates rose from 76,500 to 103,000 (see Table A-2).

Improved student financial assistance supported the enrolment growth. Scholarships and bursaries provided by the provinces rose from $2.2 million in 1957–58 to $35.2 million in 1969–70. Total loans from government for full-time undergraduates, including CEGEPs, increased from $1 million to $58.7 million over the same period. The Canada Student Loan Plan, started in 1964, with a separate plan in Québec, guaranteed loans from banks and credit unions of up to $1,000 based on need, and paid the interest until six months after graduation. Other sources of federal aid included the Canadian International Development Agency, Department of External Affairs, National Research Council, Medical Research Council, and Canada Council (Pike 1970, Hurtubise & Rowat 1970).

The university system grew in every direction. Small church-based colleges merged with each other or joined larger secular institutions. Colleges expanded, acquiring degree-granting privileges and university status. Long-established universities embarked on major construction, while entirely new institutions were built from the ground up.

More new money was invested in higher education than during any other period, in terms of capital expansion and higher operating costs. Initial cost estimates could be exceeded several times over in order to finance grandiose schemes. In Newfoundland, estimates approved in the late 1960s of $12 million to expand Memorial University surpassed $100 million by the early 1970s (Cameron 1991, Smallwood 1973).

Growth was intense between 1959 and 1969. Eighteen new universities were founded: eight in Ontario, two each in Manitoba, Alberta, and British Columbia, and one each in New Brunswick, Nova Scotia, Prince Edward Island, and Québec. One of the 18 was the Université du Québec, with eight new campuses, in Montréal (1968); Chicoutimi (1968); Sainte-Foy (1969); Trois Rivieres (1969); Rouyn (1970); Hull (1970); Rimouski (1973); and École Technologie supérieure, Montréal (1974). This far outpaced the 1950s, when four universities were established, or the 1970s, with five new campuses.

By 1965 British Columbia had four universities serving 22,500 students, compared to 14,700 just three years earlier at University of British Columbia and Victoria College. Once Québec approved statutory support for universities, grants rose from $13 million in 1959–60 to $68.7 million in 1965-66 (Harris 1966). Ontario's spending on higher education increased from under one to 11 percent of the provincial budget between 1965 and 1969 (Axelrod 1982).

During this time proposals for new programs and requests for funds were almost routinely approved by government. Some provinces even encouraged universities to table more elaborate plans for expansion than were initially proposed. Ontario welcomed initiatives from communities to found new universities and encouraged them to extend their horizons. York University's planners were persuaded by the province's Advisory Committee on University Affairs to set ambitious targets to meet long-term needs. Support was equally forthcoming for new programs. Provincial authorities routinely ratified new graduate programs approved by the Ontario Council on Graduate Studies, an affiliate of the Committee of Presidents of the Provincially Assisted Universities of Ontario (CPUO) (Neatby 1987).

Corporations lobbied for post-secondary education to meet their growing demand for college graduates. They also stood to gain from the considerable investment in campus construction. Business people were directly involved in preparing proposals for new campuses and sitting on their governing bodies. Corporate representatives dominated York University's board from its inception in 1959. Robert Winters, chairman of Rio Tinto Mines, headed the first board of governors, joined by representatives from the Toronto-Dominion Bank, Maple Leaf Mills, Wood Gundy, the Bank of Nova Scotia, and General Motors of Canada. Between 1960 and 1963 the board added members from the Robert Simpson Company, T. Eaton Company, People's Credit Jeweller's, Macmillan Company of Canada, Salada Foods, Canada Packers, Canada Wire & Cable Company, and the accounting firm of Clarkson Gordon. William Mahoney, vice-president of the Canadian Labour Congress and national director of the United Steelworkers of America, was the sole member from labour (Axelrod 1982).

Extensive corporate involvement was crucial to Brock University's 1962 formation. The founders' committee comprised 19 influential business and political leaders of the Niagara Region. Substantial corporate backing was responsible for the University of Waterloo's considerable financial success. The curriculum used a co-operative engineering model that began in 1959 with 250 participating companies. Trent University was built on a 100-acre site donated by Canadian General Electric Company. Earlier initiatives by Reginald R. Faryon, president of Quaker Oats Company, were crucial to its 1964 founding. By November 1963 private sector donors had contributed $2 million towards the founding. Business involvement was central to a $51 million expansion at the University of Toronto in 1958, to double enrolment over the following decade (Axelrod 1982).

Corporate influence extended well beyond the initial creation of a campus. Executives of major corporations influenced university policies on an ongoing basis (Axelrod 1982). John Porter noted in *The Vertical Mosaic* that 80 members of the economic elite sat on boards of governors of the 15 major Canadian universities (Porter 1965). By 1972, 240 members of

Canada's elite held governing positions in private schools, universities and other institutions of higher learning (Clement 1975).

University growth was multifarious, stimulated by money for research and teaching from government, business, and foundations. Universities were expected to educate a labour force that required far more breadth and depth of programs, many of them in expensive fields of science, engineering, and professions. Private sector employers required graduates with advanced training for executive, managerial, and technical positions. Business schools added new courses in international finance and marketing to meet demand from global corporations. Engineering and computer science programs responded to unquenchable thirst for system designers and programmers. Government sought trained teachers, social workers, and health professionals to staff expanding welfare state services. Universities required more staff with Ph.Ds for new and expanding programs in education, urban and environmental studies, computer sciences, advanced business administration, public administration, and emerging new technologies.

Universities thus became far more diversified, with new interdisciplinary programs and institutes, and varied methods of course delivery. Opportunities multiplied for research grants and consulting contracts which enriched academic careers while offering money and prestige to the host university. Funded research gave faculty authority to hire research assistants, purchase equipment and supplies, travel to conferences and research sites, and arrange flexible work schedules. They could reduce teaching loads by buying out the time with grant money.

Expansion stretched the bounds of tradition to create the *multiversity* —large, complex institutions which forever altered the face of higher education. Multiversities addressed extensive market demand for greater quantity, diversity, and quality with sprawling campuses and extensive programs. The spread of the multiversity was eclectic and pluralistic, encompassing traditional faculties, schools, departments, interdisciplinary programs, specialized institutes, and colleges.

Rapid expansion created challenges beyond the scope of traditional administration. Covering far greater territory than ever before, universities were still run by former faculty expert in various academic fields, but not in administration or management. Senior administrators still had formal authority to manage the system, but found it far more difficult to cope with the increased complexity of the contemporary campus. Management systems had not kept up with the pace of change. There was a core contradiction in the way universities were run, with a decentralized system for academic initiatives and a centralized one for administration.

Universities entered the decade with conservative, authoritarian, centralized administration geared to small, homogeneous, and stable institutions. This kind of administration was ill-suited to the transformation and diversity of the 1960s. Increasing pressure to revise traditional forms of rule, and the sheer volume of decisions in large, complex institutions, required greater participation in procedures for hiring, tenure, promotions, curriculum planning, student affairs, and expenditure management. Centralized direction was far too slow and cumbersome. Officials at the top could not stay well enough informed on all matters for which they were responsible. Many decisions could be made more efficiently at department, institute, or program levels rather than by presidents or senior officers not involved in day-to-day operations.

Changes in this direction were already far advanced in the United States. An extensive research project at Stanford University found strong trends towards decentralized administration. Investigators gathered data on academic governance from 9,500 faculty and administration respondents at 300 colleges and universities. The majority of large institutions reported greater decentralization and autonomy in academic decision-making, down to departmental levels dominated by strong chairs or small groups of professors. But slightly more than one-quarter of large institutions still reported central domination of decision-making by administrators, boards, and cliques of professors (Baldridge 1963).

Academic policy is supposed to originate with professors. Critics within academia argued that concentration of power at the top was inappropriate. In 1964 a group of professors active in the CAUT tabled a powerful critique of centralization and issued a list of demands to make administrative structures and procedures appropriate to the university. Their proposals synthesized views of faculty across the country pressing for more democratic administration. Their main proposals put the case boldly and succinctly:

> 1. That the monarchic-paternalistic position of the President or Principal be redirected by drawing the academic staff and governing Board into closer and more continuous relation. At present, the only regular point of contact between the Board and the academic staff is the President, who is thus in a position to control the volume and kind of communication that takes place and to determine to a large extent the sphere of governmental activity of both the academic community and the Board....

2. That the centre of gravity of university government be placed, as was evidently the intention of some Canadian charters, upon the Senate as the supreme academic authority and principal governmental body in initiating legislation upon every aspect of university life. This is not necessarily a suggestion that the Senate replace the governing Board, but that the Senate assume responsibility for all matters that intimately touch the academic life of the university…. The Senate should normally be a purely academic body with no lay members, unless in some circumstances the active relation between Senate and Board would be improved by some degree of joint membership.

3. That the constitution of the governing Boards be altered to include comprehensive representation of the academic community, so that although no academic issue may be "pushed through" without the scrutiny of laymen, no decision touching upon the life of the university can be passed without the scrutiny and assent of those who are intimately committed to the life and work of the university.

4.…[T]he functions of a reformed Board would be of two kinds: *(a)* highly specialized activities for which the professional experience of lay members would best prepare them, such as matters of investment, fund-raising, formal representations to government, industry, and commerce; and *(b)* formal or hieratic functions in passing *de jure* upon what the Senate and President represent as the needs and wishes of the university.…

5. That the democratic principle of election be introduced, with appropriate restraints and formalities, so that the academic community shall have a clear voice in choosing a President and in appointments to senior academic posts. The academic community should also have an increased voice in the election of members of the governing Board, beyond the election of its own representatives, this being a reasonable restraint upon inbreeding and the self-perpetuation of the Boards.

6. That all reforms of university government be codified and established by overt regulation, as far as possible within the structure and authority of existing charters; and that if any existing charter makes such reforms impossible, action be taken to revise the charter appropriately (Whalley 1964, 164–5).

By 1966 the Duff-Berdahl commission, sponsored by the CAUT and AUCC, echoed these concerns. Sir James Duff and Robert Berdahl wrote about boards alienated from the institutions they directed and dominated by members from outside the university. They observed weak and ineffective senates. University presidents were seen to be exercising excessive control and inappropriate rule. Commission proposals called for more effective senates and stronger input by academic employees (Duff & Berdahl 1966).

Faculty and students pushed for reform throughout the decade. Politically active students demanded a role in university affairs. As conditions of employment improved, faculty were empowered to demand reforms from presidents and boards of governors. The system began to respond to increasingly vocal and forceful demands for change.

Governance Reform

William Sibley aptly referred to the 1960s as an *Age of Participation*, characterized by easing of strict rule from the top. Formalizing previously ad hoc practices made administrators more accountable. They were now required to abide by written regulations and policies for conduct, grievances, tenure, discipline, and dismissal. New faculty and student rights compelled presidents and boards of governors to take their advice before making final decisions (Sibley 1976).

Reform spread quickly. One pertinent example was opening up the meetings of boards of governors and senates to observers. Until the 1960s these meetings were closed: faculty, students, or members of the public could not attend unless specifically invited. Boards and senates gradually made their meetings public, and allowed participation by faculty and students. By 1970, boards were still dominated by outsiders, who held 72 percent of all positions at Canadian universities. Administrative officers held 13 percent, faculty 11 percent, and students 4 percent. Even though their 11 percent membership was small, at least some faculty were beginning to appear on most boards of governors. Elected faculty representatives were on 43 out of 59 surveyed university boards, a considerable change from the mid-1950s when just one board in the entire country had a faculty member on it. Students held elected seats on 28 boards in 1970 and 49 by 1975, up from zero in 1965 (Cameron 1991).

Faculty had a greater presence on senate, but it was still well below an appropriate level. Professors held 55 percent of senate seats in 1965. This was a slim majority for the university's senior academic forum that was supposed to be the voice of faculty on academic policy. Administrative officers had 27 percent, students 2 percent and others 18 percent. Donald Rowat, who published these figures, claimed the 55 percent for faculty appeared to be an increase over a decade earlier, although his comparisons could not be definitive since data were collected on different bases. After 1965, the major change in senate composition was an increase in student membership to 9 percent by 1970. Faculty were at 54 percent, administrative officers at 25 percent and others at 12 percent (Cameron 1991).

Style of representation varied widely across the country. Some senates, like Dalhousie's, used a form of direct democracy. In 1990, all 400 faculty members were on the senate. This differed from how professors were treated by Dalhousie's board, which prohibited them from joining under its 1863 charter. Since there was no express ban on student membership, the board began in 1969 to include three students on its list of nominees submitted to the provincial cabinet. They could not nominate faculty until 1988, when the charter was amended to allow five nominees from senate.

Large senates were common. The University of Western Ontario's charter was changed by legislation to reduce senate from 90 to 70, giving faculty just over 50 percent with 37 elected positions, plus three elected seats for students. Western's 26-member board had four faculty elected by senate. Students had the right to elect one member of the board, but it had to be someone outside the student body. The 1968 University of Manitoba Act expanded the senate to over 90 members, including 56 elected by faculty, all administrative officers, plus six students. Its 23-member board allowed six positions elected from senate, with one of them to be a student. McGill enlarged its senate in 1968 from 38 to 69, and increased the number of elected faculty from nine to 32. Students had nine seats. The 36-member board of governors had five positions elected by senate (Cameron 1991).

The University of Toronto adopted a single governing council in 1968, with 16 government appointees, eight alumni, 12 faculty, eight students, two senior officers, two non-academic staff, plus the president and chancellor ex officio (Cameron 1991). The move from a bicameral system gave faculty and students greater representation than on the previous board of governors, but weakened their voice on academic decisions, because their numbers were smaller than on the outgoing senate. Critics of the unicameral model suggested that faculty gave up virtual control over academic programs under the old system for a minority presence on the new council (Warter 1970).

Governance could not be improved merely by increasing faculty presence on board and senate. Relative powers and functions of these bodies required reform. As faculty's voice on all academic matters, senate was supposed to complement the board, made up mainly of people from outside the university. Board power was supposed to be tempered by senate's dominance over academic policy. This supposed balance of forces was rarely attained. Boards wielded supreme overall authority. Senate remained weak, ineffective and unimportant. Duff and Berdahl's 1966 study concluded that senates rarely utilized their full academic authority. Their business was restricted to routine approval of minor matters. Duff and Berdahl recommended giving senate greater powers, including administrative and budgetary review.

Weak senates posed a serious problem for faculty. Senate was the only senior body where they had voting strength, although they did not always have a majority. Voting strength did not amount to much if senate was restricted to minor issues. Having a majority did not necessarily mean they had much power, even over the issues where senate had a say. Presidents and their administration could easily dominate the proceedings. Administrators were fully represented and held unified platforms. They were expected to vote as a bloc, on positions determined by senior officers. Faculty rarely spoke with one voice. They reflected myriad views and approached senate as a debating society, where positions could be aired and endlessly discussed.

Senate became less manageable as its size was increased to provide broader participation. A 1965 survey of 56 universities determined the average size of senate at 38 members. By 1970, a similar survey of 59 universities found an average of 52 members. Sixty or more members was not uncommon (Cameron 1991). Adell and Carter's 1972 study for the AUCC concluded senate was far too unwieldy at most universities they visited. On one campus, a senate with 150 members was practically paralyzed.

This intractable situation deteriorated over succeeding decades. In the early 1990s a CAUT independent study commission concluded that uneven powers remained between senate and board, and within each body (Independent Study Group 1993). The process was less democratic than 30 years earlier, with presidents and much larger senior administrative staff wielding even more influence. They bypassed senate by working through high level planning committees, and sending recommendations directly to boards of governors. Senate's authority was seriously eroded, by classifying administrative and fiscal matters as non-academic and therefore outside its domain, with the effect of defining educational policy more narrowly than before, and relegating senate to routine matters.

Universities also established peer review systems which gave faculty input into decisions for hiring, tenure, and promotion. This was an improvement over previous conditions when they had virtually no say in these decisions. With peer review, presidents and boards considered recommendations from advisory committees which were usually made up of faculty members. Even though professors' authority was limited to providing advice, peer review still gave them greater influence. Their advice had to be considered. This meant they had a stronger foothold on decisions that affected their careers. Nonetheless, these modest reforms did not change the balance of power in the university. Boards, presidents, and senior officers were still in charge. They had full authority to make all final decisions, with the exception of an added requirement to consider advice from faculty (Sibley 1976, Cameron 1991, Malloch 1973).

Peer participation came about partly because faculty demanded consistent, fair, and open procedures. They wanted a voice in decisions that affected their careers. Peer review was also driven by imperatives of size and diversity. Small groups of administrators could not handle the volume of decisions they faced on hiring, tenure and promotion. Professors on these committees reviewed criteria and procedures, gathered and analysed data, and rendered their decisions, thereby reducing administrators' workload.

Peer review gave faculty a greater understanding of hiring, tenure, and promotion procedures, in contrast to the system it replaced, where information was tightly held by deans and higher-level officials. Having a role meant that people seeking tenure or promotion were applying to their colleagues. It was a positive development that could be divisive when committee members were split on an application, or if members of a committee denied the tenure or promotion of one of their colleagues.

Peer review did not address other fundamental problems of tenure and promotion. The procedures still lacked adequate systems of appeal. Proceedings were just as confidential as before, which meant that the applicant was no better informed about the process or the substance of the deliberations. Peer review gave professors a role in decision-making, but final rulings were still out of their hands. Committee recommendations were just the first step in the process. Before reaching a board of governors, a committee's review of an application was scrutinized by heads, deans, vice-presidents, and presidents, who could comment on the submission and add their own recommendation. Board members gave weight to senior officers' comments, since they had far more contact with them, as regular advisors, than with professors.

Another element of reform placed faculty on selection committees for administrators, heads, deans, and presidents. Lifetime appointments for officers were reduced to limited terms, to allow turnover and improve incumbents' accountability. Heads, chosen by department members, typically returned to their teaching positions after serving fixed terms. Deans' terms of office were reduced from unlimited duration to between five and seven years. Senior administrative posts with lifetime appointment were converted to fixed term with options for renewal.

Improved participation was uncontroversial because it offered something for everyone. The limited advisory roles taken on by faculty and students gave them more influence. It also improved their access to information about administrative procedures. Faculty and student participation was acceptable to administrators because it did not challenge the status quo. The balance of power remained pretty much as it was before they had a role in the process. Senior administrators retained their formal authority, limited only by new requirements to review the advice of faculty-based peer committees.

Tenure and Working Conditions

By the mid-1960s, employers began to implement formal policies for tenure and academic freedom. Until then, practices remained informal. Protection of tenure was weak at best, and applied inconsistently across the country. There were even contradictions within campuses that had ad hoc rulings on discipline or dismissal, without guidance of policies or standard procedures. Tenure was supposed to protect professors from being dismissed for any reasons other than incompetence or neglecting their duties. Without formal tenure policies, academic freedom was at risk, since professors could be dismissed for a wide range of causes.

Tenure procedures were usually not standardized, and based on ambiguous criteria. Appeals were weak, rarely accessible as a right, and sometimes not available at all. None were binding on the employer. Presidents or boards of governors were free to ignore appeal board rulings that supported the appellant. Until the early 1970s negative tenure decisions at the University of Toronto could not even be appealed unless the president of the university first agreed that the department recommendation was flawed. At Queen's University, confusion reigned about whether an appeal could be launched on the correctness of the decision or just on the process. On many campuses, candidates had no right to be told why their application was turned down. Without full disclosure of the reasons for refusal, it was extremely difficult to launch an appeal. Possibilities for successful appeals were remote if the grounds for a dismissal were not known (Whyte 1975).

The Duff-Berdahl commission recommended a formal system based on CAUT and AUCC policies. The CAUT policy on academic freedom and tenure, that eventually was the basis for policies and procedures on most campuses, required that tenure rights be clearly stated in writing, and that academics should be eligible to apply for tenure after a suitable probationary period, with the review carried out by a committee of the applicant's peers. All stages of the application process were to be listed in writing in accordance with due process. Fair appeal procedures must be a right for every applicant. By 1970, 27 of 46 surveyed universities had adopted the CAUT policy (CAUT 1971a, Monahan 1984).

Tenure ranged from formal policies to casual procedures. Colleagues of mine at the University of Manitoba recall receiving their tenure by mail, without even applying for it. Routine tenure awards started in 1971, without a system for reviewing eligible candidates. Ernest Sirluck, president of the university, set up a temporary system that required professors to apply to faculty and departmental tenure committees. He did this without consulting anyone on criteria the committees were supposed to use. Six of the first 102 applicants were rejected. Using ad hoc appeal guidelines, the board of governors became embroiled in a bitter dispute with the University of Manitoba Faculty Association and the CAUT over the case of W.N.R. Stevens. Poor management of this case was a factor that eventually led Sirluck to resign. Relations with the association worsened after the university tried to adopt tenure quotas in 1972, even though it withdrew after a CAUT investigation committee concluded that quotas were unjustified (Sirluck 1996, CAUT 1976a).

Some universities automatically awarded tenure to full and associate professors, and required assistant professors or lecturers to wait for several years before they could apply. Applications could be routinely approved, or subjected to extensive review. When tenure was denied, some universities allowed professors to remain in their positions and others required them to leave. Of 17,950 full-time academic staff in 1970, 46 percent had tenure, with 90 percent of full professors, 76 percent of associate professors, 20 percent of assistant professors, and 2 percent of lecturers and instructors. Full professors were treated most favourably, with 100 percent tenured at Universities of Toronto, New Brunswick, St. Francis Xavier, Guelph, and Laval, 63 percent at University of Calgary, 69 percent at Simon Fraser, 70 percent at McGill, and 72 percent at York (CAUT 1971a).

Other inequities were not addressed. Hiring practices still favoured men. The number of women in full-time positions fell from a peak of 18 percent in 1953 to an average of 13 percent in the 1960s and early 1970s. Women received lower salaries and fringe benefits. A paper prepared for the 1970 Royal Commission on the Status of Women in Canada demonstrated that just over half the $2,262 difference in average salary between men and women was due solely to sex differences. These inequities remained a decade later (Boyd 1979, Scarge and Sheffield 1977, Canadian Federation of University Women 1975).

Limited progress on sex discrimination began with investigations of salaries. Gender-based salary differences were documented at the University of British Columbia in 1972 (Day 1973), the University of Toronto in 1974 (Office of the Provost, University of Toronto, 1974), and the University of Alberta in 1975 (Senate Task Force on the Status of Women

1975). A 1975 study at the University of Guelph found no basis other than gender discrimination for female lecturers' much lower starting salaries. It found no significant differences at higher ranks, owing to Guelph's effort since 1972 to eliminate salary differences between male and female faculty (CAUT 1975a, Mulcahy 1975).

In 1974 the University of Manitoba Faculty Association found average salaries of female professors were $2,897 less than men's, even though women had an average of six more years of service and were eight years older. The association requested comprehensive investigation and a commitment to equalize women's salaries. The first collective agreement for 1975–76 established an "Anomalies and Women's Inequities Fund" of $100,000. Individuals could apply to a union-administration committee that distributed the money (Masleck 1975a, CAUT 1974a). Systemic inequities lingered until 15 years later when the union finally negotiated the first fund of $100,000 to reduce systemic salary differences based on gender.

At York University, a three-year study completed in 1977 by a University Senate Task Force on the Status of Women produced more than $100,000 of awards between $600 and $1,200 to 93 of 149 women (Cinman 1977a). In 1978 the University of Alberta's Senate Task Force on the Status of Women found that salary differences favoured male faculty in all categories (Baxter 1978a). Women were also confined to lower administrative and professional ranks. After accounting for age, rank, years at the university, and highest degree, the average difference based on gender was $2,336. Salary adjustments paid between $500 and $2,000 to 51 women, from a total of about 250 female faculty (CAUT 1978a).

Women were woefully under-represented at higher ranks. For Canada, in 1969–70, they made up 3 percent of full professors, 8 percent of associate professors, 14 percent of assistant professors, and 31 percent of lecturers and instructors. They held just 5 percent of deans' positions, mostly in faculties of home economics and nursing or as deans of women. Outside these fields, there were just five female deans or vice-deans in all of Canada. Women rarely appeared on governing bodies, making up just over 4 percent of the total 2,774 senate members across Canada. As of December 1, 1970 there were only 12 women out of 1,376 members of boards of governors (Vickers & Adam 1977).

Working conditions were improved in other areas, with modest sums for travel and research, money for pension plans, and supplemental medical and group life insurance. Faculty acquired perquisites that were previously unavailable, such as offices and telephones of their own, and increased support staff services. Staff-student ratios also improved (Harris 1975, Neatby 1987).

After decades of being consistently low, academic salaries doubled during the 1960s. This still left them trailing other professionals who entered the decade with earnings well above professors and left it even further ahead. From 1961 to 1970, the median salary of university faculty rose an average of 5.2 percent a year. Incomes of doctors and surgeons went up by 8.5 percent, lawyers and notaries 6.7 percent, engineers and architects 5.3 percent, and dentists 7.2 percent. By 1970, average university professors' earnings of $13,265 compared to $33,914 for doctors and surgeons, $25,240 for lawyers and notaries, $21,253 for engineers and architects, and $21,930 for dentists (Vickers & Adam 1977).

The practice of granting paid sabbaticals became more widespread, even though they were still treated as a privilege rather than a right. Review procedures became fairer, but administrators retained authority to approve or reject an application. They also set the number of sabbaticals to grant in a year. Applications could be accepted on merit but delayed for administrative or budgetary reasons.

These reforms in the 1960s made the university a better place for academic employees. The changes were driven mainly because academics were scarce relative to the demand for their services. Sheer size of large campuses demanded academics' involvement in sharing administrative workloads.

While the additional money was real, changes in governance were largely cosmetic. They improved participation without altering power relations. Faculty's limited presence on university boards gave them the form of shared governance without increasing their authority. Larger presence on senate had little impact because of that body's weak overall influence. Peer review allowed professors to provide recommendations, but these could be overruled at a higher level.

For a while, these modest improvements forestalled demands from faculty for more fundamental change. But administrators were tightening their grip on all aspects of university management. By the mid-1970s universities faced a reversal of the improvements won in the 1960s.

Deteriorating financial circumstances threatened salaries and set the stage for increased conflict. Faculty were not prepared to give up their gains, but administration had the power to withhold them. To protect themselves, faculty would eventually have to unionize.

Chapter 5

Declining State Support

BY THE MID-1970S universities faced protracted restraint, the joint result of economic slowdown combined with a renewed wave of public sector conservatism. Instead of vitalizing the economy with state spending, successive governments in Ottawa and the provinces reverted to Depression-era monetarism. Spending cuts dealt severe blows to health, education, and welfare, and drove up rates of poverty and unemployment.

Official unemployment was more than 6 percent in 1971 and peaked at 11 percent in 1982, a level not experienced since the Great Depression. Labour costs were singled out as a cause of inflation. Bill C–73, passed in the House of Commons in December 1975, imposed wage controls between 1976 and 1978. Tight monetary policy propelled interest rates to 20 percent by the early 1980s, slowing the economy even further and driving government deficits higher. To meet rising interest costs on the public debt and balance its budgets, Ottawa imposed deeper cuts on social spending. It further undermined budget balancing by easing tax burdens on the wealthy through reduced rates on high incomes, tax holidays on capital gains, and sweetened income tax breaks for corporations (McQuaig 1987).

Education, health, and welfare were impaired by never-ending constitutional battles over finance between Ottawa and the provinces. The federal government viewed with increasing disfavour its 1967 formula for financing post-secondary education which locked it into reimbursing the provinces for 50 percent of whatever they spent. While officials in Ottawa contemplated how to change the balance, people in universities worried over any threatened withdrawal of federal money since they could not rely on the provinces to make up the losses. Universities were especially vulnerable because their share of provincial spending had ascended steadily through the expansion period, and because government provided an ever-rising portion of their income.

The federal-provincial cost-sharing program was far from perfect. For example, poorer provinces received less money because they could not spend as much as their more affluent counterparts. The program's weaknesses were flagged in 1970 by the Hurtubise-Rowat commission on relations between universities and governments. The commission proposed replacing the 50:50 formula with unconditional grants adjusted to assure fair treatment to all provinces by giving each the same allotment per student (Hurtubise & Rowat 1970). Ottawa did not even begin to address the problem for another seven years. Provinces with low per capita income systematically received lower per capita transfers until 1982 (Carter 1982).

Cost-sharing was complicated and expensive to administer. Provinces were not automatically reimbursed for every expenditure. Federal auditors scrutinized provincial accounts item-by-item, to determine which costs were eligible for reimbursement. Annual expenditure reviews involved extensive negotiations between federal and provincial officials which typically took about three years to complete. Federal bureaucrats tried to veto as many spending items as possible, while provincial officials strived for reimbursement of everything they spent.

In 1972 the first federal revision of the Fiscal Arrangements Act upheld cost-sharing while ignoring the problem of unequal distribution. Full 50 percent funding was maintained only for annual cost increases up to 15 percent; provinces became responsible for the full amount of anything above 15 percent. Ottawa next changed the arrangements in 1977 with the Established Programs Financing Act (EPF) for medicare, hospital insurance, and post-secondary education. EPF replaced the 50 percent formula with unconditional block grants. The first year's transfer was set at the average for the preceding three years. Increases thereafter were tied to growth in population and Gross National Expenditure, which rose at rates far below the 15 percent they had replaced.

EPF severed the formal connection between provincial cost and federal reimbursement. Ottawa began to base payments on each province's personal and corporate income taxes. This meant that, in principle, provinces paid for health and post-secondary education out of their own revenues. Provincial income taxes were collected by the federal government which then returned a portion as tax points. Poorer provinces remained disadvantaged. Under the 50 percent formula they could not afford to spend as much as wealthier provinces with a higher per capita tax base. To compensate, EPF provided an equalization cash payment for provinces with below average income, but it took yet another five years for per capita transfers finally to be equalized. In 1976–77 the average per capita transfer of $69.83 ranged from $57.51 in Newfoundland to $99.12 in Québec, and a year later between $77 in Prince Edward Island and $90 in Québec. By 1982 the net per capita rate was the same across the country (Gunther and Van Loon 1981).

EPF eliminated constant scrutiny by federal auditors over eligible costs. Provinces could use funds designated for health and post-secondary education as they saw fit—a reasonable compromise given that the money was theirs to begin with. This new flexibility triggered major shifts in the balance of funding. Ottawa's annual increases fell farther behind actual cost increases. The cap under EPF was less than the annual inflation of university expenditures.

EPF block funding had the effect of increasing the federal share. Once block funding replaced cost-sharing, the provinces were no longer required to spend money in order to receive it from the federal government. They took advantage of the change by spending less of their own funds and relying on EPF transfers. Ottawa's contribution to post-secondary spending rose steadily to a peak of 80 percent in 1984-85, a considerable leap from 50 percent under cost-sharing. It reached the point where Newfoundland, Prince Edward Island, New Brunswick, Manitoba, and British Columbia siphoned off part of the federal transfer for other areas (see Table A–11). Other provinces used about 25 percent of EPF payments to subsidize programs outside health and education (Gunther & Van Loon 1981).

As governments withdrew money from social spending, university funding became more erratic and unreliable. The period between 1970–71 and 1983–84 was particularly trying. Education spending as a percentage of GDP declined in every province except Québec and Newfoundland. Even though enrolment grew, universities received a smaller portion of the shrinking total for education, while primary-secondary schools received a larger percentage as their enrolment fell. University enrolment increased by more than 62 percent from 1970 to 1983, but public spending in constant dollars rose by just 3.9 percent, placing Canada tenth on a list of 16 OECD countries (see Table A–4). University funding in constant dollars per full-time-equivalent (FTE) student fell at around 15 percent in Newfoundland, Ontario, Québec, and New Brunswick, and between five and 10 percent in the other provinces (Decore and Panny 1986).

Unequal provincial fortunes meant funding for universities was irregular across the country. Modest increases in some provinces coincided with frozen grants or imposed cuts in others. Within any province, reasonable grants in one year might be followed by severe cuts in the next. Any form of planning thus became extremely difficult. It was challenging enough to maintain existing programs; starting new ones became too risky. Some provinces began to interfere with university operations in attempts to control their spending. Ontario imposed an embargo in the early 1970s on all new graduate programs because of high cost and shrinking job opportunities for graduates with advanced degrees (Adell & Carter 1972).

Funding cuts began to affect academic salaries. Québec reduced university grants by $141 million between 1977–78 and 1980–81, and a further $180 million from 1981–82 to 1984–85. The Université de Sherbrooke announced a deficit of $8.3 million on a $90 million budget and issued notices of non-renewal. The Université de Montréal, with a deficit of $13 million, issued approximately 100 dismissal notices effective May 31, 1982, to assistant professors, teaching doctors, and lecturers. Staff at McGill reluctantly agreed to reduce their increase from 16.5 to 9.7 percent (Croteau 1982).

Some provincial governments created havoc by withdrawing money in the middle of budget years. In August of 1982, Nova Scotia rescinded $4.5 million in grants already committed to the province's 11 universities and colleges for alteration and renovation. The province eventually restored $2.5 million, but spread this payment over two years. Projects had to be delayed or cancelled. The British Columbia Social Credit government's Public Sector Restraint Act of 1983 damaged regular programs by cancelling $12 million of operating grants already approved for 1982–83. The University of British Columbia lost $7.2 million, Simon Fraser University $2.7 million, and the University of Victoria $2.1 million. The province continued cuts over the next three years, with a spending freeze in 1983-84 and reductions of 5 percent in 1984–85 and 1985–86. The B.C. government encouraged universities to save money through staff reductions with a one-time grant of $14.9 million in 1985–86 for early retirement (Shore 1982, Morissette 1984b, 1985a).

Government actions varied with the ideologies of the political parties in power and strength of interest groups competing for funds, but most invoked funding chaos. Deep cuts in British Columbia under Social Credit occurred at the same time the NDP in Manitoba and Liberals in Ontario increased their grants to universities. When British Columbia imposed its 5 percent reduction in 1984–85, Manitoba approved a 16 percent increase. While academic salaries were frozen and cut in British Columbia, the University of Toronto approved 3.5 percent scale increases for 1984–85 and 1985–86, progress through the ranks at 2.75 percent in the first year and 2.69 percent in the second, and 0.5 percent for merit awards in the second year of the agreement. This was just over a year after Ontario had imposed a public sector wage restraint program (Levin 1990, Léger 1985a).

Year-to-year cycles within a province became unstable. Every province imposed cuts between 1976–77 and 1986–87. Some kept increases well below inflation; others reduced the actual amount of grants. Over the decade, total provincial operating grants in constant dollars rose by just 1.6 percent, a rate far below the increase in university operating expenses. Grant increases in British Columbia, Saskatchewan, Manitoba, and Ontario did not even cover inflation. Declines were more substantial on a per-student basis because cuts were imposed at a time when enrolment was rising. Nationally, grants in constant dollars per full-time student fell by an average of 20.2 percent. New Brunswick experienced the least decline, at 14.6 percent; the worst was in British Columbia, with 27.9 percent. Only Prince Edward Island enjoyed an increase, at 8.0 percent (Cameron 1991).

Ottawa inflicted further damage through steady cuts to EPF beginning in 1983. Post-secondary education lost $4.3 billion between1983–4 and 1984–5, from capping the basic rate increase at 6 and 5 percent respectively. In 1986 Bill C-96 removed another $5.8 billion by reducing the transfer by two percentage points a year. This marked the first cut to equalization and the beginning of its demise. Bill C-69 in 1991 removed a further $3.5 billion over the following five years by freezing the per capita rate. The equalizing portion of EPF was eliminated entirely by the mid-1990s. The total cut in federal contributions to post-secondary education between 1983–84 and 1994–95 amounted to almost $13.5 billion (see Table A–12). Another $7 to $8 billion was removed from health care (AUCC 1991).

The 1995–96 federal budget replaced cost-sharing with block grants and removed even more money from the system. Transfers to the provinces for 1996–97 fell by a further $3.7 billion. With nearly all traces of equalization gone, poorer provinces returned to proportionately smaller transfers.

Over about 15 years, between the mid-1980s and latter 1990s, the federal government withdrew the progressive funding initiatives begun in the 1950s. Cost-sharing programs had injected a considerable amount of new money into the system over a 25-year period. They were the first steps towards a system that could equalize quality and accessibility of programs across the country. Pulling the money out inflicted a huge blow to health and post-secondary education, one that continues to ripple across the country. It cast the system back to the days when each province operated pretty much on its own, without assistance or direction from Ottawa. Prospects for national policies and programs were effectively eliminated.

With government's declining contributions, universities sought other sources of money and set about trying to cut their costs. The following sections document these efforts.

Raising Tuition and Donations

Core university income comes from government and students. When government's contribution fell, tuition was targeted for more money. This reversed the historic practice that began in the late 1940s of reducing tuition fees. Until 1957, government provided between 40 and 50 percent of university revenue, and tuition covered between 30 and 40 percent (Cameron 1991). Public funding peaked at almost 84 percent of operating income in 1978. Students were major beneficiaries of this spending. Tuition was down to 13.3 percent of operating income. Low tuition improved accessibility and may have contributed to rising enrolment.

Reversing the falling rate of tuition in the 1980s brought in more money from students at the expense of reduced accessibility. It made university affordable to a shrinking pool of students. Yet presidents on many campuses publicly espoused smaller, leaner institutions with higher fees (Ham 1982, Forster 1982). In British Columbia, still the only province that allowed tuition to rise, all three universities imposed increases between 19 and 33 percent in 1983 and 1984 (McMurtry 1983, Levin 1990). The province dealt a further blow to accessibility by replacing grants to students with repayable loans.

From the late 1970s through the 1980s, tuition increases kept pace with rises in the Consumer Price Index. By 1989, tuition was up to 16.7 percent of operating income, while government's share had fallen to 80.1 percent (see Table A–5). Then tuition took off, rising by 58 percent between 1989–90 and 1993–94, while the Consumer Price Index went up by just 16 percent. Higher incidental fees and rapidly rising prices of books added to students' financial burden. Undergraduate arts tuition and fees in 1993–94 were more than $2,300 at most universities, ranging from $2,860 at Dalhousie to $1,680 at the Université du Québec. Room and board for single students added between $1,800 and $5,000 a year (Branswell 1993).

Foreign students were targeted for even more substantial increases. Until 1977 they paid the same rates as domestic students. Ontario and Alberta were the first provinces to charge higher rates for nonresidents. Québec and the Maritime provinces followed suit in 1979 and British Columbia in 1984. By 1985 Québec was charging foreign students ten times the rate for domestic students—still the lowest tuition in the country because it was frozen at 1968 rates (Cameron 1991). Manitoba was the last holdout. The Progressive Conservative government forced universities to charge higher fees to foreign students in 1993–94.

Higher tuition reduces accessibility, especially for those who must turn to student aid to pay for their education. Bursaries and loans make it possible for a few to cover tuition and living costs, but they cannot correct the problem. Income-tested bursaries provide financial relief while they create a demeaning welfare regime; loans reduce financial hardship but impose high debt loads after graduation, when careers are beginning and earnings are lowest. People from low income families are less likely to assume substantial debt because they have few supports to help repay it. Low tuition still promotes the broadest accessibility, even though it also subsidizes students from middle and upper income backgrounds who comprise the majority of students.

Raising tuition was just one method employed by universities to squeeze more money from students. They also began to recruit aggressively. By the 1980s, universities launched marketing campaigns. Guelph University used advertisements that stressed its "lifestyle" appeal. Recruiters designed appeals for people older than the usual 18- to 24-year-old category, and other groups traditionally under-represented in the system. Offerings were made more flexible, with part-time and evening studies for working people, short-term residential programs for corporate executives, and distance education programs for people unable to attend classes on campus (Axelrod 1982).

Until the early 1990s, tuition did not improve the bottom line because rate increases were limited by public policy. Tuition simply contributed a few percentage points more to revenue than at its lowest point in the 1980s. Then every province except Québec allowed universities greater discretion to set fees. Variable tuition, often at much higher rates, started to bring in more money through programs in high demand.

Tuition could not compensate for all the lost government money. To make up the rest, universities began unprecedented appeals to business, an as yet untapped source for serious money.

Spending cuts by government pose an especially serious problem for universities in Canada because they rely so heavily on public spending. In the midst of all the reductions in 1983, Canada spent 2 percent of Gross Domestic Product on higher education, a rate considerably higher than any other OECD country except the United States (see Table A–4). Eventually, every university had to face up to having less money from government. They began to appeal to alumni, corporations, students, and staff for more money.

Fund-raising appeals would have to challenge a history of low levels of corporate giving. Corporations and wealthy individuals traditionally donated money for scholarships, capital, and special programs. Business promoted higher education as a profitable investment as early as the 1950s. The Industrial Foundation on Education helped to increase corporate contributions from $2.7 million in 1956 to an annual average of about $11 million for the remainder of the decade. Business support continued to comprise a small part of university revenue. When the foundation last published its reports in 1960–61, corporate and foundation support made up just 4.7 percent of total university income, with about two-thirds for capital projects, and less than 7 percent for operating expenses. About 5 percent went to research, the vast majority of it for specific projects and targets of interest to the donors. In 1961, 98 percent of corporate contributions for research were targeted, with most of the money for tied research coming from large corporations in resource and chemical industries. Repeat giving was low. Since one-time grants were the norm, universities could not count on corporations for stable, regular support (Axelrod 1982, Byleveld 1966, 1967, Sheffield 1982).

In 1966 a National Industrial Conference Board study concluded that corporations gave money based largely on location, reputation, recruitment, and personal factors. They supported universities and colleges attended by employees and families in their communities. Large companies favoured universities with strong national reputations as good sources for recruiting personnel. Personal factors were significant when executives wished to contribute to their alma maters. These patterns of giving did not bode well for expanding corporate support, especially for universities that did not conform to their priorities. Since business avoided funding core teaching and research, the areas most in need of money, new strategies would be necessary to broaden support from business (Byleveld 1966).

Universities also had to improve support from individuals. Private funding was very low, donations and gifts making up between 0.5 and 0.8 percent of operating income during the 1970s and 1980s (see Table A–5). Most donations went to capital projects, at 3.9 percent of total income in 1977 and up to 6.4 percent by 1988 (AUCC 1991). Universities attempted to broaden their base of private sector support with large fund-raising appeals to business, alumni, staff, students, and others. But private donations could never compensate for lost revenue from government. However important for targeted capital projects, they remained a small portion of total revenue.

Borrowing as a short-term measure was rarely feasible and in some cases impossible. Universities were prohibited from doing so in British Columbia, Alberta, and Manitoba. Maritime universities were allowed to accumulate deficits no greater than 2 percent of their operating grants. Debt financing was used as a last resort in a few instances. By the late 1980s Dalhousie University had a debt of $33.4 million. By 1985–86, Concordia University had accumulated deficits of $24 million, Université de Montréal, $26.7 million, McGill, $17.9 million, and Sherbrooke, $15.2 million. By 1987, Québec universities owed a total of $129.1 million, McGill alone owing $60 million. Universities in other parts of the country rarely resorted to deficit spending (Riseborough 1987, Cameron 1991).

Even where borrowing was permitted, it could be self-defeating. Loans were extremely difficult to repay because donors could not be persuaded to put up the money. Debt reduction was hardly a glamorous project for potential contributors, who received little recognition for paying off a loan as compared to establishing buildings or scholarships in their name. Governments refused to cover deficits, fearing that this would be interpreted by universities as a green light to overspend grants without penalty. They based grants on current operating expenses, without allowing for debt repayment.

Conventional sources of money were fast disappearing. While exploring new revenue opportunities, universities desperately tried to save money in every conceivable way.

Managing Budget Decline

Budget reduction required changes not well suited to the way universities operated. Programs accumulate obligations to students, research projects, professional bodies, government agencies, foundations, and other constituents. These commitments usually extend over several years and cannot be cancelled on demand. Universities had no choice but to reexamine their commitments in the light of shrinking income.

Spending reduction required new methods of organization and decision-making within institutions previously geared for steady growth. Institutional context was an important factor—successful approaches on some campuses would fail on others (Hardy 1996). By the time restraint took hold in the late 1970s and early 1980s, academic decision-making in Canada had been decentralized. Departments and faculties generated ideas for development and eventually implemented them. They planned courses and programs, determined enrolment, and set class size. Although central bodies such as senates ultimately approved program changes, they now acted as clearing houses against overlap and duplication. This system worked well only so long as funds were in steady supply to support initiatives.

In the United States, a 1979 survey of university presidents and chairpersons at all 650 unionized campuses, and a cross-section at campuses without unions, already noted a trend to more centralized financial and personnel decision-making. Personnel decisions were moving out of academic departments and faculties into central administrative units for employee relations (Kemerer, Mensel & Baldridge 1981).

Not since the Great Depression had universities faced the prospect of spending cuts. Officials suddenly had to search for money to ensure the survival of existing programs. Maintaining services was no longer feasible. Administrators issued directives for spending reduction, creating fresh tensions between administration and faculty. Professors in decentralized units were hardly likely to offer their own programs for cuts or take kindly to being told how to run programs they themselves had created. These tensions would become a major factor in new drives to unionize.

Cost became a central component of academic planning. Class sizes were increased to save money, regardless of academic consequences. Labour-intensive teaching was eliminated where possible. Teleconferencing and distance education were promoted as cheaper and more efficient than traditional classrooms. Field supervision by full-time faculty was dropped from professional programs, widening the gap between classroom and field.

Budget estimates had to be completed without knowing how much money government was going to provide. Anticipating budget cuts required being prepared to decrease expenditures while attempting to maintain programs and commitments in case revenue remained stable. Managers could not know from year to year whether they would hire staff or be required to lay them off.

Planning for this range of scenarios spread havoc. Universities are not flexible enough to cope with large annual budget fluctuations. Calendars with course lists must be printed six to eight months before the academic year begins. Core courses are offered in cycles to ensure that students can complete degree requirements on schedule and cannot be dropped from the curriculum, regardless of budget reductions. Research programs depend on access to necessary equipment, and if purchases are suspended, such programs must be put on hold.

When anticipated government cuts did not materialize, staff breathed a collective sigh of relief, pieced their programs together, and staggered on for another year until the exercise was repeated. When cuts were imposed at predicted or even deeper levels, emergency measures were invoked to suspend hiring and halt spending. Non-academic staff and untenured instructors were laid off. Remaining faculty coped with heavier workloads, increased stress, and heightened unease about the future.

A common way to address this chaos was preparing several versions of a budget at successively deeper spending reductions. Faculties and departments submitted plans for modest increases, freezes, and cuts of varying degrees. The annual budget exercise at the University of Manitoba required units to submit scenarios showing a modest increase, a freeze, and reductions of between one and 10 percent. Final budget figures were known only after the province announced its grant. Having to identify cuts that might or might not transpire sowed confusion and insecurity, especially for support staff and instructors in marginal, sessional, and part-time positions. Full-time faculty could be threatened if cuts went deep enough.

Administrators learned from these exercises the importance of flexibility. They tried to replace retiring tenured professors with limited-term instructors who could be released at the end of their contracts. Flexibility eventually became a theme at the bargaining table, as employers demanded authority to dismiss tenured faculty for financial reasons.

When submitting plans for how they would handle budget cuts, deans and department heads had to anticipate responses by administrators and other unit heads with whom they were in competition over funds. Presenting the required cuts could be a serious strategic miscalculation if other unit heads refused to do the same: administrators might accept the cuts even if the total university budget remained intact. On the other hand, refusal to submit any reductions risked imposition of cuts insensitive to the unit's priorities. Placing high profile or popular programs on the chopping block might seem safe, on grounds that such reductions would be deemed unacceptable, yet if the final cuts were severe enough the programs could be lost, possibly forever.

Simple budgetary techniques produced unanticipated consequences. For example, fixed percentage cuts across an entire campus might appear equitable on the surface but be experienced entirely differently. Simple percentages fail to account for different program needs and capacities. Large faculties might be able to absorb percentage losses which devastated smaller units, and departments with external research income would suffer less than those relying solely on internal funds for teaching. Budget strategies were slow to address these differences.

Ranking units appeared more rational than applying across the board cuts, and possibly fairer if consensus could be reached over appropriate criteria. Though the principle was sound, implementing it required consideration of seemingly endless factors. Possible criteria included the number of courses offered, section sizes, total enrolment, student/faculty ratio, research quality and productivity, money raised through research grants, number and quality of faculty publications, and graduate vs. undergraduate programs. Each factor had inherent biases favouring the strength of different units.

Budget cuts were especially hard on programs in the midst of development or expansion. Academic programs take years to cultivate, until expert staff are hired, courses in full swing, students on board, and research taking hold. Arresting them in mid-stream can be devastating. Students in particular need assurance that the curriculum they started with will continue for the duration of their studies. Professional programs have to meet their obligations to professional associations and maintain standards for licensing and accreditation. Research projects commonly span several years and involve commitments to government agencies and foundations providing the funding.

Systematic Canadian research on the full impact of revenue decline has yet to be done, but we can derive useful information from less formal reports. Faculty and students demonstrated over low funding and declining programs in a campaign culminating in March 1982 with a Week of National Concern. They presented evidence from across the country of crowded classes, poor library support, reduced research capacity, decaying buildings and equipment, increased use of underpaid part-time teachers, new barriers to women and native people, loss of competent people, and low morale (Baxter 1982).

In spite of such deteriorating conditions, universities appeared to retain their balance of priorities. Budgets were reduced by similar percentages for each of the university's main functions: instruction, administration, student services, libraries, computing, and maintenance. Expenditures expressed as a percentage of total budget for 1987–88 (with 1977–78 in brackets) were: instruction 66.1 (64.6); library 6.4 (6.9); central computing 3.0 (3.0); administration and general 9.2 (8.8); physical plant 12.3 (14.2); student services 3.0 (2.6) (Cameron 1991).

Quality of instruction suffered because of the imposed imbalance between full-time faculty and students. Part-time instructors may perform just as well in the classroom as full-time faculty but are not paid for administrative work, consultation with students, supervision of graduate students, or research. The shift to part-time instructors meant fewer full-time professors to handle these responsibilities or to generate grant money for research.

Library services were impacted more than the drop from 6.9 to 6.4 percent might indicate. Rising costs forced libraries to eliminate journal holdings, purchase fewer books, and reduce hours of operation.

Lower maintenance of university-wide facilities and equipment reduced the quality of the learning environment. Physical plant and equipment languished as universities struggled to maintain core programs and staff. Other less obvious factors had their own detrimental effects, such as decreased funds for purchase or rental of films and videos, an important supplementary resource for lectures and classroom discussion.

Two surveys carried out in the early years of budget reduction attempted to summarize views from across the country about consequences of cutbacks, though they could not reflect the full brunt of restraint. (Findings were limited because the researchers only sought out members of the administrative hierarchy.)

A 1982 survey of senior officers at 25 of 50 universities in Canada and the United States suggested that cutbacks had minimal impact on core functions. Respondents said they cut down mainly on energy and maintenance. This small sample suggested there had been no reduction of teaching or research, or elimination of programs (Lefancous 1984).

A second survey in 1983 contacted all 625 deans, directors, and presidents of degree-granting institutions in Canada. Again the 182 usable responses were not fully representative, but comprised a sufficient number to indicate patterns. Respondents reported lower operating expenditures per student; declining value of library holdings; falling faculty/student ratios; lower ratio of support staff to faculty; declining purchases of needed equipment; increased faculty teaching load; and rising average class size (Skolnik & Rowen 1984).

Cutbacks had deleterious effects on teaching. Larger classes meant faculty became less accessible to students. They had less time to provide feedback on complex assignments, or give extensive responses on exams and papers. Professors sought labour-saving devices, for example using computer-readable multiple choice exams to replace time-consuming essay questions. Faculty were also pressed to engage in more research, which even further reduced their time available for instruction. Effort was required to prepare grant proposals, administer budgets, and supervise staff.

Since salaries were the largest component of the budget, spending reduction inevitably targeted staff. Professors, whose real earnings fell as salary increases slipped further and further behind inflation, were not prepared to accept rollbacks. Nor did they welcome heavier teaching loads. These became major factors in unionization drives.

Savings were achieved by simply not replacing people who left or retired. As their numbers dwindled through attrition, professors faced larger classes and more extensive teaching loads.

Reduced hiring also drove up the salary budget. Customary salary structures provided scale increases plus career progress increments. With regular staff turnover, salary costs should rise only by the scale increase. Increments should be financed by money saved from replacing retired faculty at high salaries with junior staff at much lower rates of pay. Low turnover in the 1970s and 1980s produced increment costs of between one and 3 percent of salaries.

A simple example explains how this works. Let us assume a model of a university with 1,000 professors and average salary of $75,000. Top salaries are $100,000 and starting salaries are $50,000. If most professors have 30-year careers, turnover would be approximately 3 percent a year. The annual impact of regular turnover would be as follows:

Table 5–1
Staff Turnover and Increments

Amount saved from 30 people retiring, at $100,000 each	$ 3.0 million
Cost of replacing retirees: 30 people at $50,000 each	$ 1.5 million
Net saving from turnover	$ 1.5 million
Cost of increments for the remaining 970 staff, at an average 2 percent 2 percent x 970 people, at $75,000 average salary	$ 1.46 million

There were no other easy ways to save salary costs of full-time faculty. Layoffs were not an option for unionized professors with tenure: universities had to face insolvency before they could be removed. Financial exigency procedures were complicated and costly. Even on non-union campuses laying off tenured professors went against the ingrained culture and ideology of protecting academic freedom. There were strong reasons for retaining faculty. Eliminating professors would mean losing research money which provided employment for graduate students, equipment for offices and laboratories, and subsidies for administrative expenses.

Layoffs were poor short term solutions. Hiring new academics is a difficult and lengthy procedure which typically takes at least nine months to a year of effort. Replacing experienced professors in middle or later stages of their careers by junior faculty may create a net saving in salaries, but it takes years for newcomers to develop their own research programs and teaching experience.

The University of Victoria eliminated 28 positions and froze faculty and support staff salaries for 1983–84 and 1984–85. Simon Fraser cut 23 full-time positions and imposed a 2.7 percent salary reduction instead of layoffs. This was the first faculty pay cut in Canada since the Great Depression. Simon Fraser was also one of the few universities to eliminate programs. William Saywell, who started as president in the fall of 1983 during a freeze on provincial grants, launched an academic review completed in September 1984, when the province cut grants by a further 5 percent. Saywell's plan eliminated the Faculty of Interdisciplinary Studies, programs in Russian and German, graduate studies in Spanish, and undergraduate studies in criminology. Savings derived from attrition of staff and faculty, elimination of vacant positions, and slashing of the university's contributions to the arts centre and athletics. Layoffs proved unnecessary (Cameron 1991, Morissette 1984b, 1985a).

The process was far less orderly at the University of British Columbia. When its operating grant was reduced by $12.6 million for 1983–84 and 1984–85, UBC's board of governors froze salaries and imposed a redundancy policy to dismiss 190 staff, including 77 faculty positions vacated through early retirement and voluntary resignation. George Pederson resigned as president of UBC in March 1985 to assume presidency of the University of Western Ontario, stating that severe cuts by the B.C. Social Credit government made it impossible for him to do his job (Morissette 1985b). In May 1985 UBC's board eliminated the Dental Hygiene program and Industrial Education, Recreational Education, and Communications and Media Technology in the Faculty of Education. Twelve professors from Dentistry and Education were dismissed, nine of them tenured, with as much as 22 years' seniority. A CAUT committee of inquiry claimed faculty were dismissed without reasons and had no opportunity to appeal the decisions. The dispute was resolved in January 1986 after the faculty association and new president David Strangway negotiated a policy requiring the board to declare financial exigency before it could lay off tenured professors. One dismissed professor was redeployed; the others took voluntary termination. Untenured faculty received a minimum one year's salary plus a year's notice. Tenured faculty received the same notice plus up to 28 months' salary based on years of service (Savage 1985a, 1985b, Gerson 1987, Malloch & Norman 1987, Morissette 1986).

These money-saving measures impaired working conditions and morale for both staff and students at UBC and Simon Fraser. Each campus lost some of its strongest faculty. William Saywell and George Pederson reported that their top professors were actively recruited by other universities, with offers of employment at considerably higher compensation. Full professors in commerce earning between $50,000 and $70,000 at UBC left for salaries up to US $90,000 at business schools in the United States. Internationally renowned researchers left for higher salaries and better research support at other Canadian universities (Morissette 1983, 1984a).

A cross-country trend started in the early 1970s of reducing labour costs by replacing full-time positions with limited-term and part-time contracts carrying lower compensation and fewer benefits. Teaching responsibilities for people with limited-term and part-time positions were similar to those of tenured faculty, but with no assurance of employment beyond the expiration date of the contract. Employers could lay people off from these positions simply by allowing term contracts to expire.

On most campuses this practice evolved without explicit planning or policies, but some universities used overt policies. For example, the University of Calgary set quotas for tenure-stream positions at no more than 80 percent of teaching staff in a department. Once a department reached the quota, all academic personnel had to be hired on limited-term contracts, even those in core programs or with continuing, long-term responsibilities.

Part-time personnel were typically paid by the course, with few benefits, and employed for nine or 10 months of the year in positions requiring annual renewal. Employers justified lower salaries by limiting job responsibilities to instruction, with no requirements to conduct research, supervise graduate students, serve on committees, or perform community service. Part-time instructors had to conduct research on their own time without compensation from the university (Malloch 1971). Foulkes (1979) noted extensive use of part-time appointments during 1978–79. At the University of Saskatchewan, Concordia, and the University of Toronto, all 20 new appointments were on limited term.

Limited-term employment could be chaotic. Employers took advantage of a buyers' market marked by a surplus of academic labour over demand.

Instructors rarely knew from year to year whether their contracts would be renewed, regardless of how well they were performing. They might not be informed about employment until soon before the term began, affording little time for ordering textbooks and preparing lectures. Staffing became divided between tenured, full-time professors and marginal, part-time sessional instructors. Despite similar qualifications to tenured professors, sessional staff tended to be underemployed and poorly paid.

Sessional employees were normally excluded from negotiated scale increases paid to full-time staff. The faculty association at the University of Calgary found that, in 1981, only 9.5 percent of part-time sessional teaching staff received regular annual increments. Close to half (45.2 percent) of the positions were held by women, who nevertheless made up just 15 percent of full-time positions. Almost three-quarters of the sessional staff had received no salary increase since their initial appointment at the university. They received no benefits, had no vacation pay, and were ineligible for funds to support research. Inequities in their pay were far more likely to reflect a department's ability to pay rather than merit or experience (Barton 1983).

Faculty unions attempted to limit use of part-time and limited-term positions. The University of Manitoba restricted term appointments to no more than four consecutive years, after which an incumbent must either leave the university or apply for a tenure-stream position. Dalhousie's 1990–93 agreement allowed term positions only where full-time positions were inappropriate, such as for short-term experimental programs, leave replacements, or visitors. Appointment renewals had to be approved by a union-management committee, unless they filled special, short-term circumstances or were funded externally. The total number of renewable positions could not exceed 5 percent of the bargaining unit.

Early retirement was another way of saving money. In 1977–78, close to half of all associate professors, and 75 percent of assistant professors, were below the age of 40. With fewer people hired in junior positions, professors' average age rose steadily. By the late 1980s, when close to 60 percent of full-time faculty were between the ages of 40 and 54, early retirement became a significant issue (von Zur-Muehlen 1987, Pfaffenberger 1989). People hired in the 1960s and 1970s were within a decade of normal retirement age. Easing them out five to ten years before 65 promised to free up a lot of money.

Professors willingly accepted early retirement buyouts, sometimes far more enthusiastically than expected by the administrators who designed the schemes. The University of Waterloo's 1996 retirement incentive was taken by 140 faculty—45 percent of the eligible pool. The University of Manitoba's 1997 early retirement incentive program was cancelled eight months earlier than planned, in April 1998, because so many had already signed up. Departure of so many high salaried individuals made a significant dent in the fiscal problem but left gaps in units which lost large numbers of productive senior people. Since replacement staff had to be hired to maintain programs, early retirement was just a partial financial fix (AUCC 1996a).

Intensive efforts to save money changed the climate in the university. Conflicts between faculty and administration occurred more frequently over an increasing number of issues. On the surface they were about money, but at a deeper level they concerned power. Faculty and administration were in an escalating struggle over who would control the university and what kind of university would emerge. Professors fought to retain an academic model. Administrators tried to use business models for preparing budgets and controlling costs. Relations between faculty and administration started to resemble worker-manager conflict in industry. The university had begun to operate like a corporation.

Conflicts Over Money   Restraint intensified age-old conflicts between employers and employees. By the mid-1970s the campus was a battleground between faculty and administration, with more than enough heated issues to ignite struggles. Salary increases evaporated, workloads rose, and hiring slowed to the point where retirees were not replaced.

In April 1971 the AUCC commissioned Bernard Adell and Donald Carter, specialists in labour law at Queen's University, to examine methods of resolving administration-faculty conflict over terms and conditions of employment. Their brief study found that divisions between administration and faculty had become serious enough to make unionization inevitable. University presidents, preoccupied with business and government, were increasingly remote from their internal community. The authors described how presidents worked through thickening layers of officials, lawyers, and special assistants hired to do fund-raising, improve relations with industry, develop publicity, and manage human resources. Prospects were dim for a strong faculty voice in this system (Adell & Carter 1972).

Adell and Carter tapped into an intensifying power struggle. Administrators controlled expanding pyramids from the top. Senior officers rejected requests from unit heads to spend money already in their budgets. Deans lost control over hiring, to the point where they needed permission from officials to replace retirees. Central departments of employee relations monitored procedures for hiring, promotion, tenure, and discipline. Loss of authority went all the way to department heads, who could only make token spending decisions without advance approval from above. Administrative control also impinged on faculty, who needed permission for funds to attend conferences, or purchase equipment and supplies.

Tension between administration and faculty became endemic. Administrators used central purchasing divisions to gradually assume control over all spending. Centralized purchasing promised savings through standardized tendering, bulk buying and economies of scale, but purchasing bureaucracies extended their control to ever more detailed levels. As academic units lost authority over purchasing, they faced increasing conflict with central departments. One bureaucratic struggle was over travel. Purchasing departments began to award campus-wide monopolies to travel agencies, saving money through bulk contracts, corporate discounts for hotels and car rentals, and agency rebates on air fares. Spending departments and central purchasing contested what shares of the rebates each would receive.

Control of unspent funds became another hot spot. Traditionally, units which did not spend their entire budget could retain the money for subsequent years. This was especially useful for special or non-recurring events, such as developing innovative teaching projects, starting new programs, supporting research, or holding conferences. Administrators now began to deny departments the right to retain these carryover funds. Even where permitted, saving budget money to use for special projects became risky. If a department spent less than its allocated budget, administrators concluded the unspent money was not necessary. Underspending could be used to justify cutting the following year's allocation, or even permanently reducing the unit's budget.

Compromises had to be worked out. On my own campus, units may now retain a portion of any unspent money; the remainder is transferred to a central fund, to which units may apply for special projects. Managing money in this way enhances the power of central authorities who set criteria for awards. Faculty are forced to compete in order to reclaim what they view as their own money.

Controlling unspent money in this way can also encourage excessive spending. Faculties may attempt to spend as much of their budget as possible, even to the point of binge spending at year end, rather than lose portions of it or admit that they don't really need it.

Research contracts and grants became another flash point. Both typically cover direct expenses such as salaries, equipment, travel, supplies, and other incidentals. Once approved, the budget is controlled by the researcher, who manages the expenditures. But contracts and grants differ significantly in their treatment of overhead. A portion of a contract is usually allocated to pay for use of university facilities and services of permanent clerical and administrative staff. Researchers try to pay as little as possible in order to retain money for direct project expenses, while officials attempt to set high fees to help offset administrative expenses.

Payment for research arrives at the end of a long process which usually commenced years earlier with the germ of an idea, followed by extensive efforts to develop proposals, seek funding sources, and prepare applications. Then there is a period of waiting until contracting agencies announce their decisions and research can finally get off the ground. Projects could be delayed even further by disputes about overhead. University policies on administrative overhead range from taking fixed predetermined percentages of all contracts to negotiating on a project-by-project basis. Professors were understandably frustrated by these negotiations.

Some researchers sidestepped overhead negotiations by funnelling money through their own private companies. This raised further complications, especially if the companies used university facilities without payment, ignored university ethics reviews, or paid out salaries beyond the limits stipulated in collective agreements or regulations.

Research grants were less lucrative since they usually did not cover overhead costs. This has been a policy of the federal granting councils since recommended in 1969 by the Science Council of Canada. The issue arose during an inquiry into federal support of university research conducted by J.B. Macdonald for the Science Council. Macdonald recommended that Ottawa should pay for both direct and indirect costs of research, since failing to cover indirect costs would impose a drain on university resources for each research grant received (Macdonald 1969).

Macdonald's opponents argued that since universities were already funded to carry out teaching and research, paying overhead costs would amount to double funding and encourage universities to try operating on the "soft" money from overhead fees. The federal government accepted the Science Council's recommendation that national granting councils should not compensate the universities for overhead costs of research (Science Council of Canada 1969).

Cost-saving measures kept most campuses intact without causing irreparable harm. Universities eliminated frills, held back on salary increases, suspended hiring, replaced full-time faculty with limited-term and part-time appointees, laid off support staff, cut back on library operations and acquisitions, put off maintenance of buildings and equipment, and sought greater efficiencies wherever possible in the use of people, plant, and equipment. Short of major surgery to academic programs, universities did everything feasible to stay the course in the most trying fiscal setback since the Great Depression.

When spending reduction techniques failed to achieve desired results, universities turned to drastic measures. The extreme was to declare financial exigency, admitting that management could not balance the books through normal budgeting procedures. This was the only way to impose large-scale budget cuts involving layoffs of tenured faculty. Boards hesitated to declare exigency not only because it could create havoc among staff, and reflect poorly on management's ability to run the institution, but because it exposed their decisions and procedures to public scrutiny. Financial exigency required review by third parties charged with ruling on the nature and extent of the exigency.

One rare instance was an exigency of $200,000 at Algoma University College in Sault Ste. Marie, Ontario in October 1979. The 12-year-old college employed 31 non-union full-time faculty, with 146 full-time and 606 part-time students. The board intended to cover the shortfall by laying off up to seven professors. The faculty association tried to avert the layoffs with a proposal for rotating leaves of absence, early retirements, internal redeployment, program changes, and wage freezes or rollbacks, but faculty rejected all these options. In the end, two professors took early retirement and another was redeployed to the library. Two others declared redundant were reinstated to their positions by a three-person appeal tribunal (Ross 1980).

Requirement of financial exigency before layoffs can occur is unique to tenured faculty—generally agreed on as a reasonable way to protect academic freedom. Nonetheless, employers seeking greater financial flexibility tried to eliminate these clauses from collective agreements. Professors at the University of Windsor were prepared to go on strike in 1980 because the administration wanted to remove the financial exigency clause from the collective agreement. Financial exigency was the central issue in the 1995 strike at the University of Manitoba, and in the tense negotiations in 1996 at Memorial University that ended one day before the strike deadline. In all these cases the unions successfully retained their protection. Had they not prevailed, an essential ingredient of academic freedom would have been lost.

The dismal years of restraint battered faculty throughout the 1980s and beyond. Professors surprised many people, including themselves, by becoming more aggressive. They unionized, even where employers vigorously opposed them. By the mid-1980s the campus scene was completely altered. Professors created new organizational forms and new forums for dealing with employers. The era of collective bargaining had begun.

Chapter 6

Collective Bargaining Era

> Nothing, by the way, so incensed us during these sessions with our Board
> —one could hardly call them "confrontations"—as the assertion or imput-
> ation by Board members that we were merely "employees" of the institution
> (Sibley 1976, 21).

TO THE NON-ACADEMIC, W.M. Sibley's statement may appear elitist. Professor Sibley spoke for thousands of professors who rejected the view that
they might be subservient to an employer. They preferred higher sounding
titles like professional, scholar, academic or colleague, and an autonomous
image, in charge of their work and careers and exercising a strong voice in
the steering of their institutions.

Sibley wrote on the eve of unionization, when professors began to
realize that they *were* indeed employees. Boards of governors had the power
to hire and fire without any consultation whatever with faculty. As senior
officers tightened their grip on the running of the university, professors
experienced the limits on their power. Illusions were dashed as they faced
threats to job security. Once they acknowledged their limited authority,
professors began to do something about it. Unionization began in the mid-
1970s and expanded rapidly.

Collective action had long been unthinkable on Canadian campuses.
Organizing against the university was self-contradictory so long as professors saw themselves as central to it. In the boom 1960s labour action
appeared especially unnecessary as pay and benefits steadily improved and
professors gained a share in governance as well.

Unionization took hold when restraint threatened their progress. Pay
was not the only matter at stake: professors needed unions to represent
them when they were dismissed, or when their rights were violated, especially when academic freedom was concerned. As we have seen, aggrieved
professors received support from the CAUT Academic Freedom and Tenure
Committee, but faculty associations had no formal standing to represent
members. Legitimate grievance procedures were virtually nonexistent.
Though it had no official or legal standing, the Academic Freedom and
Tenure Committee managed to settle cases through informal mediation and

formal investigation. But the rising number of cases soon proved far too demanding for a small national committee. Even with expanded membership, the committee could not resolve trying and contentious cases which dragged on for years.

Canadian academics unionized later than in the United States, where certification began in the mid-1960s through the National Education Association, the AFL-CIO-affiliated American Federation of Teachers, and the American Association of University Professors. By the time Canadian certification started in 1974, there were already 133 affiliated bargaining units in the United States.

The earlier start in the United States dated from 1915, when the AAUP was formed. By 1920, it was a strong voice built on experience with contentious academic freedom cases (Garbarino 1975, Ladd and Lipset 1973). Canadian experience came much later. Harry Crowe's case in 1958 finally alerted Canadian professors to strategic weaknesses of academic freedom, but timing was not yet right for unionization. Union formation was hardly mentioned in the late 1950s, when there was optimism about material improvements. The CAUT handled academic freedom violations case by case.

Professors proceeded cautiously. Sometimes the merest suggestion of organization provoked heated debate between advocates and opponents of unionization. During organizing drives, associations typically examined union options from every possible perspective. They considered reasons *against* unionization as well as arguments in favour, to ensure that their members were informed of disadvantages and benefits. Carleton University's association printed a full-page article in its newsletter on advantages and disadvantages of union certification. University of Ottawa faculty explored every conceivable alternative to unionization. Against the advice of the CAUT, the faculty association even held a referendum on whether certification should be considered. The union campaign began only after a mail-in ballot passed the referendum at 455–119 (Axelrod 1982, CAUT 1975b).

Professors resisted identifying as unionists even after they certified. With the single exception of Saint Mary's University Faculty Union, every academic union in Canada favours the neutral expression *faculty association*.

Québec associations were the first to certify, in November 1970 with L'Association des Ingenieurs Professeurs en Sciences Appliques de l'Université de Sherbrooke, followed in 1971 by campuses of the newly established Université du Québec at Montréal, Chicoutimi, and Trois Rivières. No collective agreements were yet in force. Certification in the rest of

Canada began in 1973 with the University of Notre Dame in Nelson, B.C. and 1974 with Saint Mary's University and the University of Manitoba.

By the spring of 1975 more than 60 percent of Québec professors were unionized, the highest level of any province in Canada. In late 1975 more than 25 percent of professors across Canada were members of unions on 14 organized campuses. Collective agreements were signed at the Université du Québec, Notre Dame, and Bathurst College, an affiliate of the University of Moncton. Bargaining was underway at l'Université de Sherbrooke, Manitoba and Saint Mary's. Université de Montréal, Laval, and University of British Columbia were in the midst of organizing, although UBC's campaign was stalled and never led to certification (Adell 1975, Thompson 1975).

By the mid-1980s the landscape was transformed, with over 50 percent of faculty unionized on 29 campuses. Voluntary collective bargaining outside provincial labour codes was in place on 11 further campuses where faculty associations negotiated with employers without seeking union certification (Campbell 1991).

CAUT Inquiries and Censure

Until the CAUT stepped in to support them during disputes with employers, professors had to organize their own defences. Employers announced career decisions and rarely offered the right of appeal. Tenure was a central issue. Professors had a right to apply for tenure just once, usually five or six years after starting in a job. On most campuses, denial of tenure was followed by dismissal, with no opportunity for appeal. This could seriously damage an academic career, especially when job openings were scarce across the country.

Tenure offered extraordinary job security since, in principle, it prohibited dismissal for any reason besides just cause. It protected academic freedom; professors were not supposed to be fired for what they professed. Practice veered far from this principle. The CAUT handled many violations of tenure, in which employers dismissed professors based on the views they espoused or because they were found incompatible with their colleagues or departmental norms.

Applicants for promotion also had no right of appeal. They could always submit another application—which might be reviewed by the same committee. Repeat applicants were disadvantaged by being denied information about the previous rejection.

Where appeal procedures existed, they normally comprised an internal review. Presidents or boards of governors made final rulings on appeals, usually without formal assurance of due process, fair procedure, or impartial adjudication. Such appeals amounted to the employer's second opinion. There was no provision for independent evaluation of decisions. Where appeal committees existed, they could only recommend a resolution which the employer was free to accept or reject.

Before the 1950s, the only avenue for impartial third-party review was through the courts. Faculty had to initiate their own appeals, without financial support for legal or professional services. This daunting barrier involved lengthy delays and considerable expense. Court appeals were also problematic, especially concerning academic freedom. Jurisprudence favoured employers' rights to limit freedom of speech and to define appropriate behaviour in the workplace. Courts upheld dismissal of tenured professors for financial reasons, contrary to the spirit and intent of tenure. Treatment of dismissal for cause was problematic, especially since cause was not defined in most court rulings. Courts did not usually require university boards to review internal appeals. Even though boards appointed professors, judges ruled that presidents could make final decisions to deny tenure without referring to the board. This was the precedent set by the Nova Scotia Supreme Court in *Dombrowski v. Board of Governors of Dalhousie University and College*, December 19, 1974 (Mullan 1975).

CAUT involvement gradually transformed this landscape of dispute resolution. The association began working on violations of academic freedom in the late 1950s; by the early 1970s it dealt with cases on dismissal and denial of tenure and promotion. In 1971–72 alone the Academic Freedom and Tenure Committee handled 103 appeals, compared to 100 over the entire previous decade. Many were resolved informally, after committee members and professional staff gathered evidence and visited the sites of the disputes.

Successful resolution of a grievance required careful preparation by the committee, a cooperative university administration, and an active local association. Archie Malloch, chair of the committee in the early 1970s, maintained that its success derived also from broad knowledge drawn from cases and experiences across the country. Sometimes the right approach helped to direct university and association representatives towards a workable compromise. The committee tried wherever possible to encourage local parties to use due process to reach a resolution on their own. The committee also advocated the use of arbitration. By 1974 Malloch reported that universities were beginning to accept arbitration for cases that did not involve dismissal or suspension (Malloch 1972, 1974).

Informal resolution and arbitration were successful with less contentious cases. When discussion failed to resolve a dispute, the CAUT appointed a team to investigate whether local procedures complied with its guidelines on academic freedom and tenure, and if so usually deferred to the local process. Most inquiry committees found existing university procedures inadequate. By the time a committee submitted its report to CAUT Council, satisfactory resolution of the dispute was unlikely. Members of the administration and local association had usually entrenched their positions. Publishing a report with no legal standing or binding force could not easily sway either party.

A public report was the penultimate action. The last strategy was a motion of censure, a statement that the university had violated the ethics and standards of the academic community. Malloch called censure a form of academic excommunication. Academics were urged to boycott the censured university, not speaking on or even visiting the campus. Job seekers were exhorted to avoid applying to censured universities. A list of censured universities was published regularly in the *CAUT Bulletin*.

The CAUT invoked censure ten times. The first instance was against Simon Fraser University. Governance had been contentious at SFU ever since 1965, when its first board (consisting of eight businessmen and the mayor of New Westminster) prohibited faculty and students from joining the board. Occasional flare-ups arose between the board, student activists, and the predominantly young faculty. In 1966 students and faculty protested a decision by the board to place a Shell service station on campus in exchange for a percentage of the revenue plus a $131,000 bonus towards a new men's residence.

In October 1967 the Simon Fraser Faculty Association requested the CAUT to investigate a breakdown in communications between the association and the university president. A three-person investigation team concluded, in January 1968, that the campus was undemocratic: too much power was held by the president and his ad hoc advisory committees, while the board of governors set all academic and financial policy, refusing to delegate anything to the senate. Changes were proposed to policies for appointments and tenure, composition of the senate, and relations between faculty and the board of governors (Milner, Berland and Smith 1968, Ikeda 1971).

The CAUT imposed censure in May 1968, after a second team found that SFU's board had not acted on the first team's recommendations. Students continued pressing for varied improvements: inclusion of faculty and students on the board of governors; a senate composed solely of students and faculty; election of the president and chancellor by students and faculty; due process for tenure approval; and rotating term appointments for department chairs. Except for an elected president and chancellor, these changes were already in place or under consideration on other campuses across the country (Ikeda 1971).

Censure was lifted in November 1968 after it appeared the SFU board was making an effort to correct the problems. A team visited the campus and concluded in its report to CAUT Council that

> the resolution of censure has served its purpose, in that it induced an energetic attack on the problems of university government and ensured that the role of the Board was reduced to its appropriate limits, or something near them (Macpherson, Milner and Smith 1968).

Simon Fraser was censured again in 1971, for a case dating to 1968. President Strand refused to appoint Mordecai Briemberg as chair, even though he was chosen for the position by members of the department of Political Science, Sociology and Anthropology. When department members refused to submit another nomination, Strand placed it under trusteeship. Students and faculty in the department went on strike. They demanded an end to the trusteeship and reinstatement of the department's committees on curriculum, hiring, promotion, and tenure. These committees proved controversial with the administration because students played a prominent role on them.

After the strike, the board suspended eight professors, later dismissing three of them. In the end, all eight were dismissed and never reinstated. In November 1971, the CAUT imposed censure and urged academics to boycott Simon Fraser University. This boycott was not lifted until 1974 when the university established procedures for dismissal with cause.

Censure remained until May 1977 because grievances of the dismissed professors were not settled. The CAUT removed censure after the university invited seven of the dismissed faculty members to reapply for teaching positions. (The eighth person had died in 1972.) The dismissed professors refused to apply, instead demanding full reinstatement. The Canadian Sociology and Anthropology Association (CSAA) maintained its own independent censure as well. Arthur K. Davis, president of the CSAA in 1975–76, noted the irony that even though academics were encouraged not to apply for positions at Simon Fraser, the *CAUT Bulletin* continued to publish SFU job openings (Cinman 1974a, 1977b, 1977c, Woodcock 1975, Davis 1978).

Simon Fraser's cases reveal the limited effectiveness of censure and boycott. After six years of peer pressure upon the university, not one of the dismissal cases was resolved. Removal of the boycott may have even relieved pressure on the university to address the individual cases.

Censure was next used in March 1969 against the president and board of governors of the University of New Brunswick for suspending a non-tenured member of faculty without reasons. The Université du Québec à Montréal was censured in 1970 because an entire faction of professors in the Philosophy Department was not renewed and given two months' notice, while all members of a rival faction retained their positions. The faculty unionized soon after this conflict. Mount Allison University was censured in 1970 because it dismissed Catherine Daniel, a tenured faculty member, without proof of cause or a fair hearing (Williams 1977, Cinman 1977b, 1977c, CAUT 1971b).

In 1970, the University of Ottawa dismissed professor of Religious Studies Jacques Flamand after he published criticisms of the Papal encyclical *Humanae Vitae*. He also espoused taxing church property and criticized the structure of the Ottawa archdiocese, describing the College of Cardinals as an "outdated and useless institution." The CAUT's 1972 censure of the university for this blatant violation of academic freedom was not lifted until 1977, when the first unionized collective agreement protected academic freedom and established acceptable grievance procedures. The university never admitted fault in the case of Professor Flamand, despite a cash award of $10,000 in his settlement (Cinman 1973a, 1977b,c).

The University of Victoria was censured in 1971 for refusing to renew contracts of three professors. Censure was removed in 1975 after a settlement that set up a $15,000 trust fund to compensate for damage to their academic careers, the university contributing $12,400 and the CAUT $2,600. In announcing this contribution S.J. Cunliffe, chair of the board of governors, stated that the university did not acknowledge fault in the matter, but merely wished to settle the longstanding dispute (CAUT 1975c).

The University of Moncton dismissed Firozul Islam, a tenured associate professor of chemistry, after francophone students complained about his teaching and ability to speak French, despite unanimous findings of a committee of inquiry formed under the university's procedures that the charges against him were not sufficiently serious to warrant dismissal. Censure was imposed in 1976 and lifted in 1980, after an agreement between the university, the CAUT, and the local faculty association for arbitration and cash settlement of $50,000 (CAUT 1976b, 1980a, Cinman 1977b).

The most blatantly political case was Memorial University's dismissal of Marlene Webber, a Marxist-Leninist, from the School of Social Work in August 1978 because of her political activities on and off campus. At first Professor Webber was not even sure why she was being fired. She was later informed, in a letter from the director of the School of Social Work, that she was dismissed because her political activities revealed "a considerable divergence from the philosophy and purpose of the school." A university appeals committee upheld the director's decision.

The university refused to reconsider the dismissal even after a CAUT Committee of Inquiry (chaired by C.B. Macpherson, of University of Toronto, with Jack Weldon from McGill University, Dale Gibson at the University of Manitoba and Olga Favreau from the Université de Montréal) concluded that charges of political misuse of the classroom were unsubstantiated. They found Professor Webber alerted students to her political beliefs and made a serious effort to present a balanced perspective in her classroom. No cogent evidence was produced that her political activities constituted professional wrongdoing.

Talks between representatives of the CAUT and Memorial University continued in the wake of censure but were unsuccessful. By June 1979, at its general assembly, the Canadian Association of Schools of Social Work expressed concern that actions against Professor Webber would disqualify the School of Social Work's accreditation. By May 1980 CAUT council imposed the third stage of censure, advising academics not to accept appointments at the university. The university refused to reopen Professor Webber's case. She was never reinstated (Baxter 1978b, 1979a, CAUT 1979a, 1980b, MacRae 1986, Sim 1980).

The University of Calgary was the only censured administration to have a special plan bargaining arrangement with its faculty association. In 1976, the president of the university informed Dr. George Abouna, a transplant surgeon, that his two-year contract would not be renewed. Dr. Abouna had previously been dismissed from Foothills Hospital, an affiliate of the university. Even though he won a lawsuit against the hospital for wrongful dismissal, the university refused to reinstate him. A CAUT committee of inquiry concluded that failure to renew his contract was improperly based on his dismissal from the hospital, with no other valid reasons. His employment was understood to be continuing, but set up on a limited term solely because his department had reached the university's 80 percent quota for tenured and tenure-stream staff. Professor Abouna was denied the academic freedom that came with tenure-stream appointments (Baxter 1979a, CAUT 1979c, 1980b).

Nova Scotia Technical College, later the Technical University of Nova Scotia, was the sole case of censure on a unionized campus. The case began in 1979, before bargaining commenced for the first contract, when the college dismissed John Goodfellow without giving him any reasons. Professor Goodfellow was a tenured professor of mathematics. The college's action violated a CAUT guideline on dismissal that required demonstration of sufficient cause (CAUT 1980c,d).

Censure publicized egregious cases, embarrassed university officials, and perhaps tipped the scale towards fairer procedures. Beyond this it was a limited tool for resolving disputes. None of the cases was ever fully settled. Several simply languished for years, then faded away without clearing up the issues that sparked them. The handful of cases where professors received compensation set no precedents. University officials consistently refused to admit fault.

Threat of censure may well have prevented other violations of academic freedom. Professor Robert McCarthy was terminated from Acadia University in May 1975, despite positive recommendations from three successive hearing committees. An impending censure vote by CAUT Council moved the faculty association and board of governors to appoint Professor Bernard Adell, Dean of the Faculty of Law at Queen's University, to arbitrate the dispute. Professor McCarthy was reinstated on September 1, 1979, after Professor Adell's ruling, for a three-year probationary appointment with consideration for tenure at the end of his term (Sim 1979, CAUT 1979d).

Casework on academic freedom and tenure laid a foundation for unionization. Pressure was already building among faculty to take collective action against salary cutbacks and heavy-handed treatment.

The Academic Freedom and Tenure Committee tracked these developments across the country and helped local associations to settle grievances and build on their strengths. Despite limited tools, the CAUT played an important role when no other assistance was available to protect tenure and academic freedom. But it had neither the authority nor the resources to address myriad other conflicts surfacing on campuses over salaries, benefits, working conditions, and governance Local collective bargaining was outside its scope. For this, faculty needed stronger associations with forceful mandates.

Special Plan Bargaining

When professors at the University of British Columbia voted to unionize, they started a process that eventually led to overturning their own motion. The resolution to certify was approved in February 1974, at the faculty association's meeting to discuss its annual salary brief to the board of governors. By April, 71 percent of more than 500 members at a special meeting amended the association's constitution in order to apply to the British Columbia Labour Relations Board for certification. In a rare move, then NDP premier Dave Barrett offered unsolicited support on an open line radio show in Victoria, by declaring unionized university staff and faculty a positive development. By September 11, with signed union cards from about 60 percent of eligible members, well above the 35 percent minimum required by the labour code, the association applied for certification.

Then the campaign suffered a stunning reversal. The former president of the association, who had resigned in May because of the vote to unionize, circulated a lengthy letter asking members to revoke their membership. The UBC board of governors announced in October that it would bargain with faculty only *outside* the labour code. A week later, the association's general meeting decided to withdraw the labour board application in order to investigate alternative forms of collective bargaining.

By 1975 the association and university had signed a voluntary plan—outside the labour code but closely resembling a union agreement, with the association as sole bargaining agent for full-time faculty—to cover salaries, benefits, appointments, sabbaticals, promotions, and terminations. The plan departed from a union framework on all other matters. Workload and governance were not open for negotiation. Treatment of salaries was potentially divisive, because groups within the association could negotiate subsidiary agreements for higher pay (CAUT 1974b, 1975d, AUCC 1974, Sullivan 1976, Rodyhouse 1978).

At the University of Toronto a special plan outside the Ontario Labour Relations Act has been in place since June 1977. In their first vote on unionization in the spring of 1976, two-thirds of the faculty favoured a formal bargaining relationship with the university but defeated forming a union by the same majority. The University of Toronto Faculty Association drafted positions for a non-certified collective agreement over the summer of 1976, approved them in October, commenced negotiations with the university in December, and had an agreement by the spring of 1977. Salaries were handled differently from union agreements: the Association bargained for minimum salaries, leaving individuals or groups free to negotiate something better (Smith 1978). Unions reject this approach as fostering conflict between those with higher increases and those who receive the minimum raise.

Faculty and board at the University of Prince Edward Island discussed salaries annually since its opening in 1969. More often than not the board imposed a settlement after failing to reach agreement with the faculty association. When the process broke down in 1975, faculty threatened to boycott convocation, delay submission of final grades, and set up a committee to investigate unionization unless the board negotiated for salaries and benefits. In June 1976 the association and university signed a negotiations agreement outside labour legislation, although with provisions normally found in union contracts for mediation, final offer selection arbitration, and deadlines for concluding negotiations prior to provincial budget deliberations (Hazleton 1978).

Similar scenarios played in Alberta. The University of Calgary Faculty Association obtained exclusive bargaining rights and binding arbitration in 1975 in exchange for not seeking certification. Board and faculty at the University of Alberta negotiated informally from the early 1950s until the board imposed a settlement after an impasse in the 1969–70 negotiation. A 1970 survey found faculty wanted improvements in the conduct of negotiations with the board but opposed union certification. In September 1971 the Association of the Academic Staff of the University of Alberta signed an agreement with the board of governors for negotiation outside of labour legislation with final offer selection arbitration on all outstanding items (Unger 1978, Vanderberg 1978, Cameron 1991).

Special plan bargaining lacks the assurances of unionized collective bargaining: courts have sided with defaulting employers on grounds that they were not legally required to maintain their obligations under the agreement (Adell 1970). The Brandon University Faculty Association (BUFA) in Manitoba eventually discovered that their eight years of collective bargaining had no legal standing. In 1977 BUFA appealed to the Manitoba Labour Relations Board for a ruling on the inclusion of instructional associates within the bargaining unit. The board ruled that they were not a union: the association had bargained with the employer through voluntary recognition but had not sought certification. Since the employer was therefore not required to uphold its part of the agreement, the labour board's ruling essentially stripped BUFA of its bargaining privileges. BUFA launched an organizing campaign, was certified as a trade union in January 1978, and signed its first collective agreement in March 1979 (England & McKenna 1977, Bartley 1979a, Black 1979).

Even though some special plans carry provisions similar to those in union contracts, they lack the force of unionized collective agreements. Special plans have no legal means to bring employers to the bargaining table. They lack unions' ultimate power to go on strike when negotiations go sour. Employers can pull out at any time, with no obligation to uphold the terms of an agreement. Non-certified associations do not have access to the Rand formula which allows unions to receive dues from every member of the bargaining unit, regardless of whether they join the union, on the principle that everyone in the bargaining unit benefits from union services. The Rand formula is compulsory in most provinces and may be negotiated with the employer in the others.

For many associations the non-union option was an importance advance in overcoming powerful resistance to unionized collective bargaining. Faculty were too vulnerable to proceed without any form of representation. Special plans persisted in Alberta and British Columbia, whose respective Tory and Social Credit governments prohibited academic unionization, and on a handful of larger campuses in other parts of the country. But they were ill-suited to the problems that faculty faced in the 1980s and 1990s: dealing with universities that act like corporations.

Forming Unions

Bernard Adell and Donald Carter's 1971 study for the AUCC concluded that unionization was coming because faculty faced a deteriorating job market, declining employment security, increased control of university affairs by government, worsening relations between faculty and administration, and more widespread collective bargaining on campuses in other countries. A younger and more politically radical faculty was increasingly sympathetic to unionization (Adell & Carter 1972).

Despite identifying this trend, the CAUT remained tentative about unionization, not even discussing collective bargaining in a 1970 symposium on the future of the CAUT. In the spring of 1971, a committee set up to consider collective bargaining disbanded without filing a report. Individual papers were published in the *CAUT Bulletin* as a symposium on collective bargaining, including an article by Bernard Brody favouring unionization and one by R. Dubinski opposing it (Penner 1979, Dubinsky 1972, Brody 1972).

Two years later the committee was reconstituted with union supporters, who acted as a resource centre for faculty bargaining and a catalyst for union drives across the country. This committee's work demonstrated growing commitment to unionization. The prospect of many campuses following the handful already unionized in 1974 posed an opportunity for the organization to grow and to strengthen its ties with local associations. It also faced competition from national unions prepared to organize faculty. The CAUT was well placed to provide organizing and bargaining assistance to fledgling unions. Supported by a larger budget to hire organizers and new regional offices in Halifax and Edmonton, the CAUT made certifying faculty associations a priority (Axelrod 1982).

Notre Dame University, a B.C. secular campus with a clerical, authoritarian legacy, became the first association outside Québec to unionize. Faculty sought certification in response to determination of the president and board to abolish tenure. The Faculty Association of Notre Dame University was certified in March 1973.

An organizing drive at Saint Mary's University in Halifax played an important part in accelerating the CAUT's change of perspective. The small faculty of less than 100 men considered unionizing a couple of years after Saint Mary's was converted from a Jesuit-controlled Catholic college into a lay university. Faculty were far from satisfied with the changeover, since the authoritarian rule and paternalism of the sectarian era were continued by managers of the secular university. The new lay president made matters even worse by announcing his intention to fire 14 faculty members. He backed off from dismissing anyone, but took a hard line on management rights by refusing to recognize a faculty manual that had guided administration-faculty relations during the Jesuit period. The manual was far from perfect, but removing it without consultation only aggravated relations with the faculty. Over the next two years, the faculty association referred unresolved individual and collective grievances to the CAUT. The CAUT even proposed a special plan arrangement outside the Trade Union Act, but this was rejected by the president and board.

By 1974, members of Saint Mary's University Faculty Union (SMUFU) campaigned to unionize. Even though CAUT members, some of the faculty approached the Canadian Union of Public Employees for assistance and possible affiliation. CUPE and CAUT actively courted SMUFU members divided over where to affiliate. CUPE supporters favoured the closer ties with the labour movement; opponents did not want to associate with organized labour. Some opposed any form of unionization. The CAUT won the final vote over affiliation by a narrow margin; SMUFU was certified in April 1974. An activist in the campaign commented in an interview that intense competition over affiliation probably strengthened the pro-union vote. Faced with a choice between CUPE and CAUT, even lukewarm members supported the CAUT just to prevent association with CUPE (Savage 1974, Cameron 1991, Black 1978).

Saint Mary's was a call to action. The slim margin over CUPE signified that the CAUT had to attend to local developments and strengthen its support for union organizing. Over the next decade, the CAUT was instrumental to union campaigns. It provided organizers to sign up members, and legal services to prepare applications for certification and represent associations in labour board hearings. Much-needed assistance was provided at the bargaining table, especially concerning model clauses for key issues in first contracts. Personnel from the national office offered strategic and tactical advice to negotiators, and provided negotiators and staff to bargaining committees for smaller associations with limited resources.

Assistance of this nature strengthened local associations and protected CAUT interests against competition from other unions. After one other attempt with librarians at the University of Ottawa, who affiliated with CAUT, CUPE withdrew from trying to organize faculty. Every faculty union outside Québec has since either chosen CAUT membership or remained independent (Cameron 1991).

Support for local bargaining stemmed from CAUT concern for consistent, strong contracts across the country. Smaller associations risked making strategic mistakes when negotiating their first contract. They could not afford expensive professional fees and lacked the breadth of member expertise available to larger associations. Errors at this stage could devastate key areas of academic freedom, tenure, hiring, promotion, discipline, or grievances, have serious repercussions for a union's viability, and set damaging precedents for other faculty unions. Model clauses and staff support during negotiations were meant to prevent such errors. Larger associations with more resources still required CAUT support because they were paving new ground, without any experience at unionization before 1971. The CAUT thus became the national repository of research and experience from unions across the country.

A new advance for faculty activism was marked by the establishing of the CAUT Defence Fund in September 1977. This fund pooled contributions from members across the country to cover costs of strikes and certification. Two strikes in the fall of 1976 demonstrated the need for a national fund:

Laval's professors were out for 107 days, and the strike at Université du Québec à Montréal lasted for 133 days. Both unions had to repay substantial debts incurred over the course of these lengthy strikes. By providing strike benefits from its substantial pool of money, the Defence Fund helped unions to avoid sizable debt. The Defence Fund became permanent in May 1978. Its assistance—grants for strike benefits and loans to pay for staff benefits during a strike—is still crucial to striking faculty (Woodcock 1977, Cinman 1977d, 1978a).

As union drives gained momentum, the CAUT offered annual training sessions in collective bargaining. My own first exposure to the national body was a week-long early 1980s summer session for neophyte negotiators from across the country. Strategy seminars and practice negotiation sessions with professional staff and seasoned faculty negotiators greatly enhanced our proficiency with the arcane language and unique process of collective bargaining. Faculty negotiators have been served well by these sessions before sitting down to their first bargaining table.

Compared to the authority national unions exercise over locals, the CAUT is unobtrusive. Local associations determine their own policies, finances, governance, and bargaining positions. They are urged, but not required, to use national guidelines and model clauses for bargaining. They must pay dues to the national body and meet three requirements for membership:

> (a) The faculty association must be the exclusive bargaining agent for the agreed unit; (b) the agreement to bargain must contain, in the absence of a legal right to strike, a defined and binding method of impasse resolution; and (c) the agreement must contain a recognition clause and an article guaranteeing binding arbitration for rights disputes (Penner 1979, 83).

The CAUT kept a low profile well into the 1980s. Emphasizing professional stance over union identity not only suited its members' ambivalence over certification, but served its lobbying and advocacy in the interests of higher education. Lobbying used small, low-key group or individual sessions in preference to larger public events. One notable exception was the national week of concern, March 24–31, 1982, consisting of public demonstrations in centres across the country and a mass lobby in Ottawa on March 25 with members of parliament, cabinet ministers, and senators. This was the first such event to focus solely on university funding (Baxter 1982).

First Hurdles: Certification and a Contract

Whenever faculty debated unionization, especially during the early years of certification, the issue arose of whether collective bargaining was appropriate to the university. Opponents argued that the confrontational stance of unions was unnecessary because faculty and their employers were not as clearly in conflict as their counterparts in industry or government. Opponents also suggested that unionization of faculty would encourage members to place their own welfare above the overall good of the university and its students.

This opposition to unions was understandable in light of how the university had traditionally operated. Faculty enjoyed considerably more autonomy and power than employees in most organizations. Professors might sit lower in the hierarchy than deans and senior officials but were far from subservient to them. In industry a firm's reputation rests on its products and profits; the prestige of a university depends largely on the research and publication of its faculty. Their stature, leverage, and value to the institution are enhanced with every new grant or publication (Mohrman 1989).

Opponents of unionization found it hard to imagine how a union could improve academic freedom in teaching and research. Rather, they saw unions threatening their independence by requiring uniform positions and conformity to collective agreements. Greater salary gains for the entire unit could limit potential earnings for highly productive researchers or recipients of large research grants. High-income professionals could thus be worse off with a general salary pool. Between 1970 and 1974—the years just before unionization began—faculty in professional schools, especially law and dentistry, received higher than average salary increases. Collective agreements, on the other hand, usually prohibited exceptional increases for individuals or groups (Penner 1979).

Despite considerable leverage to manage their own work, professors were still employees whose fate was ultimately determined by senior officials. Academics began to appreciate that unions were suitable to their circumstances. Collective agreements offered crucial protection for tenure and academic freedom. Professors could use their collective strength to change unwanted policies and improve conditions.

Once faculty associations addressed their members' ambivalence to unionization, they had to face defiance from employers. Uncontested applications or voluntary recognition were rare. Université Ste-Anne granted voluntary recognition in 1982. Without a challenge to certification, there was no necessity for extensive labour board hearings (Snow 1982a). Saint Mary's University Faculty Union required just three days of appearances before the Nova Scotia Labour Relations Board. But most others dragged on due to employer opposition. The University of Manitoba Faculty Association was not certified until November 1974, 19 months after it applied to the Manitoba Labour Board (Carrigan 1977).

Unions must sign up a sufficient number of members in a workplace before applying to a provincial labour board for certification. That board then defines the bargaining unit and conducts a ballot. Employer resistance usually concerned the definition of the bargaining unit—though some employers raised the more fundamental issue of whether faculty were entitled to represent themselves as employees under provincial labour law.

Although legal and technical arguments delayed campaigns while labour boards held tedious hearings and considered endless briefs, associations were always successful at certification. Compared to difficult battles over organizing unions in industry, retailing, banking, or fast food franchises, the obstacles faced by professors were mild and manageable.

Some employers tried to undermine a union's claim that it had enough signed membership cards by claiming the bargaining unit was larger than the union's estimate. This proved effective where part-time instructors did not have offices on campus and were widely dispersed, since the unions had a difficult time estimating their numbers accurately. The University of Manitoba successfully opposed an application to certify part-time sessional faculty by showing that the number of eligible staff was greater than the union's estimate. The number of signed cards therefore fell below the labour board's minimum requirement.

A few employers argued that professors were not employees as defined in legislation because they have more say in governance than workers in most occupations. The University of St. Thomas, in Fredericton, New Brunswick challenged the 1975 application for certification by the faculty association (FAUST) on grounds that faculty were not eligible to be covered by the Industrial Relations Act because they were *appointed* by the board of governors instead of being *hired* as employees. The employer claimed professors performed management functions as members of senate, board of governors, and committees for hiring, tenure, and promotion. FAUST countered that their participation was only advisory, since the board could remove them from the process whenever it wished. Ultimate power to hire, grant tenure, promote, impose discipline, or dismiss professors still resided with the board of governors. The New Brunswick Supreme Court rejected the university's claim, determined that faculty fell within the definition of employee under the act, and ruled that certification was permissible (CAUT 1975e, Adell 1975).

Industrial relations boards and the courts consistently agreed that associations could unionize because their members shared a community of interest as employees. Boards acknowledged that universities are managed differently from corporations by allowing such positions as department chair to be included in bargaining units even though they were excluded in industry. The Ontario Labour Relations Board (OLRB) included department chairmen in Carleton University's bargaining unit in July 1975, the only contested issue in the application by the Carleton University Academic Staff Association. With little Canadian jurisprudence to guide it, the board concluded that the position of department chairman differed categorically from that of manager or supervisor in industry.

The OLRB made a similar decision over the University of Ottawa's attempt to exclude department heads from the bargaining unit. The board ruled heads did not exercise managerial functions as defined under the Ontario Labour Relations Act. In industry, with authority entrenched in hierarchical structures, similar positions were part of management. University department heads were colleagues within departments that made initial recommendations on hiring, promotion, tenure, and curriculum. These decisions at Carleton and Ottawa were precedent-setting. When Laurentian University Faculty Association was certified in July 1979, the OLRB used similar logic to include directors of professional schools in the bargaining unit (Cinman 1975a, Masleck 1976, Bartley 1979b).

Mount Allison University tried to unseat a 1982 application by challenging professors' employee status. The university relied on a 1980 decision by the United States Supreme Court denying a 1974 application for certification by faculty at Yeshiva University on grounds that they exercised managerial authority. The Yeshiva decision was a major setback for faculty unionization in the United States: within a few years employers at more than 62 colleges and universities tried to decertify their faculty unions. By 1989, 25 had succeeded, while in other cases faculty voluntarily decertified in exchange for promises of increased roles in governance (Blum 1990, Gorman 1980, Lee & Begin 1984, Douglas 1981).

Mount Allison argued professors' participation privileges extended well beyond usual employee rights. The faculty association's application was stalled for more than a year while it refuted the Board of Regents' assertions. The New Brunswick Industrial Relations Board eventually rejected the employer's argument and issued a certificate to the Mount Allison Faculty Association. The Board of Regents was reported as having spent $175,000 on its attempt to defeat the certification. It also did something pretty rare in the annals of relations between universities and faculty unions. Guy MacLean, president of Mount Allison University, fired the faculty association's treasurer and chief negotiator in January 1983. After considerable protest from the faculty he reinstated the treasurer, but refused to rehire Tom Storm, the chief negotiator. The university settled with Storm just one day before a scheduled labour board hearing on unfair labour practice (Snow 1982a, b, Brunet 1982, CAUT 1983a).

Employers' actions sometimes bolstered faculty support for unionization. Carleton's faculty had misgivings about how the president of the university would handle projections in the early 1970s of low enrolment and a mounting deficit. Michael Oliver, who became president of the university in 1974, announced there would be no layoffs for 1975–76, even though senate was reviewing procedures to discontinue full-time faculty in the fall of 1974. One week after Oliver's announcement, the Carleton University Academic Staff Association met to consider unionization, based on concerns over job security and the threat of financial stringency. Relations between faculty and the president reached a new low in early 1975 when Oliver announced that he and the board of governors reserved the right to determine how they would dismiss full-time faculty, regardless of any recommendations by senate. The faculty promptly certified after a favourable vote of almost 80 percent (Cameron 1991, Mair 1977, Axelrod 1982).

Memorial University of Newfoundland Faculty Association (MUNFA) first considered, and rejected, applying for certification in the spring of 1978, after talks broke down with the Board of Regents to negotiate a special plan outside labour legislation (Morgan, Cinman & Jones 1978, CAUT 1978c).

The university opposed MUNFA's December 6, 1985 application to the Newfoundland Labour Relations Board (NLRB) on grounds that faculty were not employees as defined by Newfoundland labour legislation, and that the University Act precluded collective bargaining. The employer also submitted a lengthy list of employees for exclusion from the bargaining unit, including all directors, laboratory instructors, librarians, contract employees, research fellows, and department heads. The NLRB met for five days in May, three in August, several more in October and December 1986, and January and February 1987. MUNFA was finally certified on March 24, 1988, 28 months after it applied (Swimmer 1986a, Léger 1986a, 1987a).

Dalhousie's association proposed special plan negotiations in 1977, but the administration would not meet the association's conditions for binding arbitration on salaries, fringe benefits, and grievances, recognition as sole bargaining agent, and sharing of all information necessary for bargaining. The administration offered binding arbitration solely on salaries, recognition as primary but not sole bargaining agent, and reasonable release of information. Faculty voted 119–29 in February 1978 to seek certification under the Nova Scotia Trade Union Act. The association was certified in November 1978, and ratified its first collective agreement in November 1979, for the period July 1, 1978 to June 30, 1980 (CAUT 1978b, Bartley 1979c).

Certification was only the first hurdle for a unionizing association, and in many cases an easy walk compared to the next step: getting a collective agreement. Employers may be required by labour law to recognize a union, but nothing compels them to sign an agreement. They are inclined to delay first collective agreements because these tend to serve union interests more than employers'. Where they faced obdurate employers, faculty had either to capitulate or go on strike.

Members of the Syndicat des Professeurs d'université Laval (SPUL) struck in September 1976 over failure to reach a collective agreement some 20 months after certification. Management and union were still far apart on fundamental issues, including grievance policy and salary structure, and salaries still set by individual contracts. Laval's was the second longest faculty strike in Canadian history, lasting until December 23. With the entire first term negated, the academic year had to be salvaged with two extended semesters, from January to April 1977, and from April through July.

Laval's contract established basic rights now commonplace in union contracts. Before certification, Laval's professors could not view their personnel files. The agreement gave professors the right to see their files, add information, and remove anonymous material. It established binding arbitration for grievances, the right to sabbatical leave at full pay for associate and full professors after six years of service, and a salary structure with narrower ranges between highest and lowest salaries and between salaries at similar age and rank. Salaries had been so low that catch-up for 1975–76 was 35 percent, with another 8 percent for 1976–77 and 6 percent for 1977–78. The back-to-work agreement restored half of the pay lost during the strike, since additional teaching was required to compensate for the lost semester. The union was left with a debt of $800,000. A year later the president of the SPUL noted extremely positive results from the grievance system (CAUT 1976c, 1977a, Coté 1978, Sullivan 1976b, 1977a).

When the Nova Scotia College of Art and Design's 40 faculty unionized in early 1985, salaries were low compared to other campuses and seriously distorted internally, with differences up to $18,000 for members with similar qualifications and experience. With no salary structure they could not count on yearly increases for experience, cost of living, or merit. Full-time faculty were hired on term contracts of one to five years, with no prospect of tenure. The union struck for 20 days in the fall of 1986, after 17 months of negotiation. Their collective agreement provided a reasonable tenure system, a salary scale with substantial increases for members' salaries that were out of line with the mainstream, the right to a sabbatical every six years with an increase to 80 percent of salary from 75 percent, improvements to the pension plan, professional development allowances, grievance procedures, and a ban on layoffs except in case of financial exigency (Swimmer 1986b, Léger 1986b, Grant 1989).

The longest single faculty strike in Canada was at the Université du Québec à Montréal. The faculty association (SPUQ) faced considerable difficulties in its first round of bargaining. It held a brief strike in 1970 to persuade the administration to negotiate a first collective agreement. SPUQ's strike in the fall of 1976 lasted for four months, postponing the end of the term to April 22, 1977. To complete the academic year, the winter term ran from May 2 to July 22, 1977, creating havoc with students' plans for summer work (Savage 1974, Sullivan 1977b).

Within a short period of time university faculty established a union presence across the country. Professors drew on academic experience to build a unique form of unionism suited to their workplace. Academic employees gained significant protection in a period when job security and salary gains of the 1960s were threatened by shrinking university revenue. Organizing and bargaining experience during the first decade of unionization prepared professors well for employers' more concerted attacks that began in the 1980s and intensified in the 1990s.

Member Interests

Unionization contributes to a democratization of the workplace. My colleague Jim Silver noted, in reviewing an earlier draft for this book, that unions replace 'arbitrary' rule with the 'rule of law.' On a non-union campus, the employer has great authority over salaries, benefits, and working conditions. Whatever the employer's logic for making decisions, it appears arbitrary to employees who had no part in the process. Employers can also unilaterally alter policies without having to justify their decisions. Unionization fundamentally alters the relationship between employer and employees. Employers are legally bound by provisions in a written collective agreement. Binding arbitration and due process ensure that employee grievances get a fair hearing.

Unionization also transforms accountability. On a non-union campus the employer must absorb the full brunt of its employees' dissatisfaction. When unions enter the picture, they assume some of this responsibility. The union must have clear priorities on how to distribute money for compensation: whether to put it into lower salaries, give everyone an equal amount, allocate it on a percentage basis, or use some of it for pensions instead of salaries. No decision will please all of its members. Anger over low salaries may be displaced onto a union if it fails to do its homework on members' priorities carefully enough.

Faculty associations quickly recognized the importance of fair representation. Member support was their most important asset in negotiating with employers. Internal conflicts over bargaining positions had to be resolved as far as possible before reaching the bargaining table. Debate over bargaining strategy needed to run its full course, even if it consumed considerable time and effort. Employers might exploit rifts among the membership, but had to listen seriously to unions that boasted members' unswerving support (Sheffield 1978, Garbarino 1975).

One of the basic issues in union representation was the definition of a member. Labour boards usually excluded anyone at the level of dean or above; yet classifying them as part of management challenged collegial traditions. Association charters did not envision that administrators might one day be pitted across the bargaining table against teaching members. Faculty associations were typically open to all academics, whether faculty, deans, directors, vice-presidents, or even president. Membership rarely distinguished between senior officers and teaching faculty, but brought them together based on academic identity without regard to university position.

Before applying for certification, faculty associations had to exclude from regular membership anyone not in the bargaining unit. Some associations created special associate status for deans, senior officers, and bargaining unit members elected to boards of governors. To allow certification at Bishop's University in 1976, the board of governors created a separate advisory board without students or professors for setting financial policy and negotiating collective agreements on behalf of the board (Cinman 1977e).

In its application to Manitoba's Labour Relations Board, the University of Manitoba Faculty Association proposed to include in the bargaining unit all administrators, up to the president of the university. The president happened to be a member of the association at the time. Jonas Lehrman, an activist in the association, reflected:

> It was at this point that the senior administrators felt themselves to be quite apart from the rest of their colleagues in the academic community and instantly applied to the Labour Relations Board for the exclusion from the unit of every academic with an administrative role. It was this action that split the academic community (Lehrman 1975).

Administrators preempted a labour board decision which would have excluded them anyway. Lehrman raises the important point that legal certification brought to the surface long-standing conflicts between employer and employee. The academic *community* he refers to could be maintained only so long as faculty did not challenge management authority. Defining a bargaining unit demonstrated more clearly than before that professors as employees and administrators as managers had different interests.

Once they clarified these issues and met labour board requirements, unions had to work out how best to represent their members. Reaching consensus was obviously difficult at a time when professors were still divided on whether they should be unionized at all. Bargaining for such an eclectic group proved an ongoing challenge, as associations struggled to develop proposals that might satisfy a wide range of conflicting and competing interests.

Bargaining positions reflected a conservative defence of the status quo favouring senior professors and men. Percentage increases continued to benefit this group because they began with higher salaries. Pensions were emphasized over starting salaries, parental leave, or day care services. This was not all that surprising, in light of what professors said a few years before unionized bargaining began. The 1971 survey conducted by Bernard Adell and Donald Carter found that professors viewed unionization as a way to protect and improve on the status quo rather than effecting social change (Adell & Carter 1972).

Women drew their lower salaries from the same pool of money as higher paid males who were not prepared to relinquish their advantage. Unions responded poorly to women's concerns at first, since men could easily out-vote them by four to one or greater: in 1978, women held just 14.6 percent of 30,280 full-time positions, with median salaries at $22,888 compared to $28,049 for men. Women's salaries were lower compared to those of men at the same rank, with similar degrees, recency of degree, and field of study. Women received lower salary offers when hired, an earnings disadvantage compounded throughout their careers—especially through interruptions for childbirth and raising children. Assessment for tenure and promotion rarely considered time out for maternity or parental leave (Boyd 1979, Vickers & Adams 1977, Schrank 1977).

Employers were rarely serious about employing more women, and unions not much better. Faculty were divided over affirmative action policies: many favoured them as a way of getting women hired into the system; others opposed them on grounds that any form of favouritism or discrimination undermined selection of the best possible candidates.

Women's issues were not seriously addressed until well into the 1980s, after more than a decade of research on the matter and considerable pressure on universities and faculty associations about well-documented inequities. Even then, employers and unions were not in the vanguard for reform. One of the main catalysts for affirmative action policies was the Federal Contractors Program. Recipients of large federal government contracts were required, under threat of losing their funds, to negotiate agreements between union and management which included explicit guide-lines for hiring from designated disadvantaged groups. The prospect of losing money forced the disinterested majority finally to do something about the rights of female minorities among them.

By 1997 women made up about 25 percent of 33,000 full-time faculty positions. Since the peak employment of 37,220 in 1992, the percentage gain for women was mainly because the number of full-time males dropped by 4,500 positions. The number of women increased by just 300 (see Table A–6). This modest percentage of female faculty is in marked contrast to the huge growth in numbers of students. Women made up the majority of students, at 56.4 percent of 822,700 in 1997–98, compared with 37 percent of 465,700 in 1970 (see Table A–1). Despite considerable pressure to hire women, universities' slow response has left men with the vast majority of full-time faculty positions, even while women fill most of the seats in the classroom.

The imbalance in faculty positions reflected the entrenched system of male privilege. Exploitation of female students by male professors went unremarked in this climate. The tide began turning in the 1970s. Newly hired women were less tolerant of these abuses of power than their male colleagues. Informal complaints began to surface on campuses in the latter 1970s, but few were pursued until universities established sexual harassment policies. The CAUT first adopted interim guidelines on sexual harassment in March 1981. By 1987, most universities had sexual harassment policies and staff to implement them (CAUT 1981b, Norissette 1987). Almost every campus has had a regular harassment caseload from the late 1980s on. A few of the more public cases indicate the volatility of the issue and the contradictions of the responses (Martin 1996, Andrews 1993).

There were other differences based on seniority and privilege. Senior professors who benefited from generous pension plans and flexible options for retirement opposed salary ceilings—since their compensation was already near the top of the proposed levels—and preferred the higher raises they received from percentage scale increases. Junior professors preferred equal flat scale increases, favoured money for career progress increments over other priorities, and preferred higher salary floors to removing ceilings.

Those in professional faculties with access to consulting contracts were pitted against colleagues over the extent of their privileges. For professors in law, engineering, medicine, and business, unionization threatened their higher than average salaries that were supposed to compensate for giving up lucrative opportunities in the private sector. Union salary scales held the same rate of increase for the entire bargaining unit. Professional faculty also opposed employers' limits on outside contracting, because it was a source of supplemental income. People in the arts, humanities and social sciences, who had fewer opportunities for this sort of income, were more sympathetic to management's concerns.

Grievances could disrupt member relations. The University of Manitoba Faculty Association was once vilified by some of its members for supporting the grievance of a professor fired after being convicted and imprisoned for sexually assaulting a minor. The decision was hotly debated within the executive and throughout the association. Critics argued that supporting the grievance made the association appear to condone the griever's behaviour. When the executive council countered that the union was duty-bound to give every member a fair defence, several of its members resigned. The case was settled informally, and while the dismissed professor never returned to the university, rifts among members took a while to heal.

Unions must also deal with members who are in conflict with each other. When the University of Manitoba Faculty Association requested an arbitrator's ruling to obtain resumés of applicants comparable to a member denied promotion to full professor, the three professors in question opposed the association's request. Finding itself in conflict with these three members, the association took the unusual step of paying for independent legal counsel to represent their interests to the arbitrator. The arbitrator refused the association's request, and eventually confirmed the university's denial of the promotion (Freedman 1994).

As they worked through the task of representing a diverse membership under a labour union framework, faculty associations became adept at managing a wide variety of internal tensions. Member discord was still secondary to the primary conflict with employers that drove faculty to unionize in the first place.

Faculty Rights Employers have full authority over everything that takes place in the workplace, unless limited by legislation or contract. Every collective agreement has a clause acknowledging management rights and confirming that union power derives solely from negotiating some of management's authority for itself. This places a burden on the union contract to list every material benefit and political advantage carefully, since matters not specifically covered default to management control. Dalhousie's agreement defines this succinctly:

> The Board, consistent with its rights and obligations in law, retains the powers to manage and operate Dalhousie University, *except as explicitly limited by this Collective Agreement* (Dalhousie University collective agreement 1990–93, emphasis added).

Dalhousie's union gets power from *limiting* management authority. This raises the interesting question of why a board would agree to limit its power to manage and operate the university. *Sharing* or *delegating* would allow the possibility that negotiation might enhance power, through better management, improved participation or shared control.

The language at Queen's is one-sided like Dalhousie's, but by using the neutral term of *modifying* the university's rights it allows the prospect of enhancing overall power:

8.1 The University shall possess the rights it previously enjoyed, except as modified by the terms of this Collective Agreement. Such rights shall be exercised in a fair and equitable manner consistent with the provisions of this Collective Agreement (Queen's University collective agreement 1999–2002).

Memorial has greater balance, but it vests all powers with management, with no reference to powers in the clause on members' rights:

MANAGEMENT RIGHTS

1.10 The Association recognizes that all rights, powers and authority which are not specifically abridged, delegated, or modified by this Collective Agreement are vested in the University. The University shall exercise such rights, powers and authority in a fair, equitable and reasonable manner.

COLLEGIAL RIGHTS OF MEMBERS

1.11 The University recognizes the right, privilege, and responsibility of Academic Staff Members to participate in collegial processes of the University as set out in Senate regulations, guidelines, policies and decisions, and as specified by this Collective Agreement. (Memorial University collective agreement 1992–95)

Unions are empowered in each of these clauses by negotiating new rights previously exclusive to management.

Management rights sparked the first strike outside Québec, at the Technical University of Nova Scotia. The union was certified in February 1980 and commenced bargaining two months later, with executive secretary of the CAUT Donald Savage as chief negotiator, backed by a local team. Throughout almost a year of negotiations, the university refused to cede exclusive presidential control over tenure, hiring, and promotion, opposed granting any form of maternity leave, and vowed to retain management's exclusive right to declare extraordinary financial exigency and redundancy of academic units. In June 1981, the faculty authorized a strike with a vote of 53–2. A strike on September 21, 1981 produced significant gains for the faculty in shared governance (Snow 1981a, Savage 1981a).

Professors have also negotiated something of an anomaly for employees: in addition to their responsibilities to teach, they have rights to do certain work. Unions in non-academic workplaces usually negotiate rights *not* to do certain work, to prevent members being overloaded or taking on other peoples' tasks. They strive especially for rights to refuse dangerous or unsafe work. For academics, the work issue is a different matter. They have rights to do research that follows their interests, and engage in consulting that suits their professional calling. Virtually every collective agreement stipulates faculty rights to carry out research, engage in outside professional activity, and do community service. For example, at Manitoba:

Faculty members shall be responsible for and have the right and opportunity to carry out a reasonable amount of meaningful research, scholarly work and other creative activities (University of Manitoba collective agreement 1998–2001).

Why do professors negotiate for the right to do work? This stems from the balanced conception of academic work. One part deals with duties and responsibilities to teach, do research, and perform community service. The other part treats professors as autonomous scholars with rights and opportunities to do their own research and scholarly work. Ask any academics about what they do, and they will invariably refer to "my research" or "my work."

Unionization established new plateaus for employment security and protection against administrative reprisals. It also extended academic freedom, a key feature of academic work. Most agreements embody the spirit of the CAUT statement that serves as a national standard. The clause in the University of Manitoba agreement closely follows the CAUT model:

The common good of society depends upon the search for truth and its free exposition. Academic freedom in the University in teaching, research and the dissemination of knowledge is essential to these purposes. The university faculty member is, therefore, entitled to freedom in carrying out research and in publishing the results thereof, freedom in carrying out teaching and in discussing his/her subject, and freedom from institutional censorship. Academic freedom carries with it the responsibility to use that freedom in a manner consistent with the scholarly obligation to base research, teaching and the dissemination of knowledge in a search for truth (University of Manitoba collective agreement 1998–2001).

Dalhousie's protection is more explicit:

3.02 The parties agree that they will not infringe or abridge the academic freedom of any member of the academic community. Members of the bargaining unit are entitled to freedom, as appropriate to the Member's university appointment, in carrying out research and in publishing the results thereof, freedom of teaching and of discussion, freedom to criticize, including criticism of the Board and the Association, and freedom from institutional censorship.

3.03 Academic freedom, as appropriate to the Member's university appointment, implies protection of Members by the Board and the Association from pressure intended to hinder or prevent them pursuing their scholarly and research interests and communicating the results thereof to students, colleagues and the community at large. The Parties acknowledge this responsibility, whether such pressure emanates from inside or outside the University (Dalhousie University collective agreement 1990–93).

Academic freedom means simply that professors may say what they wish without reprisal from employers. But ensuring this protection is a complex matter. Without comprehensive job security, professors with unpopular views could be dismissed for ostensible reasons such as budgetary restraint, reorganizing academic units, or eliminating courses or programs. Allowing professors to be removed for these reasons undermines academic freedom. Troublesome professors can be dismissed, with the true reasons disguised as financial or organizational.

Tenure prohibits removing anyone for these other reasons. Dismissal is allowed only for just cause—incompetence, persistent neglect of duty, or gross misconduct. Layoff is permitted only in extraordinary circumstances, such as a financial crisis severe enough to threaten survival of a program, faculty or the entire university. Tenured professors cannot be removed just because a department is reorganized, or a dean decides to save money by eliminating a few positions.

Layoff for financial reasons requires a demonstration that the university's stability or very survival is at risk, a condition referred to as financial exigency. Financial exigency clauses define the crisis, stipulate requirements for determining whether one exists, set out a process to identify faculty members for layoff, and establish their entitlement to notice, severance pay and benefits. Every collective agreement has versions of these provisions. Until 1995, Memorial's agreement had a limited definition of the crisis:

> A state of financial exigency is defined as a situation in which the University faces substantial and potentially chronic financial losses which threaten the overall functioning of the University (Memorial University collective agreement 1992–95).

The main strength of this clause is the requirement for the threat to be university-wide. It is weak on the nature of the crisis, with terms vague enough to cover a multitude of minor, reparable situations. Memorial improved the language in 1996. Both the University of Winnipeg and Dalhousie employ stronger language:

> A financial exigency exists if, and to the extent that, far-reaching reductions are required in University expenditures, which may include expenditures on Members' salaries, in order to avoid the financial collapse of the University (Dalhousie University collective agreement 1990–93).

> The term financial exigency denotes a condition when substantial and recurring financial deficits have occurred or, on the basis of generally accepted accounting principles, are projected for at least two (2) years, and which affect the total University budget and which place the solvency of the University as a whole in serious jeopardy (University of Winnipeg collective agreement 1993–95).

Most boards of governors retain final authority to determine whether an exigency can be declared. The University of Winnipeg's board relinquishes its authority to a three-person financial commission, one member chosen by the association, another by the board, and a chair named by the two nominees. This commission determines whether an exigency exists, the amount of money involved, and the maximum number of faculty members who may be laid off. The association has the right to receive any information it deems relevant.

The board at Bishop's University relegates authority to a four-person commission, two members chosen by the association and two by the corporation. Bishop's agreement prohibits terminating anyone over 50 years of age or with 18 years or more of service. Should an entire faculty or department be declared redundant, only untenured staff may be laid off. Tenured staff within five years of retirement may be redeployed, retrained, or given early retirement (Savage 1980a).

No university has yet implemented an extraordinary financial exigency. Requirements of exigency clauses are stringent enough to discourage all but the most determined administration. Further, procedures for exigency shatter the unilateral authority enjoyed by university boards and administrators, requiring extraordinary levels of consultation and third party review. Universities must open their books to scrutiny, and officials are under great pressure to exhaust all possible alternatives to exigency—the main intent of these clauses.

Compensation

By the time they unionized, professors' salaries and benefits had improved moderately from the low levels in the 1950s, although still below professional levels outside the universities. Concern over possible loss of these modest gains played a key role in many organizing drives.

Salary packages had as many as five components. First was a scale increase to cover rises in the cost of living due to high rates of inflation in the late 1970s and 1980s. Second were career progress increments to pay for experience and productivity. Third was catch-up money where salaries were lower than at comparable universities. Fourth was a component to reduce discrepancies within the bargaining unit resulting from discrimination rather than qualifications and experience. Last was merit, promoted by employers as a means of rewarding productive employees and opposed by unions because it allowed management to exercise favouritism.

Faculty at Notre Dame University in Nelson, B.C. signed their second collective agreement on October 11, 1974 with a 16.5 percent scale increase, plus career increments and an improvement in the employer's contribution to the pension fund from six to 7 percent. Before reaching agreement, faculty served notice of a strike on September 30, 1974. The agreement set up an additional 1.4 percent in a fund to address long-standing salary discrepancies. One professor's salary rose from $9,700 to $17,400 (CAUT 1974d).

Saint Mary's University Faculty Union's first collective agreement, signed in December 1974, carried a 10 percent salary increase plus a $300 cost-of-living bonus. Sabbatical pay rose from 50 to 75 percent of regular salary. There was also a provision for justice and dignity few other associations have been able to obtain: professors filing grievances for suspension or dismissal were presumed innocent until proven otherwise and would receive full salary and benefits until after an arbitration board submitted its decision. (This is a significant benefit, since arbitrations can drag on for months or even years.) The settlement also introduced decentralized academic decision-making by creating faculty councils (CAUT 1975f, g).

Carleton University's first agreement had a salary increase of $750 on November 30, 1975, another 18 percent on January 1, 1976, and a dental plan. The agreement improved job security with a clause that allowed layoffs only in the event of a financial stringency. The board of governors could establish financial stringency only after a commission found no other possible options for saving money. The contract contained generous provisions for severance and notice (Masleck 1975b).

Negotiations for the first agreement at the University of Ottawa were settled in 1976 by an arbitration panel that chose the final position of the Association of Professors of the University of Ottawa. The increase had 12.8 percent on salary scale plus 3.8 percent for career progress increments, including $100,000 each for salary anomalies and merit (Masleck 1976).

Under the special plan at the University of British Columbia, an arbitrator's 1981 decision awarded an 18 percent salary increase for 1981–82, comprising 14.2 percent for the rise in the Consumer Price Index plus 3.8 percent for past erosion of real income. An additional 3 percent covered career progress increments, merit awards, and inequities adjustments (Léger 1981a).

A case at the University of Manitoba came at an opportune time, when lower government grant increases were squeezing university budgets. In 1979 the employer and union submitted their final salary positions to binding arbitration. The union based its package of 8 percent on scale plus

3.94 percent for career progress on historic salaries and industry comparisons. The employer's final offer of 8.51 percent argued that it could not afford to pay anything more. The arbitrator chose the union's package. He concluded that ability to pay was a consideration but not to the extent of preventing a reasonable salary increase. Giving it more weight would allow the government grant to determine the salary settlement automatically (Léger 1981a).

Union Impact

Unionization was a far sight better than the one-sided management rule it replaced. It gave professors a say in determining terms and conditions of employment; collective bargaining and grievance procedures replaced ad hoc methods of conflict management with more orderly systems.

Collective bargaining was remarkably successful. Faculty enhanced reforms begun in the 1960s, increasing their pay and benefits, introducing stronger job security, and extending academic freedom. They were fortunate in those early days to have academics as senior officers at the negotiating table: even though they represented management, many sympathized with union demands for better academic working conditions.

Strong collective agreements profited the entire system. Better benefits and working conditions attracted high quality academic staff and made it easier to retain them. Staff relations were smoother and more predictable. Conflict resolution was vastly improved. Even senior officials acknowledged these advancements. William Farr, Vice-President for Employee and Student Relations at York University, maintained that collective bargaining replaced ambiguous and inconsistent policies. It streamlined conflict resolution. Disputes were likely to stay on the issues instead of becoming more personal or political than necessary. Differences were settled more expeditiously, consistently, and clearly (Farr 1979).

Unionization increased the administration's status, size, and strength. More staff were hired to monitor and review decisions on hiring, tenure, and promotion and to handle grievances and appeals. Staff expertise expanded to include knowledge of labour legislation and academic procedures. Department and faculty level decisions about sabbaticals and other leaves were channelled through the administration to assure consistency with the collective agreement. Administrators became involved in academic decision-making, as department heads and deans consulted them for guidance in interpreting collective agreements (Buchbinder & Newson 1985, Hartnett 1980).

Even though most universities opposed unionization at the outset, and some actively fought against it, once certification was done they negotiated contracts that were sensitive to academic needs. Contract provisions are rooted in academic traditions. Tenure, academic freedom, sabbaticals, and faculty participation were old ideas. Unions realized substantial gains over modest provisions and policies that were already in place. Non-salary gains were not costly. Tenure cost nothing in the short run. Sabbaticals were virtually self-financing because salary savings covered the cost of part-time replacements.

Sabbaticals are a good example of an existing provision that was improved. In a 1974 survey of its 45 member associations, the CAUT found that 42 already had sabbatical policies that gave presidents or boards the authority to approve each request rather than having them automatically granted. Compensation during sabbaticals was far below regular salary rates, even though professors were expected to work throughout their leave. Living costs while on sabbatical might even rise since professors were encouraged to work at locations away from their home campus. Just six universities provided close to full salary; 21 paid between 51 and 80 percent, and eight paid 50 percent. Only six universities provided money to cover additional costs of travel and research. Employers defended low sabbatical pay because savings were necessary to cover replacements. Yet 13 of the 45 had no provision for replacement (CAUT 1974c).

Saint Mary's first agreement increased sabbatical pay from 50 to 75 percent of salary (CAUT 1975f). The first reported case of sabbaticals being established as a right was at Carleton University (Scarfe & Sheffield 1977). Bishop's obtained sabbaticals as a right, with 100 percent salary, in its first collective agreement in 1977 (Cinman 1977e). Benefits at these levels spread quickly through collective bargaining on other campuses.

By the latter 1980s, over 80 percent of Canadian faculty were in certified unions or covered by special plans. After more than a decade of experience they were well organized and better prepared to achieve their objectives at the bargaining table. Continued declines in funding dashed any cause for optimism. By 1985, education received 12.7 percent of total public expenditures, down from 18.5 percent in the mid-1960s, with every sign of further reductions down the road (Bigelow, Gold and Siren 1987).

As fiscal pressure intensified during the 1980s, employers and governments took a hard look at unions and collective agreements. Unions made fewer gains, as employers came to the bargaining table with salary scales revised downward and weakened articles on financial exigency. They were better prepared to confront unions at the bargaining table, with large, centralized administrative units that had worked through growing pains and learned to live with unions and collective bargaining. Struggles over salaries, pensions, and job security became ever more contentious. Faculty associations were adept at minimizing their losses. They were prepared to go on strike, and did so with increasing frequency throughout the 1980s and 1990s. The net result was a system increasingly in crisis. While faculty and administration fought their battles, provincial governments began to assist management with legislation that hampered unions' ability to press their demands. The federal government radically changed funding to create opportunities for making profit from research. University administrators began transforming their institutions to conform to governments' new priorities for a leaner system less dependent on public money and geared to raising its own revenue in the market. To meet these objectives, universities had to sell their services. Moving academic teaching and research in corporate directions required considerable change in how the university did business.

Professors were a significant hindrance to carrying out this fundamental shift in orientation: they would not willingly give up their hard-won freedom.

Chapter 7

Professors on the Line

> We're the last people in the world to do things because we think they are
> important, not because we are told to do them (Personal interview).

IN THE EARLY 1980s academic unions still sought improvements at the bargaining table, expecting that even if money for salaries was tight, other benefits would continue. But as revenue continued to fall, employers brought less money to the table, demanded concessions on salaries, benefits, and job security, and even tried to reclaim money already committed to pension plans.

Bargaining in the 1980s became marked by pitched and frequent confrontations between union and management. Unions would not accept rolling back gains achieved through collective bargaining. With employers holding fast to their positions, unions faced the harsh reality that discussion at the table was no longer sufficient to get a deal. They went on strike with increasing frequency.

Government exerted powerful influence on collective bargaining through reductions in financial support for the public sector, as well as legislation and policy changes which tipped the bargaining scale in favour of employers. The federal government imposed wage controls across the country. The provinces set limits on negotiated salary increases, dictated freezes, imposed days off without pay, suspended collective bargaining rights, and denied basic rights to form unions.

**State
Intrusion**

Economic conditions stagnated throughout the 1980s, with high rates of inflation and unemployment. Ottawa's Liberal government attempted direct control over wages and prices, something used before only during wartime. Though the unemployment rate had more than doubled over the decade, the Liberals decided to reduce inflation rather than improve the employment picture. Bill C-73, passed on December 3, 1975, allowed federal control over wage increases in large unionized workplaces. Price controls were a policy objective never clearly carried out. Wage increases were controlled by the Anti Inflation Board (AIB), empowered to review collective agreements and roll back salary settlements above its guidelines.

Wage and price controls were based on two misguided assumptions; that wages caused inflation, and that government could control prices. They did not address the major factors driving inflation in Canada: rising costs of energy, especially oil; high interest rates; and inability to control prices of the large quantities of imported goods. The program's main short-term impact was to keep negotiated wage settlements within guidelines.

The wage and price control program signalled a new era of state intervention. The AIB was more intrusive than any known peacetime policy. The provinces also began to micro-manage the rights of labour in the public sector. Unions were warned that if they stepped too far outside acceptable boundaries, government would bring them back in. This was as true for unionized professors as anyone else.

Members of the Carleton University Academic Staff Association had cause to celebrate in the fall of 1975. Salaries were so far behind other universities that a quick round of bargaining produced a first collective agreement with an 18 percent increase for 1976. The settlement raised lagging salaries, covered cost of living increases, and improved job security. But they could not justify the salary increase to the AIB, and this became the Board's first rollback of a union settlement. Carleton's professors got 14 percent, to meet the board's guideline of 8 to 12 percent for scale, and an allowance to restore Carleton's traditional pay relationship with other Ontario universities (AUCC 1976a).

Professors at the University of Ottawa met a similar fate. Their first agreement was settled by final offer selection arbitration. The arbitration panel selected the union's 12.8 percent scale increase that was later reduced by the AIB to about 9 percent (AUCC 1976b).

Wage controls affected everyone who negotiated for salaries. When union representatives met management at the bargaining table, government was a silent third party. During my first experience of collective bargaining, the administration team walked in wearing buttons with Ottawa's *6&5* slogan, an unmistakable message that government was on their side. (This was a formula imposed on federal public sector workers by the Trudeau government in 1982 and 1983.)

The federal anti-inflation program was the beginning of hard line government cutbacks across the country. When Ottawa reduced cost-sharing commitments for health and post-secondary education, the provinces pulled back even further. Funding became determined more by local politics and ideology than by sound economic policy. When British Columbia paid its first operating grant increases in five years, at 5.8 percent for 1987–88, Saskatchewan imposed its deepest cuts ever. Alberta reduced university grants by 3 percent for 1987–88, after cutting real income per FTE student by $700 over the previous eight years. Ontario raised university grants by 8 percent in 1986–87, and 7.3 percent for the following year, following a decade of wage controls, freezes, and cutbacks (CAUT 1987a, Morissette 1987a, Mandelbaum 1987, Riseborough 1987).

Government funding deadlines played a prominent role in bargaining. Employers offered salary packages conditional upon provincial funding, and which expired on the day that a province announced its spending. Unions were tempted to settle for mediocre salary offers, rather than gamble on losing even more if government grants came in below their targets.

Government removed union rights, strengthened management powers, and dictated settlements without warning or consultation. Social Credit governments in British Columbia and Alberta, Tories in Ontario, and Liberals in Québec passed more strikingly anti-democratic laws than mere wage controls. They used legislation to remove fundamental collective bargaining rights. Legislative procedures violated democratic process by proceeding without consultation.

When the B.C. Social Credit government replaced Notre Dame University in Nelson with David Thompson University Centre in 1977, the province terminated all tenured and untenured staff, retroactively decertified the faculty association, and deprived the small group of professors of successor rights on the new campus. Successor rights would have entitled faculty to retain their academic positions and their collective agreement. Granting successor rights was warranted under the labour code because the government continued to provide academic programming on the site. Despite widespread protest, the province refused to change its position (Lowe 1977, Epp 1980).

Bill 91 in September 1977 amended the Universities Act to prohibit university faculty and professional librarians in British Columbia from applying for trade union certification, again introducing the bill without consultation. Pauline Jewett, president of Simon Fraser University, publicly criticized the government for interfering in university-faculty matters. Social Credit's - 1983 Public Sector Restraint Act allowed university administrators to impose layoffs, provided their procedures were approved by the government-appointed Compensation Stabilization Commissioner (Cinman 1977f, Shorten 1983, Savage 1983, Sullivan 1977c).

Soon after British Columbia's amendment, as part of a broader assault on government employees, Alberta revised its Universities Act to deprive professors of bargaining rights under the Alberta Labour Act or the Public Service Employee Relations Act. Bill 41, enacted in May 1978, removed public-sector employees from coverage under the Alberta Labour Act, eliminated the right to strike for targeted groups of civil servants, and restricted topics that could be brought to arbitration (Lowe 1978, Vanderberg 1978).

Ontario's 1982 Inflation Restraint Act imposed 9 percent wage controls on public sector workers for agreements signed before October 1, 1982 and 5 percent for contracts signed between then and September 30, 1983. Draconian provisions of the act froze all other terms of collective agreements over the control period, and suspended binding arbitration and the right to strike (Shore 1982, Snow 1983a, CAUT 1983b).

Québec suspended public sector collective bargaining, imposed salary cuts of almost 20 percent for January 1 through March 31, 1983, and set ceilings for salary increases over the following 33 months. Québec teachers and members of the Québec Common Front responded with a limited general strike in January 1983. Bill 111 forced them back to work and suspended all trade union rights. Employees could be dismissed with just a written notice. Arbitration was allowed on some dismissals, but with a reverse onus of proof on the person who was fired. The legislation empowered the government to suspend dues checkoff for six months for each day the strike continued. Striking employees were automatically fined one day's pay and loss of three years' seniority for every day of work missed. Additional daily fines were set at $50 to $100 for individuals, $2,000 to $10,000 for union officials, and $10,000 to $50,000 for unions. The Québec Labour Code was transferred to the criminal courts. It heard evidence given in other proceedings without the witness's presence, and suspended the federal and provincial charters of rights (Levesque 1983).

The latest innovation—legislation for public sector employees to take days off without pay—was first an option in the Ontario NDP's 1993 Social Contract Act. Manitoba's Progressive Conservatives, under Premier Gary Filmon, shut down most government services for ten to twelve "Filmon Fridays" each summer and sent their employees home without pay. Manitoba's legislation also authorized universities, school boards, hospitals, and community health centres to impose unpaid days off on their employees. Unions were forced to accept these conditions, and employers took swift advantage of the option. So eager was the University of Manitoba to use these new powers during 1994 negotiations that it started deducting money from pay checks for 12 unpaid days several months before the bill was even passed in the legislature.

Premier Gary Filmon made no secret of his disdain for Manitoba's unionized professors. Not long after the faculty's 1995 strike, his government amended the University of Manitoba Act to allow mandatory retirement for members of the faculty association. This provision was extended in 1998 to faculty at other Manitoba universities. Mandatory retirement is forbidden for every other employee in the province under a Human Rights Act prohibition on discrimination based on age. Legalizing mandatory retirement dealt the University of Manitoba a huge bargaining card in 1998 contract negotiations.

Why have successive governments suspended public sector workers' bargaining rights and weakened professors' union and human rights? Cost containment and convenience are major factors. Legislation forces wage cuts quickly and effectively, bypassing complex, drawn out bargaining that may produce more costly settlements.

Concern over cost may explain why governments have acted this way, but it does not justify their actions. By unilaterally imposing their will, governments have sacrificed democratic process for political and bureaucratic expediency.

Governments have asserted their control by undermining union rights. Otherwise they would have to negotiate and endure the occasional strike like any other employer. No matter how politicians may depict unions as greedy and unreasonable, strikes show that government is not fully in control of its employees. Governments have taken extraordinary measures to avoid embarrassment. Legislation may be a shameful alternative to genuine negotiation, but it has the advantage for elected governments of showing that they are in the driver's seat.

The control issue is even more deep-seated with professors. Their labour-intensive work is costly. Government pays the bill for their salaries, but has no direct control over what they say or do. Academics are immune from retaliation even when they openly criticize government policies and practices. A province would have to push a university to financial exigency before professors could be laid off.

Throughout the latter 1970s and 1980s, Ottawa and the provinces altered the climate of collective bargaining on campus. Removing money from university budgets made negotiations difficult enough. Additional measures by government strengthened management's hand and limited union options. Employers' escalating demands for concessions began to threaten fundamental aspects of unionized collective agreements. Professors who would never have dreamed of labour militancy began to consider the final avenue for a union under fire—strike action.

Faculty on Strike

When employers attempted to inflict government-imposed budget reductions on faculty, unions had to act. Universities tabled meagre salary offers, reduced job security, and even went after pension surpluses to shore up sagging finances. Professors found themselves on the defensive as never before. Some accepted salary reversals because they were worried about public perception of privileged academics fighting for more money while the rest of the labour force endured layoffs and earnings setbacks. But acquiescence was risky business. Gaining concessions in one bargaining round only encouraged employers to demand more rollbacks the next time they came to the bargaining table. Employers became relentlessly uncooperative. Professors found strike action the only way to have their demands taken seriously.

The threat of a strike can be as potent as a strike itself. The last few days before picket lines are set up may be the most productive period of bargaining. Once a strike begins, it may take weeks until conditions ripen for settlement. Many negotiations are settled on the eve of a strike, the moment of greatest leverage for the union.

On March 3, 1980, administration and union representatives at the University of Windsor settled just 45 minutes before professors were scheduled to go on strike. The administration wanted to remove the financial exigency and redundancy clauses from the collective agreement. Faculty were convinced this would allow arbitrary dismissal and spell an end to tenure and academic freedom. The final agreement contained a strong clause requiring the board to demonstrate a bona fide financial exigency to an independent three-person commission. A redundancy clause prohibited layoffs where departments or faculties were eliminated, unless affected professors refused reasonable options for retraining or redeployment (CAUT 1980e, Savage 1980a, Snow 1982a).

Memorial University settled on February 6, 1996, just one day before a strike date. The administration wanted to weaken financial exigency measures already far below the norm, and to replace the collective agreement with a much weaker administrative handbook. The final agreement established a much stronger financial exigency article which required verification by a five-person union-management committee (CAUT 1996a).

All told there have thus far been 25 strikes by Canadian faculty unions on 20 campuses involving some 7,000 professors. Two took place in the 1970s, seven between 1981 and 1986, and 16 after 1987 (see Table A–10). Striking became more frequent and intense in direct proportion to employers' increasing pressure for concessions.

When the call comes to report to a picket line, union members confront one of the most difficult decisions of their careers—whether to strike and, if so, how active or visible to be. As the usual machinery of the university ceases to operate, striking employees step out on their own, without the security of pay checks or the comfort of daily routines. Members are required to do unfamiliar work and assume new responsibilities. Many who have never been close to a picket line are now required to walk one, and to encounter the wrath of people wanting to cross. But strikes can also be liberating. Participating in job action is as close as most workers ever get to democratic self-management.

Strikes concentrate an enormous amount of positive energy. Students and members of fellow unions march with picketers to show their solidarity. Money and messages of support arrive from campuses across the country, assuring strikers that they are not alone. A strike is a momentous turning point in the life of a union. Contrary to images in the popular press of violent and aggressive militants on picket lines, a strike is in essence an act of passive resistance, a refusal by employees to abide by the usual rules of the workplace on the employer's terms. Strikers learn valuable lessons about individual and collective strengths that serve them well in successive rounds of bargaining.

A 1988 strike at the University of Saskatchewan took an interesting approach to withdrawal of services. Their collective agreement had an unusual feature that allowed faculty to strike only in their teaching capacity. Accordingly, professors stopped teaching but still worked in their offices, conducted research, and took breaks to walk the picket line. Striking faculty at most universities vacate the campus, unless they need to care for animals and plants or monitor laboratory experiments. Saskatchewan's setup diluted participation in the strike, since striking professors carried on with much of their regular work. The strike came to an abrupt end on April 8, when the province legislated professors back to work to ensure they would administer final exams and submit course grades. This is the only instance in Canada of a government forcing professors back to work (Fairbairn 1988, McManus & Byfield 1988, Stobbe 1988).

Lakehead: Union Maturity

At Lakehead University the union's stage of growth may have been more significant than the actual issue which sparked a strike. Lakehead's compact campus sits in a tranquil section of Thunder Bay near the north shore of Lake Superior, and boasts such amenities as a lovely stream running into a small artificial lake behind the main building complex, and a student pub claimed to be the second largest of its kind in the Commonwealth. Union support runs high in this working class town whose livelihood depends on grain handling in the port and on pulp and paper manufacture.

Lakehead was about 12 years old when its professors began serious talk of forming a union. The first attempt failed by a two-to-one vote. Frustrated by successive salary settlements imposed by the administration, a condition described by an association executive member as "binding supplication," faculty indifference to unionizing shifted to interest and eventual support. The president of the Lakehead University Faculty Association (LUFA) at the time recalled that he opposed unionization when taking office in 1976, but gradually changed his mind when rounds of reasoned discussion failed to achieve agreements between the association and administration. Two years later LUFA was certified as official bargaining agent for the university's professors, and he became chief negotiator for the first agreement.

Bargaining was the dawn of a new era for Lakehead's professors. For the first time they could negotiate salaries instead of waiting for the employer's edict. Though they did not get large increases, they improved other aspects of their work through deliberate compromises between money and non-monetary benefits such as the right to inspect personal files. The contract established due process, a great improvement over the arbitrary and inconsistent treatment previously meted out in tenure and promotion.

A decade later, on January 15, 1988, Lakehead's faculty went on strike during an unseasonably mild spell for normally frigid Thunder Bay. More than 90 percent of voting professors favoured striking. The union wanted Lakehead's salaries to rise by at least one notch from its position at 11th in the province. Other unresolved issues included maternity leave, patents and copyrights, and pensions. It eventually became necessary to strike for negotiations to progress.

In an interview a few years later, a member of the bargaining team said:

> I don't think the university ever expected a strike. Neither did I. To this day I don't know how we fell into it. We were all drawn into it. Some of it was in a way beyond the parties' control.

Others have speculated that the strike was simply part of the growing pains and maturation of a union in a labour-oriented town. The strike was over in 10 days, with reasonable settlement on the outstanding items. Another member of the negotiating team commented on the social and political value of the experience:

> People got to know each other, people felt much better about one another, from opposite ends of the campus. "We showed them," was very often said. All of the little injuries that we daily suffer from administrators or our colleagues, all of that was washed away or ameliorated. We felt healed. It was marvellous.

LUFA's strike bolstered its confidence and strength. Its members returned to work feeling they had achieved something significant. When LUFA and the administration next went to the bargaining table in 1990, they achieved a collective agreement after nine sessions.

Dalhousie and Trent: Pensions and Attrition

Professors at Dalhousie University are some of Canada's most seasoned unionists, with three strikes between 1985 and 1998. The first, after 10 months of negotiation, lasted for one day. Beyond salary issues, the main point of contention was the employer's withholding of $5.1 million in contributions to the pension plan, on grounds that the plan had a surplus. This strategy has been attempted by other employers with defined-benefit pension plans, when actuaries estimate that the accumulated capital is more than necessary to cover all commitments. Dalhousie's faculty maintained they were entitled to this money. Payments were restored to the plan after the strike.

Withholding pension contributions is possible only with defined-benefit plans which pay a fixed rate, typically 2 percent for each year of service calculated on the average of the final few years of salary. More flexible money-purchase plans cannot have a surplus—they vest all accumulated contributions plus investment income with the employee. Retiring employees receive the entire accumulated cash in their accounts.

Dalhousie's 1987 negotiations included a compromise that divided the members. In exchange for a salary increase, the union gave up a clause that required the university to replace faculty members who left. Negotiated in the first collective agreement, this clause made it very difficult for the employer to eliminate a vacated position. At the time union members thought they had obtained "an absolute prohibition against non-replacement," but in practice the clause was difficult to enforce. The university did not fill vacant positions, even though this violated the spirit of the agreement. An active member of the association described the union's strategy:

> That absolute prohibition didn't work because what you actually got was deals under the table, deals between deans and the administration, where they would say, "We won't fill this right now, we haven't lost the position but we're not going to fill it right now, and besides that you're going to get another person with a scholarship over here." It was impossible to control. So we gave that up for a clause which required them to name what they were going to do, just say out loud what they were going to do so we'd keep track of it.

Members of the executive and bargaining team misread the views of a large number of members who railed against this move as abandoning an important principle.

Dalhousie professors struck for 12 days in November 1988, over salaries, workload, and pay equity between men and women in the bargaining unit. The board was prepared to offer comparability for female faculty, but not for librarians, counsellors, or instructors in the bargaining unit. Before the strike, the administration announced they would cut off strikers from research grants and refuse reimbursement for costs of attending academic conferences. This initiative backfired, especially among faculty in the medical school and science departments. People in these fields relied extensively on research grants, resented what they saw as unreasonable administrative controls, and became strong supporters of the strike (CAUT 1985a,b, 1988a).

A decade later, Dalhousie's faculty were again on the picket line, this time to stem a 15 percent attrition since the last strike. Enrolment had risen by 15 percent, but the administration had not replaced 113 faculty who had retired or left the university since 1987. The union sought full replacement of all professors leaving during the new contract, and to narrow a 15 percent salary gap with comparable institutions. After striking from March 25 to April 1, 1998, the union gained a 13.5 percent financial package over a 44-month term, plus strong assurances to replace early retirees and develop a process for dealing with attrition in the future (CAUT 1998a,b).

Retirement and replacement are thorny issues. Faculty have taken advantage of early retirement bonuses paying between one and one-and-a-half times annual salary for professors over the age of 55. This practice ranks financial considerations above academic priorities. The age group contains the university's senior scholars and some of its finest teachers just reaching the zenith of their careers, yet universities dangle a retirement carrot because senior professors also receive the highest salaries in the system. A short-term strategy to release much-needed money could impose a significant cost to the educational quality of the system if replacements are not managed carefully.

Early retirement creates a challenge for academic planning. Whenever large groups leave at the same time, distortions are bound to occur. Departments with many senior faculty stand to lose a large portion of their staff, including specialists in key programs. Research programs suffer, courses cannot be taught, and graduate students lose the expert advice they need to complete their studies.

Despite the planning problems they create, faculty associations have favoured early retirement incentives—they allow renewal, with money to hire young, newly trained faculty, and provide bonuses for retiring professors.

Departments must get permission from administrators to hire replacements. Control over these decisions allows administrators to exercise considerable power over academic priorities, refusing replacements in some areas while allocating them to others. Experiences at Dalhousie and Trent offer examples of strategic use of retirement to eliminate positions. Both unions took a firm stand against retirement as attrition, and management on both campuses refused to change their policies until the faculty went on strike.

Trent's faculty struck late in 1996. After seven months of bargaining, union and management remained far apart on the use of a pension plan surplus, on raising salaries to par with other Ontario universities, and on replacement of faculty. Over the previous four years the number of full-time faculty had declined by 14 percent, as positions of retirees and others leaving were left vacant. The agreement that ended a two-week strike included a process for resolving differences on the pension surplus, a mechanism for achieving salary parity, and a commitment from the university to maintain the complement of full-time faculty. By Spring 1998, the association reported that use of the pension surplus was resolved, and salary parity adjustments continued (CAUT 1998c).

Manitoba: Academic Freedom   Professors at the University of Manitoba unionized in 1974 when relations with the university's president were bitter, especially over authoritarian style, unilateral changes to the process for granting tenure, and a foiled attempt to introduce a tenure quota system.

For more than a decade the University of Manitoba Faculty Association (UMFA) was reasonably successful at the bargaining table, achieving collective agreements on par with others across the country. Bargaining deteriorated with the government budget cuts of the latter 1980s. The administration brought very little money to the bargaining table, and attempted to limit job security. In the spring of 1990, just days before final exams commenced, UMFA held its first strike vote, with a strong majority of 517 to 223 in support of a full-scale walkout. Concerned about the consequences to students of delaying exams, and the fears of strike action expressed by many association members, the executive decided to wait until fall. The agreement was settled in August.

Five years later UMFA did go on strike with a vote of 635 to 206. There was no money on the table. The union's team accepted salary reductions in the form of up to nine days off without pay in each year of the proposed agreement. The most contentious item was a proposal to allow administrators to lay off individual faculty. This would gut tenure's protection against laying professors off unless the university faced an extraordinary financial exigency. Even in an exigency, Manitoba's agreement, like most others, prohibited senior administrative involvement in layoffs because this interfered with academic freedom. A victory for the administration would be a watershed for campus labour relations. UMFA's strike began on October 18, 1995.

Frost was in the air at 6:00 a.m. on October 18, as picketers assembled in the dark at the four campus entrances. By 7:30 the line was a hive of activity. Police physically restrained picketers from the roadway while cars entered the campus. They ordered my picket line to move away from a crosswalk location to a spot that would ease the flow of traffic and make picketing far more difficult. Reached by cell phone over his morning coffee, our lawyer confirmed that we need not move. A bus driver who refused to cross the picket line was suspended on the spot by his supervisor. Even with their union officials present at the picket line, sympathetic drivers were forced to cross the line under threat of discipline.

The small body of picketers distributing their leaflets restrained hundreds of steaming cars in the morning rush. By 9:00 the cars slowed to a trickle, police departed, the air was calm, and picketers dug into doughnuts and hot coffee. The intense order of the picket line gave way to professors strolling casually about the area. The picket captain reminded them to spread out and walk single file. Someone muttered that he would have more success herding cats.

The outward calm of the picket lines by this time in the morning belied the pandemonium of their support system. Strike headquarters, a store front in a strip mall near campus, was bedlam. Telephones rang incessantly with queries from members and the media. People ran from phone to phone, supplying whatever information they could, writing messages on slips of paper and sticking them to the wall in the hope that someone would find them and respond. In the back room a small group built picket signs. Others huddled over drafts of a news release and a newsletter to members. With no one apparently in charge of organization, everyone tried doing everything. Doughnuts and coffee, the staple of strikes, disappeared as fast as they arrived.

Within days the strike organization was transformed. One of the first to establish order was a professor from Middle Eastern and Judaic studies, a vocal and articulate opponent of strike action who nonetheless arrived at headquarters early on the first morning prepared to support the democratic will of the majority. He immediately set up a badly needed protocol for incoming and outgoing messages on the overheated fax machine. This pattern of quickly identifying and filling needs was repeated continuously. Librarians set up a system to organize up to 500 picketers at four sites for six shifts a day. A cartographer improved picket line decor with elegantly hand-lettered signs. Music students and their professor, self-proclaimed "Minstrels of Redundancy," lifted spirits with rousing renditions of labour songs at formal and informal gatherings. Bands of lawyers and economists were on call for research and analysis or advice required by the bargaining team.

An Internet page set up by a mathematics professor reaped electronic mail support from around the world. The faculty association published an open letter addressed to the premier of the province from A.G.W. Cameron, professor of astronomy at Harvard University and a Manitoba graduate, stating that first-rate scholars and students would shun the university if the administration should prevail. This letter sparked considerable public debate and even drew a response from Premier Filmon, who attempted to discredit the author of the letter as a poorly informed astrologer. Even trifling tasks drew upon appropriate expertise. Manure deposited overnight on a picket site was scooped up by a botanist delighted with this treasure for his plants.

Manitoba's professors felt the full range of first-time strike emotions. Pre-strike terrors of the picket line evaporated as participants experienced joy, anger, fear, and boredom in their daily excursions. Old friendships were renewed, new ones were formed, and some relations frayed irreparably. High expectations when the negotiating teams met plunged to despair when negotiations broke off. Colleagues crossing the picket line drew responses ranging from wrath to indifference.

Direct involvement by the premier of Manitoba added to members' woes. He stated publicly that the union's demands to retain the article on extraordinary financial exigency were unreasonable, since these provisions did not exist in any other collective agreement in the country. More worrisome than his ignorance of the facts was the premier's alignment with management against the union. By taking sides on the issue at the very heart of the dispute, he endangered the province's ability to help the parties reach an agreement. The union appealed to the province to appoint a mediator after the university repudiated calls for arbitration or mediation. At first the premier and his minister of labour rejected the request because an arbitrator's ruling or a mediator's report might favour the union, but the province eventually relented and appointed a mediator who helped the parties reach an agreement.

Manitoba's professors returned to work after 23 days on the picket line, having achieved an agreement that restored the protection they sought and even improved job security over the previous agreement. As with all good settlements, each side claimed success. The strike was hailed as a victory by the union, while university president Arnold Naimark said the agreement provided a model for maintaining academic freedom and integrity of programs.

These positive utterances do not mean that relations were entirely smoothed over or that conflicts were ended. Strikes are battles, after which both sides need time to assess their gains and heal their wounds. Professors faced difficult but manageable hurdles of restructuring courses and re-scheduling assignments and exams. Repairing frayed relations took rather longer; some could not be patched and remain hostile to this day. Eventually the campus returned to normal, although it would never be quite the same. No matter how much anxiety it provokes, the prospect of another strike will never again evoke fear of the unknown for those who went through it.

Strikes are the culmination of conflict between faculty and administration over job security, salaries, pensions, workload, tenure, copyright, technological change, and even parking. Once a strike is on, every issue is scrutinized in the press. In Manitoba's case the sides bargained in the pages of the *Winnipeg Free Press* through rival advertisements about contract proposals. Such campaigns provide limited information about what really takes place during the strike. They rarely change anyone's opinion, but do alert the public that all is not well between professors and their employers. The public sees only the tip of an iceberg. Below the surface lie a multitude of grievances over rejected promotion or tenure applications, denial of performance increments, charges of sexual harassment, allegations of unprofessional conduct, reprimands, suspensions, or firings.

Mount Allison and York: Rollbacks

In 1991 the president of Mount Allison University and the Mount Allison Faculty Association (MAFA) struck a parity committee to examine the president's contention that only layoffs and salary rollbacks could solve a budgetary crisis. The five-member committee unanimously decided that the problems could be solved over three years without layoffs or rollbacks, and the university senate endorsed their recommendations. Nonetheless, when negotiations for a new collective agreement began in August 1991, the university demanded salary clawbacks of up to $3,700 per faculty member, sabbatical entitlement reduced to just once every 20 years, and elimination of a policy allowing faculty to continue working past the age of 65. The president threatened to lock faculty out after examinations unless they accepted the rollbacks. MAFA struck from April 3 to 18, 1992 after more than six months and 32 sessions of unproductive bargaining. The three-year agreement stipulated no rollbacks, froze salaries in the first year, and paid cost-of-living allowances for the next two. The administration dropped its proposal on sabbaticals, and the union agreed to mandatory retirement at 65, with an option of continuing to age 67 at half time (CAUT 1992a).

York University is a large commuter campus, with 28,430 full-time students, 9,470 part-time, 8,460 in non-degree courses, and 1,125 full-time and 702 part-time faculty (York University 1997, 1996 figures). Barely 30 years old, York is the culmination of a 1959 corporate vision. The layout is strikingly similar to office buildings in its suburban surroundings. The campus has its own mall, York Lanes, complete with franchise food outlets and other shops typical of commercial shopping malls across the country. Business mentality has so infused fund raising that in 1997, without even consulting the faculty, the dean of Atkinson College sought $10,000 in corporate donations in exchange for official sponsorship of new multimedia high-tech courses bearing the name or logo of the donor company. This proposal was withdrawn after considerable protest. York's corporate-dominated board and its continuing drift toward business interests became an issue during the 1997 strike (Klein 1997).

York University Faculty Association was unionized in 1975 in one of the few uncontested certifications in Canada. YUFA's first major job action was withholding of grades for one week in 1981 to improve the salary settlement. Four years later, YUFA struck for two days in October 1985, again to improve a salary offer. Ending mandatory retirement, the other major item on the table, was settled in principle before the strike began. Negotiation for one of the best retirement packages in the country was completed during the 1987 round. York's professors were the only ones in Canada who had successfully bargained the right to work past the age of 65. They could also receive as much as 2.25 times their salary for retiring before 65 plus options for part-time teaching past retirement (Léger 1985b).

Gaining the right to work past 65 was a major achievement. Except for Manitoba and Québec, where it is prohibited in human rights legislation, retirement is mandatory at 65 everywhere in Canada. In the latter 1980s, the CAUT supported a challenge to mandatory retirement in Ontario launched by professors at the universities of Guelph, Toronto, Lakehead, and York—using a provision of the Canadian Charter of Rights and Freedoms prohibiting discrimination on the basis of age. The Supreme Court upheld mandatory retirement in its December 6, 1990 decision in *McKinney v. University of Guelph*.

In 1996 negotiations York's administration proposed to cancel the retirement package. In June, after four months of bargaining, the administration called for conciliation, a step that has serious consequences in Ontario.

The conciliator filed a "no board report" in July, signifying that an agreement could not be reached. Ontario labour law permits strikes or lockouts 15 days after a report is filed. In August, the administration used a provision of Ontario labour law allowing employers to abrogate a collective agreement once a strike or lockout is permitted, regardless of whether they actually take place. The administration also attempted to impose a salary settlement outside of collective bargaining.

Few issues unite faculty more than authoritarian or arbitrary edicts from management. YUFA's strike ballot was supported by 71.3 percent of the 620 voting members (the bargaining unit had 1,073 members), a notable increase from the 53 percent vote for the 1985 strike. Cancelling the collective agreement without consultation struck fear in the hearts of some professors, and drew anger and militancy from others.

Professors were less united over retirement. Opponents criticized the YUFA leadership's determination to retain the entire retirement package. Others insisted that the package should be preserved until the administration offered reasonable compensation. Having sacrificed monetary benefits in the 1980s to obtain flexible retirement, they now wanted some of the money back. The issue divided people on the left who were usually united on union issues. Many people also criticized the union's insufficient attention to equity. York's record for employing female academics was higher than the Canadian average, with women at just over 32 percent of full-time faculty. But their salaries lagged behind men's. During the strike, YUFA eventually incorporated pay equity into its salary position.

Faculty returned to work on May 14, 1997, the day after they ratified the three-year contract proposed by a mediator, and eight weeks after the strike began. Retirement became mandatory at 65, and bonuses for retiring early were markedly lower than before. Modest salary improvements were supplemented by close to $3 million for pay equity adjustments over the life of the agreement. The agreement now includes class size and total student load in calculation of workload—a matter of note for academics who face rising class size and falling faculty: student ratios. The contract also establishes a joint committee to study and develop recommendations on impacts of technological change.

Strikes rarely end neatly. Few people are completely satisfied with the final contract, evidenced by the 75.6 percent approval in the ratification ballot. In York's case, the biggest issue was losing the right to work past the age of 65. The loss is unfortunate, but defending it had become untenable. Everyone else in Ontario's labour force faced mandatory retirement. Drawing salaries past 65 pitted younger against older faculty, an understandable division in the short term when money for salaries is so limited, but short-sighted since younger professors will one day themselves face retirement with no option to continue past 65. Mandatory retirement is a gain for administrators. It saves money and improves their ability to predict when professors will leave the system.

Returning to work did not ameliorate the harshness of the strike. Statements made at the height of tension are not easily forgotten or set aside, nor are damaged relations between union and administration easily repaired. York has its share of unresolved conflicts amongst faculty who took opposing sides during the strike. YUFA members showed their continuing anger by voting a lack of confidence in York's administration at the ratification meeting. Of the 570 people voting, 79.6 percent supported the motion.

Consequences of Strikes

What can we learn from these experiences? From the union standpoint, strikes have become a necessary part of the bargaining process. Employers are now far more aggressive at the bargaining table, refusing to budge unless a union can at least pass a strong strike vote. Strikes range in duration from just a few days to several weeks.

What kinds of unions are likely to strike? The simple answer is that strikes have already been held by virtually every type of union across a broad spectrum: specialized institutions like the Technical University of Nova Scotia, small liberal arts campuses like Mount Allison and Trent, medium size universities like Lakehead, and large, complex regional institutions like Laval, Dalhousie, Windsor, York, and Manitoba.

Some novice unions went on strike in order to get a first collective agreement. Others had already weathered decades of bargaining before a defining impasse that lead to a strike. No union ever takes a strike vote lightly. But even associations which agonized over each step in the process that led to their first strike vote rarely hesitated to call for striking when they faced another deadlock.

Who goes on strike? Militants bent on confrontation, radicals organizing for change, or disgruntled professors fed up with setbacks and losses? There are no clear patterns or stereotypes. Faculty members on every campus hold a wide range of political and ideological perspectives. People on the left usually provide leadership, support, and active involvement, although there are exceptions where they are divided during a strike. Many people on the right may be just as involved in all aspects of a strike. Even those who oppose unions may support their association if they see no other avenues for a reasonable resolution.

Field of study is not a reliable indicator of who will support a strike. Social scientists and humanists tend to provide more than their share of participants, but engineers, lawyers, and business professors, wrongly type-cast as steadfast holdouts, are just as likely to be picket captains, organizers, and strategists. During its 1995 strike the University of Manitoba Faculty Association was well served by former deans from law and science.

Successful strikes require member solidarity. Academics set aside their differences when basic rights are threatened because they agree on certain fundamentals about their work, especially the primacy of academic freedom, tenure, and quality of education. Perceived threats in these areas are almost certain to unite professors. Withdrawing prior commitments and rolling back benefits already in place are other unifying causes. When employers attempted to take pension contribution holidays they reneged on an understanding that they would always pay in as much as the employees. Using actuaries' estimates of surplus to stop their payment was a mistake. This was money already committed, and taken on faith as part of the compensation package. Removing it was tantamount to seizing a basic entitlement.

Material conditions defined the context for these battles, and in the end were their root causes. University presidents and members of their boards are not inherently mean-spirited. They are not inclined to introduce harsh measures bound to draw the ire of their faculty, unless pressed by severe financial and political circumstances. Still, they have alternative approaches at their disposal, and imposing extreme penalties was seldom if ever necessary. Before any strike was over, each employer had rescinded the initiatives that resulted in the walkout. Unions did not get everything they were after, but they did manage to eliminate the devastating consequences of their employers' demands. Employers' claims of impending disaster were groundless. Every one of these universities has survived with the compromises they worked out.

Have most strikes been necessary? With hindsight, it is easy to claim that astute, sensitive managers could have prevented the conflicts by introducing workable compromises at an earlier stage of negotiations. But this ignores the powerful influence that extreme conditions exert on adversarial relations. Management and board see their hands as tied by tight budgets and unmanageable salaries. They are sorely tempted to hold out, even if it requires pitched battles with faculty. Winning promises to lower costs and buy a great deal of flexibility. But these supposed benefits are illusory: no employer has ever succeeded in imposing their conditions on a striking union.

Strikes are costly, over and above students' lost teaching time and employees' foregone wages. Some less tangible costs are possibly more expensive in the end. Employees usually decide to strike because relations with management have already deteriorated. Strikes heighten the tensions, bringing out the best and worst from participants. Pitched battles over issues can spill over into personal brawls, leaving shattered relations that are difficult to mend. Insults pitched by either side can poison the academic atmosphere for some time to come. Union members do not easily forget or forgive colleagues who crossed their picket lines. Trust between union and management is difficult to rebuild. In some circumstances senior officers have left an institution in the wake of a strike.

Unions almost always walk away from a strike stronger than they were before it started. They build unimaginable solidarity among members, many of whom discover each other for the first time through discussing ideas, sharing personal fears. and building on others' complementary strengths. During a strike, a union is unequivocally in charge of its members' actions. This may be a first time that they have the same purpose with fellow employees, and do serious collective work. After meeting on picket lines, and depending on each other in ways rarely found in the academic workplace, professors leave a strike knowing how well they can work together.

Union Strength

Unionization began because faculty were at risk of losing perquisites and salary improvements acquired in the 1960s. Their persistence has prevented university boards and administrators from weakening academic freedom and the autonomy of universities.

In just over two decades faculty unions developed into a seasoned force in grievances, at the bargaining table, and on the picket line. Through collective bargaining, faculty strengthened their position in the university at a time when their influence through senate was being eroded. Faculty associations became the main body for representing faculty interests.

Faculty unions managed to retain and sometimes improve working conditions against onslaughts from universities and the state through the 1980s and 1990s. These were major accomplishments, especially in light of the powerful forces shaping the corporate university.

Universities for Sale

At the turn of the 21st century universities are under extreme pressure to commercialize and privatize. Most faculty unions recognize that these changes would work against their interests. The bargaining table has become a forum for the future of the university. The following chapters discuss these forces and the kind of university they are producing.

Chapter 8

Capitalist Research:
A Marriage of Convenience

[O]f all the types of institutions which gather people together in a common effort, the university remains the least inhibiting to variety in ideas, convictions, styles, and tastes (Kingman Brewster 1972).

UNIVERSITY AUTONOMY began to falter in the 1980s, as governments withdrew financial support. Canada's universities were following a path that was already well paved by universities in the United States. Sheila Slaughter and Larry Leslie argue in *Academic Capitalism* that commercialism developed more slowly in Canadian universities than in the United States, Australia, or the United Kingdom. Only in the 1980s and 1990s did lack of public support for core programs made them vulnerable to the enticements of private sector money.

Over their history, universities have served business at arm's length, supplying trained graduates, independent studies, expert advisers, and contract research. Government now acts as matchmaker to marry business and university interests in seamless research enterprises.

Developing a Research Infrastructure Until 1919, government support for business-related research was largely in mining, fishing, agriculture, and forestry. Modest beginnings for the mining industry dated as early as 1842, with the Geological Survey of Canada housed at McGill University. After Confederation, its world class research was closely linked to industry through a division of the federal Department of Mines. University-based research remained modest, with few direct ties to industry, yet its value for commerce was already recognized. By 1900 the Canadian Manufacturers Association lobbied for closer relations between industry and universities (MacAulay 1984).

Until World War I industrial research was still virtually nonexistent in Canada. People in federal government circles saw this as a serious problem:

substantial industrial research was needed to stimulate domestic production and reduce Canadian dependence on equipment and technology imported from Europe. At the same time interest grew in collaboration between university-based scientific research and industry. Support for industry-university cooperation came from prominent industrialists, the Canadian Manufacturers' Association, leading academics, and university officials. Corporations subsidized the training of future researchers as early as 1916, paying most of the graduate fellowships at the University of Toronto (Enros 1981, 1991, MacAulay 1984).

Federal strategies emulated the British Department of Scientific and Industrial Research, established in 1915 to mobilize corporate and university research for the war effort. In Ottawa, a 1916 order-in-council established the Honourary Advisory Council on Scientific and Industrial Research, later known as the National Research Council (NRC). The council's initial appointed membership of 11 men included four university-based scientists, three senior university administrators, two senior corporate executives, and two consulting engineers (Gingras 1989, Eggleston 1978, Neatby 1987).

Between the wars, federal support helped to increase the number of corporate research laboratories from 37 in 1918 to 998 in 1939. University and government research capacity expanded as universities trained the growing body of research staff. Graduate enrolment rose from 423 in 1920 to 1,569 in 1940, and degrees and licenses rose from 248 to 837. The NRC supported 711 fellowships and bursaries for masters and doctoral students on large campuses. Eighty-six percent of these awards went to physics and chemistry, concentrated at the University of Toronto with 325 fellowships, McGill with 232, and Queens with 52. But scholarship and research were still far from first-rate. Libraries were in poor shape, there was a dearth of learned societies and journals, financial support for students and research was at low levels, and faculty were both underpaid and overworked (Harris 1976).

World War II was a watershed. The federal government intervened at all levels of economic planning through a judicious mix of crown corporations, government agencies, and regulation of private industry. Federal investment in munitions manufacturing spawned a staggering growth of applied university-based research in radar, explosives, atomic energy, land, sea, and air warfare, metallurgy, food technology, and medical applications. Ottawa greatly expanded NRC infrastructure: the number of staff rose from 153 in 1935 to 2,000 a few months after the outbreak of hostilities. The

NRC's $7 million budget supported 21 new laboratories conducting wartime scientific research, including an explosives experimental station at Valcartier, large nuclear research laboratories in Montréal, an atomic energy plant at Chalk River, large radar research laboratories and a field station near Ottawa, naval research stations on the East and West coasts, and a large complex for aeronautical and engineering research just outside Ottawa (Gingras 1989, Thistle 1966). By the end of the war, applied research had a strong foothold on larger campuses.

Post-war federal institutions were larger and stronger than ever before, adept at managing the economy, producing goods and services, and conducting and coordinating research. But Ottawa dismantled the substantial public infrastructure developed during the war, abolishing national planning, scaling back government-run programs, and privatizing publicly-owned enterprises. It also encouraged new foreign investment, even though Canada had managed a vibrant wartime economy entirely with domestic capital.

Turbo Research Limited is one example of privatization. It was made a crown corporation in 1944 to take over an NRC project to develop gas turbine and jet aircraft engines. This entire field of research was turned over to the private sector. Turbo Research was closed in 1946, and its work on design, development, and manufacture of jet engines handed over to A.V. Roe Canada Limited (Eggleston 1978).

Opportunities for basic and applied military and domestic industrial research expanded considerably after the war. The NRC became a key player in encouraging government-industry-university cooperation in science and engineering (Eggleston 1950). The NRC trimmed its 13 research divisions and extensive laboratories by spinning off separate agencies: the Defence Research Board in 1947 under the Department of National Defence (Goodspeed 1958); Atomic Energy of Canada as a crown corporation in 1952 (Harris 1976); and the Medical Research Council in 1960. By then Ottawa was supporting university research with $15 million from the NRC, $1.7 million from the Defence Research Board, $3 million from the Department of National Health and Welfare, and about $1.5 million from other agencies and departments (Glassco Commission 1963, Report IV).

But Ottawa had still not managed either to coordinate research or develop clear policies to guide spending. Practical industrial research promoted by the NRC was not being taken up in universities or corporations. Canadian companies were reluctant to develop costly in-house research, which required lengthy lead time and produced no immediate payoff. The number of branch plants in Canada probably hampered the development of domestic industrial research. Parent corporations with their own research centres outside Canada could provide information and product more cheaply than could Canadian subsidiaries.

Corporate-university cooperation got a boost in 1956, at a national gathering of academics, business executives, and government bureaucrats in St. Andrews, New Brunswick. They formed the Industrial Foundation on Education, the first national body outside government devoted to cooperation between industry and university and financed entirely by industry. Discussion at the gathering went beyond its initial purpose of supplying more graduates to business and government, and the IFE spawned more regular and intense collaboration between university, business, and government (Pilkington 1984, Bissell 1974).

During the 1950s, recommendations from three royal commissions reinforced business and government interest in universities. The 1951 Massey Commission on the Arts, Letters and Sciences argued Canadian universities were threatened by severe funding shortages. Massey recommended increased spending on universities to strengthen the liberal arts. Ottawa responded later that same year with $7 million in direct payments to universities.

The Massey Commission had less impact on research policy. Massey found excessive concern with scientific research and professional training at the expense of liberal arts. (His recommendation for a Canada Council finally saw the light of day in 1956.) Massey's voice was an exception among the rising tide driving government money toward materialistic ends. Universities were on the verge of far more extensive ties to capitalist production, and Massey's eloquent defence of the humanities got a weak reception compared to the scientific, professional, and business lobbies.

The 1957 Royal Commission on Canada's Economic Prospects urged further spending on universities because Canada's economic fate depended on high quality accessible education. The Commission pressed for closer coordination between industry and university to serve national research objectives (Axelrod 1984).

The 1960 Glassco Royal Commission reproached Ottawa for being too lax in directing scientific research. Glassco said the NRC had far too much autonomy and an academic orientation towards basic research, rather than supporting applied research and the needs of industry. Glassco's recommendation for a central agency to advise Parliament on national science research priorities had an impact on federal policy. The Science Council of Canada was eventually formed in May 1966 to advise government on applying science to Canada's economic and social problems, and became an influential advocate for use of university research to serve industry (Glassco Commission 1963, Eggleston 1978).

Two major 1967 investigations of national policy on university research helped focus federal direction. A Senate inquiry chaired by Senator Lamontagne argued that research efforts in science should serve national economic and social objectives. It recommended more support for applied and less for fundamental and basic research, and favoured a comprehensive national science policy to coordinate research (Canada Senate 1970).

J.B. Macdonald, a former president of the University of British Columbia, questioned this trend towards serving industry in an inquiry co-sponsored by the Science Council of Canada and the Canada Council (Macdonald 1969). Macdonald favoured strengthening university autonomy, ensuring faculty independence to determine their own research. He wanted more federal support for research, graduate student assistance, and university libraries. The Science Council rejected Macdonald's recommendations. Members of the council argued that the granting councils should instead support mission-oriented research and increased cooperation between university and industry (Science Council of Canada 1969).

Gradually the federal government committed more money to university research. Close to $100 million a year was paid out in the late 1960s, 80 percent from the NRC, MRC, and Canada Council, and the remainder from government departments, the Defence Research Board, and the Atomic Energy Commission of Canada. Almost 63 percent was in science and engineering, 21 percent for medical research, and only 15 percent for humanities and social sciences (see Table 8–1 below).

Table 8–1
Federal Council Support of University Research, 1967-68

Canada Council	$	11,208
Medical Research Council		20,500
National Research Council		45,400
Total Councils Support		77,108
Mission-Oriented Support*		
Sciences		16,459
Humanities & Social Sciences		$4,104
Total Federal Expenditures	$	97,671

SOURCE: Davidson 1985.
*All government departments and agencies funding research
in the universities.

The national granting councils were reorganized in 1976, by expanding the Medical Research Council's mandate, folding the NRC granting functions into a focussed new agency, the Natural Sciences and Engineering Research Council (NSERC), leaving fine and performing arts with the Canada Council, and forming the Social Sciences and Humanities Research Council (SSHRC). Ottawa did not develop a national science policy (Cameron 1991).

Social sciences and humanities received virtually no government support before World War II. Between its 1940 inception and 1957 the Canadian Social Science Research Council (SSRC) became the main source of money for research, graduate student assistance, and conferences. About 85 percent of the $720,000 it paid out over these years came from the Rockefeller Foundation and Carnegie Corporation, with the remainder from universities and colleges, private individuals, and organizations. Even when the Canada Council was formed, SSRC had to get a $150,000 grant from the Ford Foundation to manage the transition.

The humanities fared no better. From its 1944 beginning, the Humanities Research Council of Canada received no money from government, and relied on Rockefeller and Carnegie for more than 80 percent of support totalling about $350,000 (Harris 1976).

Natural sciences fared far better. Total research and development in 1971 was $1.2 billion for the natural sciences, compared to $157 million for humanities and social sciences. By 1983, natural sciences spending was up by 19.1 percent, in constant 1971 dollars, while social sciences and humanities fell by 22.7 percent (see Table 8–2 below). Social science and humanities research in universities was financed chiefly by internal university money, which made it vulnerable to fluctuations in university funding. Most research funding for natural sciences came from external sources.

Table 8–2
Research and Development Expenditures in Canada
by Scientific Field

Year	Natural Sciences[a]			Human Sciences[b]		
	$	% of R&D[c]	% of GNP	$	% of R&D	% of GNP
1971	1,160	88.1	1.23	157	11.9	.49
1975	1,686	88.2	1.02	226	11.8	.14
1980	3,204	90.4	1.08	340	9.6	.12
1983	4,969	91.5	1.28	459	8.5	.12

SOURCE: Davidson 1985 Table 1.
[a]Includes science and engineering
[b]Includes social sciences and humanities
[c]Total Canadian R&D

Linking Universities to Industry

By the 1980s government had scaled back core funding and was striving to harness university research to business needs. Government programs encouraged partnerships aimed at enabling business to exploit the full market potential of findings from university research. These partnerships marked a significant turning point in business approaches to universities. A business executive member of NSERC explained it in 1985:

> Industry can no longer afford to do all of the long-term research it needs to survive; thus it is no longer looking at universities simply as an inexpensive source of trained people, but also as a vast reservoir of expertise which can perform that urgently needed long-term effort (NSERC 1985, 74).

At the time Canada's industrial research was weak. OECD studies showed Canada lagging behind other member countries in encouraging university-industry ties (OECD 1984). Despite government efforts through the Science Council of Canada and NSERC, industrial research and development in Canada was just one percent of GNP, compared to an average 2.5 percent for other OECD countries. Part of the problem was industry's poor research record. Corporations carried out just 48 percent of the Canadian total, concentrated among a few very large firms, compared to between 60 and

70 percent in other OECD countries. Federal government research consisted of regulation and provision of in-house information.

University research was thus a vital part of the Canadian mix. In 1981 universities accounted for about 26 percent of total R&D expenditures in Canada, as compared to 14 percent for the United States (Doutriaux and Baker 1995). Ottawa attempted to redirect the priorities of university research towards the needs of industry. The Science Council played a lead role: its chair, Geraldine A. Kenney-Wallace, issued a "call to intellectual arms," imploring Canada's universities to transfer their knowledge and findings to corporations (Science Council of Canada 1988, x).

During the mid-1980s the Science Council promoted the concept of the *service university*—one that would directly provide scientific benefits to industry and government through entrepreneurial, technical, research, training, investment, and management services. The council stepped beyond the boundaries of its science mandate to prescribe service roles for social scientists and humanists: market research, personnel management, and study of the social impact of corporate actions.

Slow response from university scientists displeased the council, which criticized universities for underplaying the transfer of knowledge and technology to industry. It urged university presidents and administrators to encourage faculty and student commitment to this mission (Science Council of Canada 1988, Davidson 1988).

Business responded favourably to government's support for partnerships. In 1985 university and corporate presidents established the Corporate-Higher Education Forum to advocate a new model of partnership over the old one of corporate patronage. Forum members exhorted university researchers to define projects according to the needs of business, and corporations to seek profitable returns from closer partnerships with universities. Placing corporate interests on the research agenda drew favourable nods from university officials who saw opportunities for new income (Corporate-Higher Education Forum 1987).

Giant corporations like IBM already sought concrete benefits from their donations. The company had traditionally given small arms-length donations to a large number of universities. Now IBM replaced them with a smaller number of negotiated arrangements with greater visibility and closer relationships with university staff for training, hardware, and software development. IBM committed close to $50 million of in-kind contributions over the first three years of the program. Recipient universities were required to put up an equal amount of money (Maxwell & Currie 1984).

The federal government took up the partnership cause with a host of new but ill-defined granting programs that required university researchers to demonstrate how outcomes would benefit business with new products, expanded markets, or more efficient production. Academics could hardly ignore these programs as other sources of money disappeared. Government poured public money into private companies on the assumption that recipients would make good use of it. It also offered money to researchers prepared to meet industry's requirements. There was no comprehensive planning other than emphasizing research for business. Promises for grants and subsidies were supposed to motivate potential applicants.

Program requirements were confusing, and delivery poorly organized through an ad hoc mixture of agencies. One review in the latter 1980s identified no less than eight separate special programs promoting university-industry linkage in the National Research Council alone. It located another six in the federal Department of Industry, Trade and Commerce, and numerous initiatives in other departments. The federal Department of Supply and Services gave preference to private industry in its annual $2 billion for engineering services contracts. Contracts with universities had to show how the resultant technology would be transferred to industry. Provincial research councils and programs also targeted support for home industries (MacAulay & Dufour 1984).

Although these initiatives followed the huge withdrawals of money from university core budgets, they did not replace the lost money or repair damage from cuts. They merely redirected some of the lost money to targeted programs benefiting the private sector.

We can get a flavour of changing priorities by looking at a few of these programs. Many were in the Department of Industry, Trade & Commerce. Industrial Innovation Centres focussed university resources on aiding small and medium size technology-based firms. The centres were supposed to develop products, processes, and businesses; provide courses; conduct research on entrepreneurship, management, and innovation; and develop spin-off companies. Between 1970 and 1982 Centres of Advanced Technology sponsored 15 centres to apply university teaching and institutional research to higher-risk industrial technologies (see Table 8–3 below). Most centres were on university campuses, but the more successful ones had additional support through parent provincial research organizations, where facilities were already established for specialized industrial technology, technical information services and active industrial networks (MacAulay & Dufour 1984).

Table 8–3
Centres of Advanced Technology 1971 to 1982

Centre	Parent Institution	Amount	Start-ed	Term
Powder Metallurgy	Ontario Research Foundation	$450,000	1971	3 years
Systems Building	University of Toronto	$300,000	1971	3 years
Canadian Institute of Metalworking	McMaster University	$830,000	1969	6 years
Ocean Engineering	BC Research	$1,225,000	1973	3 years
Technologie de l'environ-ment	Université de Sherbrooke	$300,000	1974	3 years
Ocean Technology	N.S. Research Foundation Corp	$1,075,000	1974	7 years
Systems Analysis, Control & Design	University of Western Ontario	$1,195,000	1973	7 years
Biomedical Instrumentation Devnt Unit	University of Toronto	$875,000	1976	5 years
Canadian Food Products Devnt Centre	Manitoba Research Council	$55,000	1974	5 years
Health Industry Development Centre	Manitoba Research Council	$225,000	1976	3 years
Waterloo Centre for Process Devnt	University of Waterloo	$1,000,000	1978	5 years
Measurement & Control of Particles & Vapours	McGill University	$1,000,000	1978	5 years
Advanced Instrumentation	Saskatchewan Research Council	$1,000,000	1982	5 years
Fisheries Technology	Technical Univ of Nova Scotia	$1,000,000	1982	5 years
Atlantic Coal Institute	Univ College of Cape Breton	$1,000,000	1982	5 years

SOURCE: MacAulay 1984, Table 2. Funding is from Industry, Trade and Commerce

Another departmental program, Industrial Research Institutes, set up institutes on 11 campuses between 1967 and 1980 to market university research to industrial firms. After initial grants these Institutes were expected to be self-supporting from fees for overhead and program management. At least four achieved this objective. In his summary of a departmental review of the program, James MacAulay (1984) notes that except for a successful program at the University of Waterloo, the other 10 had limited accomplishments.

Industrial Research Associations (IRA) was a multi-year, multi-million dollar program for companies in an industry to contract with universities for academic expertise. Associations were established for sulphur, welding, gas, masonry, and plastics. The Welding Institute of Canada sponsored a Masters of Science degree in welding engineering with the Universities of Toronto and Waterloo that became part of Waterloo's cooperative on-the-job training program. Associations had minimal appeal for researchers because competing companies protected proprietary information on products and production processes (MacAulay & Dufour 1984).

In early 1980 Industry, Trade and Commerce set up a special electronics fund which received $93 million by 1982 for major projects in proven firms. The fund supported a university centre in every province, at $1 million each, to develop microelectronics applications for manufacturing and processing industries in its region. Centres were run jointly by representatives from industry, government, and university.

The provinces also supported technology transfer. Ontario's Board of Industrial Leadership and Development (BILD) matched grants for university-based, corporate-sponsored research. BILD started in 1981, with $5 million over two years for projects in the natural sciences and engineering. Each project required a contract between the host university and a corporation to "facilitate the successful transfer of research results from the university laboratory to industrial production in the future and thereby contribute to the continuing development of the province" (Bell 1990).

BILD matched corporate contributions to a maximum of $50,000 per contract. More than 85 percent of $4.27 million spent on 167 projects went to large universities: Queen's received 8.6 percent; McMaster 15.9, University of Toronto 28.3, and University of Waterloo 32.5. Seven universities shared the remainder.

BILD program findings reveal the notorious weakness of using matching grants to influence business investment. A survey of corporations whose research contracts at Ontario universities were awarded BILD matching grants suggested that the majority would have participated in university research without government support. Nonetheless, BILD was followed by more ambitious initiatives. The University Research Incentive Fund, set up in 1984, paid out $3.3 million to 29 projects in its first year and another $17.8 million on 215 corporate projects between 1986 and 1988 (Bell 1990).

Federal experience shows similar patterns. The national granting councils spent close to $400 million in 1987–88 to match cash or in-kind contributions from corporations, foundations, trusts, nonprofit organizations, and crown corporations, provided the money went to a council or university. A 1988 review by the Senate Committee on National Finance deemed the program unnecessary, since most of the projects it supported would have proceeded without the matching funds. The program did little more than subsidize private companies for contributions they were already prepared to make (Cameron 1991).

Ottawa also reorganized government agencies to focus more directly on research assistance to industry. In 1990, the federal government created the department of Industry, Science and Technology by absorbing the more science-focussed Ministry of State for Science and Technology and the Industry, Trade and Commerce Department, which had been relegated to a branch of the Department of Regional Industrial Expansion. The new department's mandate was to direct science policy towards the concerns of industry.

Research councils were reorganized. Between 1976, when it was spun off from the NRC, and 1981, NSERC paid out $1.2 billion in grants to encourage closer ties between corporations and universities. NSERC became a leading player in Ottawa's drive to shape university research to the needs of industry. By 1984–85 annual grants of $656 million accounted for 36.1 percent of all money received by Canadian universities for research in the natural sciences, engineering, and medicine. The Medical Research Council was second at 21.8 percent (NSERC 1985).

NSERC has paid sizable sums to university researchers for serving industry interests. Corporations have contributed very little new money. NSERC's second five-year plan noted that "university-industry interaction existed long before the specific targeted programs and would exist today without those programs." Universities attract corporations because they offer profitable investment, regardless of whether government adds money. Matching grants do not improve the level of corporate contributions (NSERC 1985, 1991).

The federal Networks of Centres of Excellence program (NCE) took commercialization further. In the first competition in 1988, each application had a 20 percent weight for demonstrating linkages amongst industry, university, and government, and 20 percent for showing that results would lead to new products or processes for commercial exploitation. Quality of the proposed research program counted for 50 percent, and 10 percent was reserved for proof that an adequate management structure was in place.

The first 15 projects, funded in 1989–90 for $240 million over five years, involved 32 universities and 168 corporations. One centre was in the social sciences, a network on aging based at the University of Toronto. The other 14 were scientific. An interim review of the program noted increased collaboration between scientists in universities and industries, and called for more of the same (Canada 1989). Most of the network involvement went to large universities that assembled the myriad required participants and prepared the complex applications (see Table 8–4 below). The bias towards major universities reflects the extensive resources necessary for preparing costly time-consuming proposals.

Table 8–4
Networks of Centres of Excellence Phase I

University	No. of Networks
British Columbia	13
Toronto	12
McGill; Laval	9
Alberta	8
McMaster; Ottawa; Calgary; Queens	7
Montréal; Saskatchewan; Victoria;	6
Concordia; Western Ontario; Manitoba; Waterloo ; Guelph	5
Simon Fraser	4
Ecole Polytechnique; Dalhousie; York	3
Carleton; Trent; Technical University of Nova Scotia; Sherbrooke; New Brunswick	2
Memorial; Mount Allison; Lakehead; Windsor; Univ of Québec at Rimouski; Univ of Québec at Trois Rivière	1

SOURCE: House of Commons 1993, Appendix B: "Description of the Networks."

A favourable review of Phase I by the House of Commons Standing Committee on Industry, Science and Technology, Regional and Northern Development recommended retaining the criteria and weights (House of Commons 1993). Phase II, for three-year projects starting in 1994/95, increased emphasis on commercialization, explained in five equally weighted criteria. *Excellence of the Research Program*, stressed "areas of research with high economic and social impact." The criterion for *Highly Qualified Personnel* required expertise "in research areas and technologies that are critical to Canadian productivity and economic growth." *Networking and Partnerships* expected "links among academic institutions and public and private sector participants." *Knowledge Exchange and Technology Exploitation* required developing "new products, processes or services for commercial exploitation," and transferring technology to private and public sector partners. The final criterion required evidence of sound *Network Management* (Networks of Centres of Excellence 1995).

A report prepared for the NCE suggested the changes were designed

> to increase private sector involvement in all network activities, *including the establishment of research priorities*. One premise of the program is that strengthening the linkages between university, government, and private sectors will facilitate the exchange of information and technology, stimulating the private sector's ability to capitalize on frontier research and accelerating the commercialization of research results from the network (Networks of Centres of Excellence 1992, 12, emphasis added).

Within a short period of time, eligible academics have put considerable effort into working with industry and designing projects for commercial outcomes. Some—in fields such as engineering and computer science—are already amenable to working with business. Others—in medical and social sciences or humanities—do not have the business orientation necessary for commercial applications, spin-off firms, and equity fund-raising. This may be the most significant impact of the networks: shifting the focus in these fields away from research for teaching and professional development towards commercial research for corporations.

Over the course of about 25 years government has replaced university grants with programs targeted for commercialization of research. The result is a considerably transformed university system in Canada. Reduced core money from government has meant that universities can less easily set their own priorities, but must instead meet the requirements of targeted funding programs. In the process their priorities are driven more by external markets and less by internal academic criteria. Research is being run like a business, with projects designed to take advantage of commercial opportunities. This is one of the essential elements of the emerging corporate university.

Table 8–5
Networks of Centres of Excellence
($million)

	Phase I	Phase II*
PHASE I NETWORKS – RENEWED		
Canadian Bacterial Diseases Network (CBDN)	18.2	15.3
Canadian Genetic Diseases Network (CGDN)	17.5	15.1
Canadian Institute of Telecommunications Research (CITR)	14.7	12.7
Concrete Canada	6.4	5.5
Inspiraplex	12.3	10.6
Institute for Robotics and Intelligent Systems (IRIS)	23.8	20.5
Mechanical and Chemi-Mechanical Wood-Pulps Network	14.6	12.6
MICRONET	10.8	9.3
NeuroScience Network	25.5	22.0
Protein Engineering Network of Centres of Excellence	20.0	16.8
PHASE I NETWORKS – NON-RENEWED		
Canadian Ageing Research Network	5.0	Did not apply
Centres of Excellence in Molecular and Interfacial Dynamics	18.5	Not renewed
Ocean Production Enhancement Network	23.9	Not renewed
Insect Biotech Canada	9.5	Not renewed
Canadian Network for Space Research	17.0	Not renewed
NEW PHASE II NETWORKS		
Health Evidence Application and Linkage Network**	n/a	8.6
Intelligent Sensing for Innovative Structures	n/a	9.5
Sustainable Forest Management	n/a	10.8
Telelearning Research Network	n/a	13.1

* Projected funding for Phase II; ** (75% MRC and 25% SSHRC)
SOURCE: ARA Consulting Group Inc.1997.

Chapter 9

The Corporate University

The descent of the university into the market place reflects the lie in the soul of modern society. (Harold Innis 1946)

THE CORPORATE UNIVERSITY replaces the traditional learning centre concept of providing services with a profit centre model of selling commodities—a fundamental change in the values and priorities of the university.

Trafficking in Intellectual Property

The traditional university produces knowledge through research, and distributes it freely in the public domain through teaching, publication, and community service. To the corporate university, knowledge is intellectual property, a commodity to be bought and sold.

Intellectual property changes the incentive system. With public money in short supply, university researchers are drawn to commercial opportunities. Administrative and business studies attract contracts and grants through their close affinity to corporations. Research in disciplines close to the market, such as technology fields, agriculture, engineering, and biological sciences, can produce considerable commercial value (Slaughter and Leslie 1997). Academics in these fields have worked closely with industry for some time. A 1986 survey of science and engineering faculty at the Universities of Montréal, Waterloo and Alberta found 90.2 percent of engineers, 76.5 percent of computer scientists, and 66.0 percent of biological scientists engaged in consulting. Of these, 81.5 percent had done work for Canadian firms, 32.1 percent for United States firms, 58 percent for the federal government, and 50.6 percent for the provinces. A survey in the same year of 100 spin-off firms found that most professors voluntarily returned 10 percent of the revenue to their respective universities (Science Council of Canada 1988, 1986).

Administering the corporate university requires importing sufficient corporate money for people in these fields while attempting to orient academics in other areas towards business. Universities providing necessary support services tend to have more academics working closely with business. Specialty services exist in university-industry research centres, offices for technology transfer, science and industrial parks, and centres of entrepreneurship. In the fall of 1997 NSERC posted a list on the Internet of some 25 Canadian universities with offices of industrial liaison, industrial partnership, and technology transfer, with large institutions making up more than half the list.

The University of Alberta expanded its facilities once it embraced technology transfer as part of the academic mission. Staffing in the industrial liaison office rose rapidly, to 22 in 1996. The university spent more money on industrial liaison even though core funding for the university over the preceding three years fell by 20 percent. The industrial liaison office expected to create more than 50 spin-off companies by the year 2000 and increase revenue on industrial contracts from 10 percent of externally funded research to 15 percent (NSERC & Conference Board of Canada 1997).

Academic staff associations and the Canadian Association of University Teachers have been drawn in because their members stand to benefit. At first, the CAUT leaned towards supporting closer ties with business, without paying sufficient attention to the disadvantages. In April 1983 it cosponsored with other academic and business organizations a conference in Edmonton, Alberta on *The Business Community and the University: The Need for Collaboration*. York's faculty association protested this kind of sponsorship (Newson 1983).

By 1987 the CAUT had taken a more balanced approach, publishing a guide to university-business relations for universities and researchers (CAUT 1987b) whose theme was safeguarding university independence. It stressed the importance of ensuring that research and development contracts with the private sector should be public, and opposed secret research of any kind, even for military purposes. It proposed that researchers should have free reign over publishing the results of research, without any market-oriented influence by industrial sponsors.

By 1999 the CAUT was openly criticizing the corporate university. It announced plans for a fall conference on "Universities and Colleges in the Public Interest: Stopping the Commercial Takeover of Post-Secondary Education" (CAUT 1999b).

Universities usually support entrepreneurship, and some academic entrepreneurs initiate their own ventures despite recalcitrant administrators, even breaching university policies to support their business activities. In 1982, Ray Valentine, a plant biologist and cofounder of the biotechnology firm Calgene, was asked to leave the University of California at Davis unless he relinquished his contracts with Calgene (McDonald 1982). At one major Canadian university, a dispute arose in the mid-1990s between the administration and food scientists over a private firm set up to avoid paying the university's overhead fees of 35 to 50 percent on every research contract. This firm contracted with companies in the food processing industry, hiring graduate students and faculty members to do the work using university equipment and facilities. Unprepared for these kinds of arrangements, and unable to capture any of the revenue that went to the consulting company, the university charged the professors with breaking university rules (private interview).

Canadian universities are built on a core foundation of noncommercial academic disciplines. The Universities of Waterloo and École Polytechnique are exceptions, technical universities built on an engineering foundation without the arts and science core disciplines that form the basis of most universities. These institutions favour specialized programs with a nucleus of engineering and related subjects, and hence are more adaptable to market competition. They have fostered commercial activity and offered an expanding range of services to industry (MacAulay & Dufour 1984).

The University of Waterloo supports entrepreneurship and actively encourages professors to set up their own private companies to generate income from products or processes they develop. Some of its arrangements blur the distinctions between university and business. A 1995 case covered in the media described how university funds were used to benefit a privately held company. This involved the Earth Sciences Department, the Centre for Groundwater Research, and EnviroMetal Technologies, a spin-off firm partly owned by a professor with appointments in both the department and the centre. The latter was part of Ontario's centres of excellence program for transferring marketable knowledge from universities to business. A research associate professor in the department was paid by the Centre for Groundwater Research to work on a process designated for exclusive marketing by EnviroMetal Technologies (Saunders 1996).

McGill compensates for the cost of setting up separate firms, sharing revenue equally with the developer if the university commercializes the invention, and taking 20 percent from professors who use their own firms. The University of Calgary set up University Technologies International Inc. in 1989 as a for-profit corporation to commercialize the university's intellectual property (Grigoroff 1996). By 1997–98 Canadian university researchers had created 312 spin-off firms to develop and market their inventions, with equity in 42 of the firms for a total of $17 million (Statistics Canada 1998).

Universities in the United States have gone further. Entrepreneurs had access to university facilities and faculties by the early 1980s. David Dickson (1981) describes a project at the Massachusetts Institute of Technology at which a professor who sold a lucrative medical instrument company created from the proceeds a family-run biomedical research centre on campus. The centre employed one-third of the biologists on faculty and owned all the intellectual property they created.

A study of articles published in 1992 by authors from Massachusetts in 14 leading science and medical journals found that more than one-third of the authors had a financial interest in their research. In 20 percent of the articles the lead author served on the scientific advisory board of a biotechnology company. Lead authors in 22 percent held or had applied for a patent related to the subject of the article. Seven percent had a lead author serving as officer, director, or major shareholder of a biotechnology corporation. Professors following the traditional academic model would usually disclose these ties and discuss how they tried to maintain their objectivity. In the commercial context of the 1990s this was apparently deemed unnecessary: not one of the 267 articles disclosed the authors' financial interests (Krimsky et al. 1996).

Studies sponsored by drug companies can be severely limited in scope, sometimes to merely comparing one brand to another. Results may be biased: Barbara Mintzes (1998) describes studies suggesting that research done by recipients of corporate money inordinately favours their sponsors. A 1994 review analyzed 56 industry-sponsored studies of non-steroidal anti-inflammatory drugs to treat osteoarthritis whose results were published between 1987 and 1990. In every case the sponsor's drug was found either equally or more effective than the comparison drug (Rochon et al. 1994).

Canadian universities are starting their own venture capital firms and taking equity positions in others. Tremendous gains are possible from companies listed on public stock exchanges. Guelph University Alumni Research and Development Inc. (GUARD) was founded in 1994 with $500,000 from friends and alumni of the University of Guelph to manage potentially profitable innovations developed on campus. In 1996 the university granted exclusive rights for commercial exploitation of intellectual property to GUARD, in exchange for a significant equity position in a $9 million share offering on the Alberta Stock Exchange. About one-third of GUARD's shares were reserved for university and alumni supporters, with the rest distributed among banks and venture capital firms (AUCC 1996d).

Profit derived from intellectual property is the cornerstone of the corporate university. Academics in potentially lucrative fields are encouraged to search for money at all stages of their research. Obtaining grants to do their studies is just the beginning. Higher stakes are involved in marketing the products of their work. These issues are taken up in chapter 10.

The Student as Customer

Within the corporate university, students become a profit centre. Tuition fees traditionally covered only a moderate portion of operating income. Until the 1980s, provincial governments committed to increasing accessibility by minimizing financial barriers either froze tuition or allowed modest increases when revenue from other sources was rising. Improved finances from the 1950s through the early 1970s allowed the provinces to cover the greatest part of university operating costs. Low tuition was part of the equation that produced steadily expanding enrolment by making it feasible for people from families with modest means to attend university.

After the early 1980s, the provinces shifted the financial burden back to students. Tuition has risen faster than increases in the cost of living, while government grants are holding the line or falling. Every province except Québec has compensated for reduced government revenue by freeing universities to set their own fees. For 1996, Ontario expected a minimum 10 percent tuition increase from every university, allowing raises of up to 20 percent, while considering a model for charging fees based not only on program costs but upon students' expected lifetime earnings. Between 1990 and 1995, average tuition across Canada rose by 62 percent in real terms (Lewington 1996, Little 1997).

By 1997–98, student fees in Canada accounted for 31.6 percent of operating funds, compared to 13 percent in 1979–80 (see Table A–5). Higher tuition, combined with reduced provincial grants and increased federal loans to students, places a high debt burden on graduates (AUCC 1999). A federal task force on youth estimated in 1996 that personal educational debts for many students would reach $25,000 by 1998, compared to $8,700 in 1990 (CAUT 1997a).

Raising tuition in itself cannot guarantee an increase in total revenue, since higher rates drive away potential students. Mindful of this, universities are experimenting with market pricing structures to maximize income from student fees, raising tuition only so long as total revenue increases. This approach ignores social factors such as the impact of higher fees on accessibility of lower income groups. Tuition must eventually reach an upper limit where total revenue falls due to costs discouraging too many people from attending, but such upper limits have never been tested in Canada. As tuition in Canada is still considerably lower than at most comparable universities in the United States, considerable increases may be possible before they impair revenue.

Tuition varies more by province than by institution because provinces regulated across the board rates. For 1998–99, Ontario universities were in the $3,300 to $3,600 range, and Nova Scotia between $3,800 and $4,400. Most Québec universities charged $1,668 for in-province students and $3,168 for Canadians from other provinces (AUCC 1996b). Now that the provinces no longer control tuition, fees may begin to vary by program and institution. It is conceivable that prestigious universities may charge higher prices and still retain a large student base.

Recruitment takes on a different character when students are viewed primarily as market customers. Advertising and marketing campaigns emphasize convenience, service, lifestyle, and reputation. In 1996 Augustana University College in Camrose, Alberta used an airline marketing model to attract students with the headline *"We're Having A Seat Sale."* For a limited time students were offered a fee of $499 for a three-credit course, a 38 percent saving on the regular price of $806 (AUCC 1996b).

Higher tuition combined with fewer students may be good business strategy, provided one views the university as a *seller* rather than a service provider, and students as customers, valued for the revenue they provide. When the university begins to act as a business entity it must concentrate on narrow financial interests, at the expense of its broader mandate to service the community and to provide fair access to its benefits.

Full-time enrolment peaked at almost 576,000 in 1994–95 and fell back to 573,000 by 1997–98. Part-time enrolment declined from a peak of 316,000 in 1992–93 to 249,000 in 1997–98 (see Table A–1). Universities now compete for shares of a declining market with personalized services and aggressive campaigns to attract top candidates. Communication technologies allow them to invade each others' geographic markets. Winnipeg was one of 20 Canadian cities targeted by Queen's, with a newspaper advertisement geared to technophiles. An advertisement in the *Winnipeg Free Press* appealed to locals to "Get a Queen's University MBA in Manitoba."

Readers were invited to attend one of four one-hour information sessions, have a free lunch, and learn about the Queen's Executive MBA:

> [P]articipants meet in small, cohesive learning teams and attend class via state-of-the-art interactive videoconferencing technology. Classes are real-time, fully-interactive, multi-point sessions, with advanced communications technology that lets you see, hear, and talk with your classmates across the country.

Recent declines in enrolment may be harbingers of a smaller, leaner university system as the result of contradictory pressures. The labour force of the future requires more university graduates, yet the twin policies of withdrawing public money from universities and encouraging higher tuition can only hinder enrolment.

Exploitation of Teaching

Control over the teaching labour force is a major challenge for the corporate university. Almost unique among employees in advanced capitalist societies, academics control most of their own labour process. They operate essentially as semi-autonomous craft workers, free to set procedures and methods of work provided they teach assigned courses, conduct an acceptable amount of research, and maintain an adequate publication record. Within the boundaries of the curriculum and the length of scheduled courses, professors determine the content and pace of their teaching. They are free from supervision in the classroom or when they prepare lectures, and may work at any time of day, at different locations, without constraints of time clocks or dress codes.

Professors pretty much control all aspects of the curriculum. Collectively, they determine what courses to offer, the size of sections, and whether they are to be delivered as large lectures or small seminars, or through supervised practical experience. They design their courses, choose textbooks, prepare lectures, and assign and grade examinations.

This traditional model of teaching prevails for sound pedagogical and professional reasons. The model makes less sense from a corporate perspective. Course delivery can be labour intensive and costly; small seminars may be productive for the mind, but don't generate huge profits for the institution.

Teaching is under pressure to bring in more income at lower cost. New markets are available, as people seek degrees, certificates, and training to survive in the information economy, but reaching them means changing the way universities run their teaching enterprise.

Competition from universities owned by large corporations demonstrates that teaching can produce handsome profits. Major new institutions in the United States are challenging Canadian universities in their home markets through on-line services. The University of Phoenix, a subsidiary of Apollo Group Inc., has an enviable 20 percent annual growth rate. In just a few years, the on-line university attracted 48,000 part-time degree-credit students by 1998, each with a full-time job elsewhere and paying average annual tuition of $6,500. Faculty, all are part-time and untenurable, are paid between $750 and $1,000 per course. Apollo Group, also owner of several other colleges and universities, reported quarterly profits in early 1998 of $12.8 million on sales of $86.5 million (Marchese 1998).

Another for-profit enterprise, Chicago's DeVry Institute of Technology, had 48,000 students in 1998 at 15 campuses across the United States and Canada. Western Governors University, founded in 1996 by 17 state governors and 14 business partners, including IBM, AT&T, and Microsoft, is a broker for on-line courses, without any faculty of its own. WGU aims to have 95,000 students by early in the 21st century (Marchese 1998, Hammonds et al 1997, Garson 1996).

In "Digital Diploma Mills, Part II," an article widely distributed on the Internet, David Noble (1998) elaborates on how electronic technologies are used to convert the instructional process and classroom teaching into products. CD-ROMs, Web sites, and courseware separate the course from the professor and make it available for sale to companies already in the business of selling information and entertainment. The University of California at Los Angeles (UCLA) sells exclusive production and distribution rights for electronic courses to The Home Education Network, a private, for-profit corporation. The University of California at Berkeley licenses to America On Line (AOL) rights to market, distribute, and promote electronic courses. Professors are paid an honorarium for developing a course, but must sign copyright over to the university and waive any rights to royalties. AOL receives 10 percent of all royalty revenues.

There are powerful economic reasons for developing these options. Using communication technologies for distance education allows universities to offer new products to an expanded customer base. Revenue is no longer limited by physical capacity. Use of electronic media vastly expands potential markets even as cost of production is trimmed because the professor who wrote the course is paid just once for preparation. Electronic distribution lowers costs; buildings and classrooms become unnecessary as students do their work at home and email it in for grading.

With these new technologies faculty lose control of the curriculum to administrators, who assign coordinators to contact students, distribute materials, and hire readers paid on a piece work basis. There is no need for a salaried full-time professor when instructors can be employed for occasional on-site seminars and examiners hired as needed to grade assignments. In 1998, the rate for graders at the University of Manitoba was $75 a term per student for reading and grading assignments submitted by mail.

Distance education provides the means for proletarianizing teachers. Managers assume control over teaching as professors become alienated both from the course and the students who take it. Distance education has the added advantage for employers of almost entirely removing the human element. Teacherless courses become products that management can deliver without worrying about labour relations, and pose no threat of strikes during academic terms or exam periods.

Courses conducted via mail, television, or the Internet disadvantage students, who are cut off from each other and the person who prepared the course. A university course involves more than just reading texts and handing in assignments. Outlines, reading lists, and examinations are only the basic framework. Course delivery is supposed to be tailored to students through discussions in the classroom, the halls, and instructors' offices. Distance education severely curtails the debate and discussion that normally take place in these locations, and robs students of opportunity to develop skills through interaction.

Courses run by administrators are not automatically reviewed each year for developments in the subject matter, as professors ordinarily do when revising outlines to incorporate new research. Reviews of this nature are far less likely when they necessitate hiring someone to do the work.

Expanded use of part-time instructors exploits the teaching staff. Part-time teachers already make up more than one-third of all Canadian faculty, typically at less than half the lowest rate for an assistant professor. The University of Manitoba's 1997–98 collective agreement set part-time rates at $5,960 per course, or $17,880 for the equivalent of a full-time teaching load, compared to the minimum salaries for full-time lecturers ($31,746) and assistant professors ($40,868). An Ontario study showed that for 1989–90 part-timers comprised more than 32 percent of all faculty in the province, performed 20 percent of teaching, but received only 7.6 percent of salaries. Fringe benefits were 4.5 percent of salaries, compared to between

12 and 13 percent for full-time faculty. Part-time staff are rarely covered for supplementary health, disability insurance, dental plans, group life insurance, or leaves for sickness, parenting, or vacation (Rajagopal & Farr 1992).

Employment of part-time instructors alters the fundamental character of university education. Teaching is supposed to be informed by research, on the premise that good researchers keep up with developments in their fields and bring them to their classrooms. Part-timers who are full-time professionals can enrich teaching in their fields, but others cannot keep up with research in professional and academic fields while busy trying to supplement meagre teaching stipends. Not only does separating teaching from research inevitably compromise the quality of teaching, it reduces the services available to students. Part-time instructors are rarely paid to advise students, and even those who volunteer on their own time lack basic supports such as offices on campus.

These assaults on the rights and privileges of academic workers create a divided instructional staff. Full-time faculty have comprehensive duties that give them control over their courses and the opportunity to do research. Casual and part-time instructors only have part of the job, and are expected to deliver similar course content for markedly lower pay and benefits, no job security, and no freedom to do research as part of their assigned duties. Distance education creates an even lower level of appointments: people who prepare courses without delivering them, or who administer courses they have not prepared. Students thus face the prospect of paying ever higher fees for lower quality products.

Fund-Raising Fund-raising drives have become a growth industry, one widespread and noticeable enough to capture the attention of popular publications. *Maclean's* 1997 annual review of universities carried a lead article, "Academia Inc.," on how universities are "turning themselves into sleek new profit machines." Every university uses appeals to corporations, foundations, alumni, staff, and the public for buildings, scholarships, endowed chairs, expansion, and a host of special projects. Slick, professionally-run campaigns emulate the model of major universities in the United States whose largest campaign targets now exceed $1 billion. For 1998 Yale boosted its endowment to $5 billion with a $1.7 billion capital drive. Harvard's endowment was $9 billion (Jackson 1997).

Not long ago Canadian campaigns above $100 million were unheard of. The University of Toronto broke this record in 1991 by raising $125 million, some two years ahead of and some $25 million over its target. Early successes lead to more ambitious aims. Big universities have distinct advantages: large pools of potential donors, and resources to staff extensive fund-raising operations. The University of British Columbia's development office had a staff of 32 in 1995, when its World of Opportunity Campaign raised $262 million from alumni, corporations, and contributors in Asia and the Pacific Rim. McGill raised $208 million in a three-year drive ending in 1996. The University of Toronto places great stock in private fund-raising. John Dellandrea, director of fund-raising, received $250,660 compensation in 1995, compared to president Robert Prichard's $199,500. The vice-chair of the university's governing council maintained Mr. Dellandrea was well worth this sum, since he brought in more than $30 million in donations for the previous year (Galt 1996). The University of Toronto's campaign was well ahead of its plan to raise $400 million by 2002, with more than $350 million already collected by the summer of 1998.

Like other volunteer, nonprofit, and non-governmental organizations, universities have transformed how they raise money. It is no longer possible to seek generous donations and contributions without offering something in return; official recognition is usually the minimum incentive for high-end donors. While it does not cost anything to name a building or laboratory after a donor, only a limited number of physical assets can be used in this way.

Arts organizations have proved themselves adept with donor packages, awarding prizes and privileges in proportion to the contribution. Small donations receive pins or other tokens of appreciation; large contributors receive rights to name part of a building, concert series or exhibition, enjoy advance tickets, priority seating, and invitations to special openings and receptions, and assume seats on governing boards. Universities are similarly well-placed to develop custom packages. Wealthy donors get their names on buildings, faculties, academic chairs, and institutes. Middle range contributors can name lecture halls, classrooms, lounges, and cafeterias. Lower level donors' names are placed on lockers, water fountains, seats, or commemorative plaques.

The Asper Centre for Entrepreneurship at the University of Manitoba owes its name to a $1 million donation from Issie Asper, chair of CanWest Global Corporation. York University's Schulich School of Business was named after a $15 million contribution from Seymour Schulich, chair of

Franco-Nevada Mining Company. Joseph Rotman, chair of Clairvest Group Inc., a Toronto-based merchant bank, donated $15 million to the University of Toronto for the Joseph L. Rotman School of Management. Rotman was alleged to attain the right to influence school policies in exchange for his donation. Investors' Group purchased the right to name the University of Manitoba's new Gymnasium for the 1999 Pan American Games. For smaller contributions, donors' names were engraved on seats or lockers (Giberson 1997, University of Manitoba 1997).

Toronto's approach offers up more of the university to its donors. George Bush received an honorary degree in 1997 despite protests by faculty and students that his actions while United States president and director of the CIA made him an inappropriate candidate. Twenty-eight professors walked out of the convocation that awarded his degree. Mr. Bush is a close associate of Peter Munk, president of Barrick Gold Corporation, Canada's second largest gold producer, who donated $6.4 million to the university for the Centre for International Studies. The initial agreement for Mr. Munk's contribution—altered in response to protest once its contents became public—set up a Council on International Studies to receive advice from the Barrick Gold advisory board (Cole 1998). This is a rare intrusion, but a dangerous harbinger of increased corporate influence on university policy. The Centre for International Studies may not openly compromise its work, yet members may well feel constrained from criticizing the gold mining industry, where Canadian corporations such as Barrick are major international players.

Universities are now designing investment-style packages which don't fit the traditional profile for arm's length donors, blurring the distinction between donations and research contracts. Packaging of this nature not only camouflages business arrangements as donations, it also threatens academic freedom by turning professors into off-site research staff for donor corporations (Cole 1998).

David Strangway, president of the University of British Columbia during its 1995 fund-raising drive, noted that capital campaigns were lucrative for the university because they tapped donors' interests in name recognition. Successful capital campaigns can be costly in the long run, since paying for operating expenses had less appeal. Maintaining facilities financed by donations forces up operating costs without providing additional income to cover them.

UBC used its campaign revenue to expand physical plant, arguing that improved facilities would attract more students who would eventually become generous alumni. Proceeds of the campaign were used for 15 new buildings, including a library, art gallery, theatre complex, laboratories, parkades, and a recreation centre, together with more than 50 new endowed chairs. Students recruited from Asia and the Pacific Rim paid tuition that covered the entire cost of their education, at about $7,300 for arts undergraduates, compared to $2,295 for domestic students, and up to $43,000 for medicine. Special attention was given to these students because current alumni in the region have proved to be generous donors (McInnes 1995, Giberson 1997, Sweet 1997).

Although it may be a financial necessity, elaborate fund-raising impedes the independence of the university. Peter Desbarats describes how corporate donations influenced his behaviour while dean of journalism at the University of Western Ontario:

> The moment of truth arrived for me in 1995, when Rogers Communications granted my request for $1 million to endow a chair of information studies, for which I was extremely grateful. When journalists subsequently asked me to comment on the Rogers takeover of Maclean Hunter, all I could do was draw their attention to the donation. They understood right away that I had been, to express it crudely, bought.

> This had nothing to do with Rogers. I had begged for the money. It was given with no strings attached. It will serve a useful purpose. But unavoidably I gave up something in return. No one should pretend, least of all university presidents, that this experience, multiplied many times and repeated over the years, doesn't damage universities in the long run (Desbarats 1998).

Desbarats can be congratulated for the honesty of his reflection. Nonetheless, one must note that while dean, he voluntarily refrained from speaking out on a matter on which he held valued opinions informed by considerable experience and expertise—even though the donor did not overtly restrict his speech. The "chilling effect" of self-censorship of this kind is infectious. Often it stems from nothing more than ordinary polite reluctance to criticize a benefactor, especially if there is a continuing relationship and prospect of future support. Some corporations expect no further returns for their contributions; but this does not alter the psychological obligations that clients typically assume towards patrons. Many corporations know that they need not overtly demand returns, or control over how their contributions are spent.

Corporate-Friendly Practice

Operating universities like businesses changes their essence. Gearing to the market means redefining relevance. Social values that have shaped higher education are replaced by measures of financial viability. Research and teaching are assessed in narrow market terms. Profit becomes the guiding principle for deciding which services and products to offer.

Corporate conversion favours professions and professors whose work may prove valuable to a corporation, industry, or market. Compromising their independence may seem a small price to researchers scrambling for support for their work.

Support is less likely for scholars doing basic scientific research, or for social scientists, philosophers, or historians whose value to business is not so readily apparent. Studies geared to political analysis or understanding social dynamics may never find corporate sponsors; nor will inquiries that question capitalist values, criticize corporate practices, or advocate for the poor and downtrodden. Money to support research and practice in these endeavours is shrinking. Interested private sector buyers for social sciences and humanities research are few and far between. Business is not interested in supporting its critics. Poverty research is out of fashion. Professors in these fields face the prospect of bigger teaching workloads with lower pay, less time for research, and expectations that they will finance their own replacements by retiring well before their productive years are over. The message for people in these fields is clear: either change their research and practice so it will serve corporate interests, or remain on a relentless downward slope.

Corporations draw faculty into a search for sales rather than truth, favouring projects with strong market potential over theoretical or basic research. Inherent value of the work is less important than its potential to generate revenue. For example, drug companies spend a lot of money on clinical trials, and carefully orchestrate how the work is done. They regularly hold conferences in fashionable resorts, to which they invite physicians and spouses. These meetings amount to mutual courting events: the companies try to convince physicians to prescribe their drugs, or seek co-operative researchers for drug trials, while medical researchers use these sessions to get lucrative drug trials for their campus. Brand-name drug companies gave $84 million to university and hospital researchers in 1991, most for clinical trials of known drugs (Helwig 1992). The money helped to employ researchers and keep university departments afloat, but offered few opportunities for basic research.

Teaching is being marketed as a commodity. Successful marketing follows conventions rather than challenge them. Designing and packaging courses for what will sell puts them at risk of pandering to the broadest common denominator. This does not bode well for teaching fundamental disciplines or challenging conventional assumptions and ideas.

The key to developing corporate-friendly practices lies in managing a university like a business. Trends in this direction are evident, with pyramids at the top, presidents being redefined as chief executive officers, and businesslike merit incentives for faculty. This kind of business management is inherently hostile to the purposes of the university (Rowat 1964). Tight managerial control attempts to maintain uniform purpose, constant effort, and consistent product throughout a business organization. Policies issue downward from the top. Management treats employees as factors of production, a resource to be exploited. The individual becomes a commodity, purchased when needed and discarded when unnecessary.

Universities cannot thrive under this kind of regime. University education is supposed to nurture independent thinking rather than conformist opinion. Policies emanating from the top do not foster creativity from professors at the front line of teaching and research. Creative intellectual production requires diversity rather than uniformity, with critical and informed debate from all points of view. Universities must create an atmosphere for challenging the status quo and supporting it. Outrageous and unacceptable perspectives should coexist with conventional ones. Esoteric research and pragmatic projects should all be supported. Conditions must be ripe for testing untried ideas.

The corporate university reinforces inequalities. Those who cannot pay are less likely to receive services from universities that direct their resources to business partners with deep pockets. Nonprofit and poverty organizations cannot pay for information or research they need. If universities rely on corporate funds to replace lost public revenue, those sectors with fewer resources will receive less service when they need it most.

Academic freedom cannot be part of the corporate agenda, because it exists to protect professors from the influence of market forces. Business-minded administrators cannot dictate to tenured faculty the terms or content of their research. Professors are free to forego opportunities for large grants if not required for their research. They need not seek licensing contracts if their independence may be compromised. This level of freedom conflicts with commercial priorities that define academic productivity in monetary terms.

The threat to academic freedom extends to the very independence of the university. It is supposed to serve as broad a range of interests as possible, without prejudice. This includes providing resources for people who criticize business and government and for interests that are less well represented in political and economic circles. The university can counterbalance the market that gives priority to those who can pay. Social critics should have as much legitimacy to do their work as defenders of the status quo. Without this autonomy the university may cease to be a place of independent inquiry. Those who cannot pay will not be served. In a climate like this, a voice of reason and balance will be silenced and business partners will triumph. Faculty unions are resisting pressures of corporate universities where they interfere with academic freedom and tenure. Their members require independent universities. The next chapter examines how faculty are responding to the prospects of the corporate university for the 21st century.

Chapter 10

Universities for the 21st Century

[If the university]... denies its intellectual and moral purpose, the complete
conception of the common good is lost, and Canada, as such, becomes a
materialistic society (Massey Royal Commission 1951).

UNIVERSITIES ARE CAUGHT in the wake of a global wave of privatization.
Crown corporations in transportation, gas and oil production, manufacturing, and telecommunications are already in private hands. Governments are
now applying the process to public utilities, health care, education, and
social services—stripping assets from the public sector and transferring
their benefits to select groups of shareholders.

In order to appeal to corporations with a broad selection of investment
options, cash-starved universities are putting aside traditional barriers to
private sector entry. Businesses now routinely obtain access to university
staff and facilities, and control over information.

Social and political costs of academic-corporate fusion are incalculable.
Universities are crucial repositories for independent inquiry and the capacity
to see beyond the horizons of conformity. Investigators in all disciplines
ask questions, challenge accepted wisdom, foster creative thinking, and
expand the frontiers of knowledge without concern for whether the results
might be profitable. Loss of such institutions threatens us with societal
stagnation.

Commercialization puts an entirely different spin on academic institutions. Commercial research aims to develop commodities, and values
ideas that lead to saleable products. No innovative or brilliant new idea will
interest corporate buyers unless it eventually earns a profit. Corporations
such as Bell Laboratories, Intel, Microsoft, IBM, and the major pharmaceutical companies work on product development and improvement and
carry out proprietary market research, where investigators have appropriate
specific targets and boundaries on what they can and cannot do. This
approach to research is much too narrow for the university.

One reason why Ottawa encourages university-based industrial research
is that Canada has far less corporate-based research than the United States
and other OECD countries. The crux of the Canadian problem is that

although money is needed for applied research in new technologies, health care, education, social management, and industrial development, little new funding is being allocated to these sectors. Rather, public money for basic or independent inquiries is being diverted to support applied corporate research. Universities are being enlisted to assume the work of corporations.

Universities were less willing to sacrifice their independence while government paid the bills. But as government support pulled back, university executives turned eagerly to the corporate path, and many academics followed suit. Others are doubtful. Becoming commercial undermines their independence, transforming their occupation from knowledge worker to employee in a research and teaching factory.

Professors' positions at the union-management bargaining table reflect fierce attachment to independence and the satisfactions of a craft occupation. It is still too early to tell how they will resolve differences between collective interest and individual opportunity. Professors could very well pose the major obstacle to privatization of the university.

Doing Industry's Research

Not long after I joined the University of Manitoba's School of Social Work in 1977, Seagram's Corporation offered to support research on employee assistance programs. Such research was not only consistent with the school's mandate, it also fit nicely with the company's desire to be seen as doing something about the adverse effects of excessive drinking. But the school turned down the offer, arguing that taking research money from a sponsor with an interest in the subject matter might appear to compromise its programs.

Two decades later, by contrast, the University of Toronto's Faculty of Social Work came under fire for actively pursuing corporate contributions. By the summer of 1998, the Faculty's endowment campaign had surpassed $14 million. Allan Irving, Associate Professor of Social Work, documented some $6 million obtained from four corporations (and one corporate foundation) to endow several research chairs and a centre for applied social research. But the corporate sponsors were well-known supporters of neo-conservative agendas aimed at destroying social programs and privatizing higher education, and were accused of questionable employment and environmental practices. Irving argued that accepting this money compromised the faculty's mission to promote social justice, human rights, and equity (Irving 1997).

Was Manitoba's School of Social Work more politically correct than Toronto's in refusing corporate money? Or has the passage of almost 20 years transformed co-option into just another sensible business opportunity?

Social work has relatively little to offer business sponsors: some legitimacy, good public relations, and expertise in services of interest to the donors. Social service fields ripe for privatization—such as caring for children, the elderly, and the disabled—may draw potential investors, but the returns are not yet that high. This will change if governments continue to transfer money from public to private providers of services.

Stakes are higher in fields where industries stand to profit directly from academic research. Studies during the early 1990s of university-industry linkages in the United States noted that most corporate patents were in biotechnology, pharmaceuticals, medical technology, electronics, optics, and nuclear technology. Tentative findings suggested that corporations with university research ties had higher rates of return from R&D spending than companies without university connections (Link and Rees 1990, Mansfield 1991, Berman 1990).

Biotechnology and pharmaceutical companies in the United States form an advanced corporate-university complex for research and development. At a February 1997 conference on *Financing the Biopharmaceutical Company*, the consulting firm McKinsey & Co. described how universities, biotechnology firms, and pharmaceutical companies are linked for commercial drug innovation. Academics advance basic knowledge in biological systems and identify new concepts for disease intervention. Concepts with commercial potential are sold or licensed in their early stages for further development by biotechnology companies. Major pharmaceutical companies enter the picture at the last stage to develop and market drugs. The latter invariably have extensive ties with both universities and biotechnology firms (Edwards 1998).

In 1996 universities spent $12 billion, roughly one-third of the $36 billion disbursed in the United States on research and development for pharmaceutical innovation. In comparison, biotechnology companies spent about $8 billion, and major pharmaceutical companies $16 billion. But Mark Edwards' studies of royalty payments found universities receive a disproportionately low share of the profit—only 6.25 percent—whereas biotechnology firms get about 18.75 percent, and 75 percent goes to major pharmaceutical companies which spend just 45 percent of the total (Edwards 1998).

Edwards describes numerous cases of universities receiving short shrift. A license agreement between UCLA and the biotechnology firm Xoma concerned monoclonals for diagnosis and treatment of septic shock. UCLA received about $100,000 in pre-commercial payments, and up to a 3 percent royalty on net sales. Nine months later Xoma signed a development and license agreement with pharmaceutical giant Pfizer for $2 million in up-front payments, 33 percent royalty on net sales, and reimbursement of some $28 million in development costs. UCLA's share was thus between 5 and 10 percent of the "total pie" shaped by Xoma and Pfizer (Edwards 1998).

Industry profits are distributed through a complex web of contractual arrangements. Some are relatively straightforward, such as payments to biotechnology companies for compounds used in DNA research, or royalties to universities for techniques or procedures. One of the most lucrative academically was for an idea, a pivotal process in recombinant DNA research discovered by biologists Stanley Cohen at Stanford University and Herbert Boyer at the University of California. The Cohen-Boyer process earned the two universities more than $200 million over a 17-year patent life that ended on December 2, 1997. When the patent ran out, the process had 370 licensees, each having paid $10,000 to sign up plus $10,000 a year for the right to apply the patents, and royalties of between 0.5 and 3.0 percent of sales of recombinant DNA products that used the process. Licensees' financial obligations ceased when the patent expired (Edwards 1998).

Competition is intense for the high profits in these industries. A striking example is reach-through agreements, an invasive form of capturing revenue from developments not foreseen when a deal was struck. Companies providing a technology, research tool, or compound demand the rights to negotiate licenses for any inventions or discoveries arising from their use. Discoveries even marginally related to the original work are covered if the licensed tool or product was used *at any stage* of their development. Reach-through agreements result in a "stacking up" problem of licensing commitments made during product development. University and corporate developers may pay up to 50 percent of final product revenue to a string of companies which negotiated percentages for items provided. Some of these payments will almost certainly be for tools with slim connections to the outcomes (Hamilton 1997, Freundlich 1998).

The National Institutes of Health in the United States argues that these developments are counterproductive for research, using the example of pharmaceutical compounds which are necessary "research tools" for university scientists. Firms providing these compounds force universities to provide what amounts to an equity position in the research process. Instead of selling compounds for a price, they take a portion of all future revenue (NIH 1998).

Trading in royalties and licensing fees is expensive, yet researchers can hardly opt out if they want the procedures and products necessary for their work. Universities must hire staff expert in technology transfer to work out these complex arrangements. Lengthy negotiations delay research projects until contracts are signed, and administering the contracts will be costly.

Prospects of private contracts will inevitably discourage academic traditions of open publication and debate. Researchers will not publish their results because corporations are unlikely to pay for findings in the public domain; financial rewards accrue from selling confidential information. Studies in the United States found significant reductions in the number of scientific publications during the 1980s, despite an increase in R&D expenditures. The authors argue that this indicates a growing tendency to seek private opportunities in lieu of publication (Doutriaux and Barker 1995).

Some universities frown on professors discussing work that might have commercial potential. The University of Manitoba's Industrial Liaison Office provides the following table of best and worst practices for handling inventions (understood as any idea, process, or item that can lead to developing new commercial products). Faculty are encouraged to file invention disclosures with the industrial liaison office, and to patent inventions before publishing or even discussing their findings. This is listed in the column for "best" strategy in Table 10–1 below. The column for "worst" practice lists the traditional sequence for good research, in which investigators discuss their ideas and publish tentative findings before they finalize anything.

Table 10-1
Invention Disclosure Strategies
Industrial Liaison Office

Worst	Better	Best
1. Invent	1. Invent	1. Invent
2. Publish or talk	2. File invention disclosure	2. File invention disclosure
3. File invention disclosure	3. Publish or talk	3. File patent protection
4. File patent protection	4. File patent protection	4. Publish or talk

SOURCE: Strang 1997.

Invention disclosure strategies in this table give commercialization the highest priority. They undermine the best practices for academic research, which rely on sharing findings through publication and discussion. The best practices listed in the accompanying table could be the worst for advancing good research.

Similar policies are advanced by semi-independent bodies like the Canadian Institute for Advanced Research. Founded in 1982, the Institute supports some 150 program members, mostly university-based researchers. The federal government funded one-third of its $11 million budget for 1997–98, matching one dollar for every two dollars of other contributions. Fifty-two percent came from corporations, foundations, and private individuals, and the remaining 15 percent from the governments of Ontario, British Columbia, Manitoba, and New Brunswick.

In 1995 the Science Promotion and Academic Affairs Branch of Industry Canada commissioned the Institute to produce a model for the "transfer/commercialization of university research in Canada." The Institute's report advocated fundamental value changes to give new meaning to intellectual property. Since (it was argued) these products of the intellect have only *potential* value, not realized until commercial products or services incorporating ideas are proven successful in the marketplace, the Institute called for university reward systems which would give proper credit for commercialization as opposed to the standard, "still largely based on academic excellence, teaching and publication in learned journals" (Canadian Institute for Advanced Research 1998). A proposal to abandon academic excellence in favour of profit is surely not the route to a better university—restriction of value to commercial terms threatens the entire foundation of university research.

Conflicts between corporate interests and university policies raise serious ethical issues. In March 1999, Monsanto Company announced it would build its first crop development centre in Canada at The University of Manitoba (McNeill 1999). Monsanto is one of the world's largest agrochemical corporations, with 1998 revenues of US $8.7 billion from agricultural, nutrition and consumer, and pharmaceutical products, including the herbicide Roundup® and the artificial sweetener NutraSweet®. The company's commitment to spend $9 million Canadian on the $10 million research centre (the provincial government committing the remaining $1 million) is considerable compared to the university's annual research expenditures of just under $50 million (Office of Institutional Analysis, 1997), but for Monsanto the cost is minor in light of its US $939 million spending on research and development in 1997 alone.

Based on the university campus and run by Monsanto, the research centre is supposed to focus on developing new strains of grains and oil seeds. Monsanto specializes in genetically altering crops and agricultural products. For example, its patented Roundup Ready® soybeans are engineered to contain a bacterial gene that resists the herbicide glyphosate, the key ingredient in Roundup®. This gives Monsanto a huge marketing advantage by virtually requiring farmers to use its herbicide and its seeds: more than 18 million acres of Roundup Ready® soybeans were planted in the United States in 1998. The technology has spread to other crops. In 1998, close to 50 percent of canola planted in Canada was genetically engineered to be either herbicide- or pesticide-resistant (Crouch 1998).

Monsanto has become notorious for its U.S. Patent Number 5,723,765: "Control of Plant Gene Expression," commonly described as terminator technology, used to engineer crops which kill their own second-generation seeds. A toxin is activated just before sale by soaking the seeds in the antibiotic tetracycline. This forces farmers to buy fresh seeds every year from Monsanto, since harvested seeds cannot produce new plants. Use of terminator seeds raises serious unanswered health questions. Little is known about how much tetracycline may enter the food chain, or of the potential damage from bacteria that become resistant to the antibiotic.

Manitoba's experience with grains and oilseeds offers Monsanto tremendous opportunities for commercial exploitation. Grains genetically engineered with terminator technology can create entirely new markets. A 1998 release by the Canadian-based Rural Advancement Foundation International (RAFI) notes:

> Historically there has been little commercial interest in non-hybridized seeds such as wheat and rice because there is no way for seed companies to control reproduction. If commercially viable, the new (terminator) technology could mean huge profits in entirely new sectors of the seed industry. For farmers, the patented technology will undoubtedly mean greater dependence on the commercial seed market, and a fundamental loss of control over germplasm. If widely utilized, farmers will lose the age-old right to save seed from their harvest (RAFI 1998).

The company also announced its intent to develop fat-reduced versions of canola, an oilseed developed at the University of Manitoba.

Monsanto's example should prompt any university to tread carefully before allowing companies on campus. Monsanto has not taken noticeably great care with other toxic products. It produced virtually all the PCBs in the United States until the 1976 ban, and manufactured Agent Orange, now linked to cancer and reproductive problems in Vietnam War veterans (Ivins 1999).

For companies like Monsanto, the main issue is gaining influence over what is produced in university laboratories in order to reap the proceeds. Even where academic freedom is strongly protected, companies exert considerable leverage through distributing research grants targeted for the work they want done.

The pharmaceutical industry offers abundant opportunities for academic researchers to carry out drug trials. But companies funding research are not always prepared to accept negative findings. In 1995, the Canadian generic drug manufacturer Apotex clashed with Dr. Nancy Olivieri, a respected researcher at Toronto's Hospital for Sick Children (affiliated with the University of Toronto). Investigating the effects of the experimental drug deferiprone in treatment of thalassemia, an inherited blood disorder, Dr. Olivieri published promising results of a three-year study of 21 patients in the *New England Journal of Medicine* (Olivieri et al 1995). This pilot phase was financed by the Medical Research Council of Canada.

A larger study was needed to prove deferiprone safe. Unable to obtain sufficient government support, Dr. Olivieri accepted Apotex's 1993 offer of $120,000 a year over 2 ½ years. Even though Apotex spent more than $83 million a year in research and development (Apotex Inc. 1999), virtually all of its products were generic drugs; this project offered Apotex the prospect of a brand name drug. Its agreement with Dr. Olivieri gave the company commercial rights, ownership of the data, and a confidentiality clause so tight that even providing basic information to patients involved in the study required company permission (Daly and Boyle 1998).

Problems surfaced in fall 1995, when early results in the larger study showed that deferiprone might cause liver scarring in some patients. Dr. Olivieri wanted to pursue the study with the remaining patients, who might still benefit, but only after informing them of the new findings and the consequent risks they faced. She drafted a new consent form, and sent it to Apotex in May 1996. Dr. Michael Spino, Senior Vice-President of Scientific Affairs at Apotex, disagreed that the patients were at risk. Apotex terminated the study, firing Dr. Olivieri as chair of the study's steering committee, and threatening her with legal action if she expressed her views to patients in mid-treatment. Neither the hospital nor the University of Toronto supported Dr. Olivieri.

Her findings were published more than two years later in the *New England Journal of Medicine* (Olivieri et al 1998). She received no assistance from her employer during the controversy, and was forced to cover the legal costs of defending herself against threats from Apotex. At the time of the case, the University of Toronto was negotiating for a donation of between $20 and $30 million from Apotex for a new medical building. Dr. Olivieri claimed the Hospital for Sick Children was too closely entwined with Apotex. In December 1998, Professor Olivieri was dismissed by the hospital from her position as Director of the Haemoglobinopathy program. She was reinstated on January 26, 1999, in a settlement with the Hospital for Sick Children brought about through the joint efforts of the University of Toronto Faculty Association (UTFA) and the CAUT. The settlement allowed Dr. Olivieri to continue her clinical research and receive indemnification by the hospital for her legal costs. The controversy continued, with grievances filed by the University of Toronto Faculty Association on behalf of Dr. Olivieri and three of her colleagues. The CAUT was considering an independent inquiry into the entire matter (Taylor 1998, Foss 1998, University of Toronto Faculty Association 1999).

In 1995, Knoll Pharmaceutical Co. forbade Professor Betty Dong at the University of California, San Francisco, to publish the results of a study financed by the company. Professor Dong had found that Synthroid, a hypothyroid drug made by Knoll, was equivalent to competing generic drugs, and thus that switching to the cheaper drugs could reduce health care costs by $356 million. Professor Dong had made the mistake of signing a contract that required company approval for any publication (King 1996, Vogel 1997). Knoll finally allowed her to publish the article in the *Journal of the American Medical Association* in 1997, only after the case had been widely publicized (Dong et al. 1997).

To satisfy business demands, universities and corporations seek far greater influence than ever over academic employees, to the point of overt interference in their research. But university researchers are supposed to be—indeed, are *required* to be—disinterested in their results. This holds for drug trials as much as any other inquiry. Research is compromised the moment an academic acquires a material interest in the results. Professors Olivieri and Dong got into trouble with their corporate funders precisely because they maintained academic independence by refusing to cross this line.

Corporations have legitimate material interests in the results of research. They seek profitable returns from investment in new products, and negative findings require a return to the drawing board and the spending of more money. But pharmaceutical companies would be in serious conflict of interest if in-house researchers carried out all drug trials. They need the moral authority of independent university-based researchers to ensure studies are free of contaminating material influences which would undermine public confidence in their products.

Drug trials should be financed entirely by government through special taxes on pharmaceutical companies. In this way the companies would still pay for the research, but with no direct connection to the investigators. Precautions should be instituted to guarantee the independence of research from potential abuse, for example by corporate officials attempting to influence government distribution of grant money.

Academic systems are premised on information being made freely available in the public domain. Tenure, promotion, and prestige stem from publishing as often and as widely as possible. Access to information from other studies allows researchers to replicate their peers' work, a crucial aspect of testing out new theories and methods. The route to academic success is the antithesis of corporate secrecy designed to prevent competitors from stealing ideas, replicating work, or copying products.

Cases like the examples described above underscore the importance of academic freedom. Without it Professors Olivieri and Dong, and others in similar situations, could not challenge their corporate sponsors.

Bargaining Under Commercialization

Corporate sponsorship threatens academic integrity. Subtle pressures act upon administrators and faculty alike not to offend important corporate donors. Obtaining business support requires approving research projects that promise commercial benefits. New policies influence the direction of academic research by making working conditions more amenable to commercialization. Three initiatives have a significant bearing on collective bargaining: performance indicators; technological change; and intellectual property.

PERFORMANCE INDICATORS are systems used to rank departments and faculties, similar to quantitative systems already well established in business to identify projects for investment, using measures such as the amount of contract and grant money they bring in, or the number of patents, licenses, and new products they develop. Units with the most points are rewarded with extra money, as offering the best returns on the university's invested dollar.

Reliance upon performance indicators has already devastated some of the U.K.'s finest institutions in areas such as community development and international development studies. Their public funding shrank as they lost the competition for funds with institutes that were more successful at raising private money (De Benedetti 1995). The Australian government has used performance indicators to reallocate funding among universities. In Spring 1994, a committee on quality assurance in higher education distributed $76 million to the half of the country's universities judged the most effective (Ford 1994).

Forewarned by these examples, Canadian faculty have brought performance indicators to the bargaining table. Queen's 1999 agreement acknowledges that professors have a legitimate (albeit limited) role in designing and implementing new performance indicators. The contract gives the union grievance rights if it has grounds to believe a new performance indicator is invalid. Management still has final authority to adopt the indicator, but only after the grievance has been settled. Performance indicators were a major issue at the University of Manitoba in the 1998 round of collective bargaining. After failing to reach a compromise, the university agreed to not impose performance indicators until after the next round of bargaining. Union and management established a committee to continue examining the issue between bargaining.

Using performance indicators highlights a central point of conflict between faculty and administration over who really runs academic programs.

Administrators claim they are necessary tools for allocating resources. Faculty claim that performance indicators give administrators far too much influence over academic priorities. By controlling the purse strings, administrators can use indicators to justify spending money on favoured programs, without submitting their decisions to lengthy senate debates over academic priorities. Budget matters may bypass senates entirely.

TECHNOLOGICAL CHANGE is the second issue. Before the 1990s academics had few concerns about the impact of technological advances on their work, other than keeping up with changes in software and hardware. Computers tended to ease their work, by facilitating data analysis and writing, improving literature searches, bringing electronic mail, and providing direct access to libraries around the world via the Internet. Control was a key factor with all these changes. Academics determined how and when they used the technology. Computers did not adversely affect their independence. If anything it gave them greater freedom to work where and when they pleased. Computers were not used to eliminate faculty, or to downgrade their work.

For most other workers, computers were used to reduce the skill requirements of their jobs, and allow greater control and monitoring by managers. Computers also made it easier to replace workers with machines. This happened with university support staff. As secretarial support was reduced, professors assumed the additional work of producing their documents directly on computer.

Computerization facilitated academic work, opened up new areas of research on the impacts of technological change, and provided consulting opportunities to install computerized management information systems. Academics were some of the more influential writers on the subject, showing how technologies were used historically to increase output, lower production costs, de-skill jobs and reduce wages (Braverman 1974, Noble 1977). Academics wrote about how computers were used to transfer control of labour processes from workers to management, in the factory and the office (Edwards 1979, Garson 1977). Struggles over control took longer with craft occupations than assembly line labour. Production that relied on workers' judgement and skill posed greater challenges to computerization. Management eventually won even in these areas, as the technology became sophisticated enough to automate the trades of machinists and printers (Cockburn 1983).

Until the 1980s, intellectual work was presumed immune from computerized control, because it relies so deeply on the mind of the worker.

This is no longer true. David Noble (1998) describes how electronic communication is used to remove professors from the teaching process. Modular courses may even eliminate the need for academics to prepare the content. Corporations in the United States are already operating universities with modular courses. Companies buy components on the open market and package the courses for students.

Unions are beginning to address technological change at the bargaining table. York University Faculty Association negotiated a clause in 1997 that allowed the union to oversee the use of technology, gave members a voice in decisions to convert courses to new technologies, and assured copyright protection over their courses, regardless of the format in which they were delivered. Article 18, on "Workload of Faculty Members" spells out professors' rights regarding how technologies will be used to deliver their courses. Unresolved disputes are submitted to a joint union-administration committee.

> Assignment of courses using alternate modes of delivery shall be consistent with the pedagogic and academic judgements and principles of the faculty member employee as to the appropriateness of the use of technology in the circumstances. Furthermore, it is recognized that not all courses are appropriate for alternate delivery. Normally, a faculty member will not be required to convert a course without his/her agreement.

Manitoba's 1998 agreement requires a faculty member's consent to the information technologies in courses, and gives professors copyright and intellectual property rights over the contents.

The third issue, INTELLECTUAL PROPERTY (IP), is a cornerstone of the new corporate university. Robert Gorman (1998) notes that IP is shorthand for "legal rights in products of the mind." Ownership of the fruits of scholarly work was rarely contentious when they were limited to publication of books or articles in journals. Academic publications seldom achieve any commercial success, with the exception of occasional best-selling textbooks. Authors traditionally retained copyright for their material and enjoyed any commercial benefits that might accrue from selling or licensing.

Today's academics make money from selling computer software, courseware, and multimedia works on CD-ROMs, and universities have become proportionately more interested in revenue as a product of scholarly work. Employers now seek ways to capture value from the professors who develop the products, chiefly by changing their protocols on copyright. Some simply assert rightful ownership of scholarly publications, teaching notes, and materials as products made for hire (Gorman 1998).

Universities in the forefront of commercialization offer elaborate schemes to induce faculty to work for business. MIT's Industrial Liaison Program (ILP) serves hundreds of corporate members that pay annual fees in the tens of thousands of dollars. Faculty earn points for serving ILP members. In 1997 they received one point for each unpublished article that was given to an ILP member, two points for a phone conversation or brief campus meeting, and 12 points for visiting a company's headquarters or laboratory. Each point was worth about $35 that could be exchanged for prizes such as office furniture, computer equipment, or travel to professional conferences (Soley 1997).

Canadian policies are driving universities in a similar direction. In May 1999, a committee of the Prime Minister's Advisory Council on Science and Technology released a report urging that universities receiving money from the federal government adopt "innovation" as a fourth mission. The committee defined innovation as "the process of bringing new goods and services to the market, or the result of that process" (Expert Panel on Commercialization of University Research 1999).

The committee recommended a national IP policy fashioned after the 1980 Bayh-Dole Act in the United States. The Canadian version would require universities to hold the rights to commercialize all IP that results from federally funded research, and to make their best efforts to commercialize the IP, by either doing it themselves or assigning it to industrial partners. The committee proposed that universities should provide incentives for faculty to create intellectual property. This would include making commercialization a factor in tenure and promotion policies. Ottawa would monitor their progress by requiring universities to file annual performance reports on commercialization strategies.

Implementing these recommendations would establish unprecedented government interference in universities. Until this development, Ottawa's requirements of grant recipients were mainly to abide by federal policies for ethics reviews or affirmative action. This initiative threatens to alter the university's core priorities by adding commercialization to teaching, research, and community service. The CAUT denounced the report. Its president, Bill Graham, commented that the recommendations would make "the profit motive the number one priority of research" (CAUT 1999a).

Resisting Privatization

Campuses have become more adversarial than ever, with heated negotiations and strikes over matters affected by privatization. One of the most contentious issues involves university boards demanding greater flexibility to dismiss professors. Unions have adamantly refused to allow layoffs for any budgetary reasons as undermining the essence of tenure and academic freedom. Manitoba's professors went on strike over the issue in 1995. Memorial's administration tabled far more pernicious demands, proposing to eliminate faculty rights by replacing the collective agreement with a hastily drafted "Handbook for Academic Staff Members" that allowed targeting professors for layoff with focussed budget cuts. The administration withdrew its demands in February 1996, just over a day before the faculty were set to go on strike. Manitoba's and Memorial's administrators seriously underestimated professors' determination to defend their rights. So did York's in 1996 when the administration tried to abrogate the collective agreement.

Conflicts like these are becoming more frequent on campuses across the country. Senior university officers have replaced their mandate to support academic services with drastic actions to save money and increase their authority, even where these initiatives damage relations with faculty or impair the health of the institution. Professors increasingly distrust their employers, while students in turn worry about how they will be affected by faculty strikes, and how the quality of their education may suffer through threats to academic freedom.

Conflict with employers has moved staunchly non-union campuses to certify. From the mid-1970s through the 1980s, when the majority of faculty associations unionized, professors at several southern Ontario campuses—some of Canada's larger, more prestigious universities— refused to form unions. This was no longer true by the mid-1990s. Deteriorating circumstances drove faculty at Queen's University to certify in November 1995. The University of Western Ontario's certification campaign started in October 1997, after nine months of discussion failed to reach a non-union agreement. Western's administration wanted its board of governors empowered to impose most of the articles in its proposed comprehensive non-union agreement, rather than negotiate with the faculty association. 1,250 full-time and part-time faculty were certified in May 1998, and unionization restored a semblance of faculty autonomy (CAUT 1998d).

Faculty have rarely found administration allies against government spending cuts. University boards and presidents seem unable, or unwilling, to defend the independence of their institutions. Profiting from the market with corporate contracts and grants seems more important. Reflecting on his 15 years as dean of the journalism faculty at the University of Western Ontario, Peter Desbarats argued that university presidents caved in "without a whimper" to the Ontario government's right-wing philosophies (Desbarats 1998), as did university presidents in other provinces. Some presidents complain about cutbacks, but none oppose the drift to what Desbarats terms the "Americanization of our universities"—embracing deregulation of fees and private sector financing, and competing for students and corporate partners.

Academic unions are well placed to confront privatization, since their self-interests coincide with what is necessary to salvage university autonomy. Tenure and academic freedom require institutional independence from private sector influence. By defending their rights, professors are also defending universities from becoming subservient to the market.

Faculty unions have occasionally taken overt political positions. During its 1997 strike, York University Faculty Association identified the corporate university as a source of its problems. The Manitoba Organization of Faculty Associations planned a conference on university commercialization for the spring of 2000. The CAUT gave the issue high priority with its fall 1999 conference on "Universities and Colleges in the Public Interest: Stopping the Commercial Takeover of Post-Secondary Education" (CAUT 1999b). It is too early to tell if this stance will be taken up by other unions. Faculty unions traditionally hold moderate positions because their members' views cover a broad spectrum from left to right—and some of those members are especially well placed to benefit from market-oriented research.

How unions use their bargaining strength in the 21ˢᵗ century will be decisive for Canada's universities. Commercialism is directed by forces in government and business far more powerful than those in academia; nonetheless, union actions may help to steer societal change in a more balanced direction.

Academic freedom still has strong protection in every collective agreement. Even though corporations have gained a foothold in shaping university research, the vast majority of professors still set their own agendas. To continue, they must preserve academic freedom.

Preserving Academic Freedom

So far we have painted a picture of universities training their sights on corporate money and becoming corporate-like in the process. Administrators have centralized and sought increased control for this transition. Faculty remain the chief obstacle. Greater administrative authority threatens their autonomy, income, academic freedom, and tenure. They are protecting their rights through increased union militancy.

Where universities head in the 21ˢᵗ century will depend on how well the non-corporate core prevails. Universities have always adapted to changes in their environment, inventing their own futures in response to altered government priorities, changing demographics, shifting demands of labour markets, and new opportunities for research and teaching. But the corporate university is cause for more concern than previous transformations. It threatens institutional autonomy and academic freedom—core foundations of free teaching and research.

In the past, strong and unfettered public funding protected university autonomy. Though responsive to market forces, universities were less vulnerable to commercial influences. Strong revenue growth enabled the vast expansion and many improvements of the post-war decades, especially increased access to university education. Reduced tuition rates allowed entry by disadvantaged groups who previously had minimal access. Affordable and accessible universities became more pluralistic as they responded to issues raised by new groups joining the university community. Programs in women's studies brought new perspectives on gender relations, identified male bias in science, humanities, social science, and the arts, and offered alternative explanations. Aboriginal studies contributed to more balanced interpretations of Canada's politics and history, even as improved access created opportunities for Aboriginal students to train as teachers, lawyers, engineers, social workers, and health care professionals.

Growth fostered expansion of traditional academic research, introduction of new professional disciplines, and activist programs in the community. For example, labour studies adds much needed perspectives to the study of politics, economics, and history, and prepares people for work in industrial relations professions. Institutes on ethics promote independent research and commentary on behaviour in politics and industry, and on appropriate use of new health and environmental technologies.

Public funding was a key element in all of these developments. Reliance on funds from private, vested interests can destroy the essence of the university. How readily will anyone do critical research on the pharmaceutical industry if their department receives support from large corporations like Apotex or Pfizer? Will people in basic health research be able to do independent work if grant money stems from corporations for product development and drug trials? Will scientists at the University of Toronto feel as free as before to study or comment on environmental practices of gold mining companies now that the university has received more than $6 million from Barrick Gold? The University of Toronto's Faculty of Social Work has a $1.5 million grant from the Royal Bank of Canada for its centre for applied social research. Will the centre be free to take positions on bank profits (Irving 1997)? Will it support research on Canada's low corporate taxation rates that benefit the banking industry? Can it criticize the way small depositors are treated, paying higher service fees than wealthy customers?

When academics don't voluntarily restrain themselves, administrators may pressure them with either subtle comments or overt reproaches. The culture of private corporations produces disturbing consequences on some campuses. In the late 1980s William Mackness, dean of the Faculty of Management at the University of Manitoba, reprimanded a professor for challenging a statement made by a representative of Xerox Corporation during a reception on campus hosted by the company. This sparked a lengthy academic freedom grievance by the faculty association. Prior to joining the university, just a few years before he issued the reprimand, Dean Mackness held a senior executive position at the Bank of Nova Scotia. For a dean with such strong corporate ties, free critical expression seemed as unacceptable in the university as in the banking industry.

Corporate influence poses greater problems with research. Donor control can hamper free flow of information. Corporations paying for research often expect exclusive rights to the results, and frown on publication that makes the information available to competitors. A typical compromise between business and academic interests is to delay publication until inventions are patented, or until marketing studies are completed or products are ready to roll off the assembly line. Research contracts may require secrecy where sensitive data are involved, such as in military research, biotechnology or other highly specialized sectors.

How will commercialism ultimately affect the university? A pessimistic scenario has universities becoming businesses which train student customers and serve corporate clients. Free inquiry gives way to selling of research. Education narrows to focus on what sells. Universities eventually lose their balance. Lower revenue programs in arts and humanities lose ground to cash-rich faculties in business, engineering, and computer science. Stagnant starting salaries in publicly funded fields fall behind compensation in units with stronger revenue from the private sector. Starting salaries in arts departments already lag as much as 30 or 40 percent below amounts paid by business faculties.

Privatization threatens the tradition of education in a wide range of fields. Programs in the liberal arts and humanities provide crucial preparation in advanced literary knowledge, social analysis, and critical thinking. Theatre, music, and fine arts explore the cutting edges of creative expression. These areas are jeopardized by private market orientation. Without them, education may prepare graduates for jobs in industry, but leave them less equipped for changing careers in volatile labour markets. It also robs society of the creativity and innovation nurtured by flexible and varied curricula.

Universities driven by market priorities provide a limited contribution to democratic processes. They cannot foster the kind of debate and social criticism that thrives in an independent academy (Readings 1996). The university is supposed to be a forum for open debate from all perspectives. Economics departments are home to monetarists and marxists. Sociology departments house materialists and post-modernists. Specialized programs supported by commercial interests do not encourage competing ideologies. Business faculties have little room for critics of capitalism.

Progressive Partnerships

While the drift to the market may be understandable in the era of privatization and fiscal restraint at the end of the 20th century, it is neither reasonable nor desirable. The university must be available to all sectors of the community, not just those with the most money. Business has less need for service or support than other parts of the community. Serving the strongest is difficult to justify when so many areas are wanting.

The poor and disenfranchised should have at least as much access to university services as corporations and the wealthy. Problems of economic and social inequality are in dire need of attention. The widening gap between rich and poor is now a serious problem affecting virtually every country in the world. Poverty is endemic to the core areas of large cities. People in universities can address these problems with educational, professional and research services. They can form progressive alliances with organizations already working in these areas. The United States government encourages universities to form partnerships for urban renewal. At the end of 1996 the Office of University Partnerships, Department of Housing and Urban Development (HUD), supported over 325 community development projects involving 225 universities, colleges and community colleges in partnership with local governments, community-based organizations, school districts and public housing authorities.

The Social Sciences and Humanities Research Council of Canada (SSHRC) has a similar initiative on a smaller scale. Community-University Research Alliances (CURA) require equal partnerships between universities and organizations in the community, with components for research, education and training, and knowledge sharing. The initial four-year $10.5 million project supports up to 16 CURAs, each one with up to $200,000 a year for three years. SSHRC's statement of context describes the problems they expect to address:

> Shifting employment patterns and skill demands in a knowledge-based economy, the growth of poverty and homelessness, an ever more diversified social fabric, transformations in family-life, changing values, the marginalization of young people concerning the workforce, budget reductions affecting organizations and public services, increasing urbanization and depopulation of rural areas, and the new rules of business competitiveness are among the phenomena transforming communities and the lives of their inhabitants (SSHRC 1999).

This is a modest budget for addressing such substantial problems, especially in light of the much larger sums Ottawa makes available for supporting business. Nonetheless, the program creates opportunities for progressive partnerships.

Prospects for doing this work will be eroded if universities drift more deeply into corporate waters. Supporting community development, studying progressive taxation systems, examining fair methods of income distribution, or improved systems of welfare are difficult in a system supported by opponents of these policies.

Funding must be more balanced, to preserve the university's independence in research, teaching and service. This requires making a strong case for increased public support for core university services. Government is the only source of funds that allows this level of flexibility.

Business practices are not yet the dominant force in the Canadian system. Faculty have managed to retain autonomy through collective bargaining; some university presidents officially defend institutional rights to self-determination; paths are still open to preserve independence and integrity rather than relinquishing them to the priorities of the paymaster. These paths need not be created or started from scratch. They already exist. Strengthening them is crucial, because virtually no other institution in society possesses this degree of independence.

Even the press, despite its proud self-image of fighting for freedom of expression, long ago surrendered independent practice to tighter corporate control. The number of newspapers is steadily shrinking, and most are owned by a handful of corporations. The only Canadian newspapers to claim national status, the *Globe and Mail* and *The National Post,* devote a substantial portion of their daily coverage to business. No other sector —not even sports—receives anything near the same emphasis. But these newspapers rarely publish anything critical of capitalist institutions. There is little coverage, positive or otherwise, of labour, environmental, or other social movements.

Preserving independence of the university becomes all the more important in light of these strong biases. Universities are uniquely placed to foster critical debate. Erosion of university autonomy hampers the capacity of our entire society to develop new ideas and to challenge existing paradigms.

University research encompasses all the pure and applied sciences, humanities, social sciences, and professions. Scientists address far-ranging questions about the origins of the universe. Engineers meet practical challenges to design better computers and bridges. Philosophers pose enduring social, existential, and ethical questions. Historians, economists, and social scientists analyze social, political and economic change, and develop solutions to social problems. Health scientists seek to prevent and cure disease.

Basic requirements must be met to preserve this range of work:

INSTITUTIONAL AUTONOMY is necessary for researchers to pursue these questions without interference.

ACADEMIC FREEDOM is required to retain highly trained professionals who devote their life's work to specialized research. Freedom reinforces their commitment to delving into uncharted territory, or experimenting with new answers to old questions.

TENURE is a third essential condition for pursuing long-term research. Enduring problems may require years of study before showing results. Academics require employment security for investing long-term efforts. Short-term corporate models of productivity threaten this system.

Even with these fundamentals in place, basic research can flourish only with adequate funding for staff, state of the art equipment, and supportive infrastructure. Shortages of research personnel have become a considerable problem. Trimmed budgets reduce the capacity to hire expert staff, and resultant rising teaching loads leave faculty with less time to do research. Even when they are able to recruit faculty, universities cannot compete with industry for the best and brightest researchers. Industry can offer higher salaries, better equipped laboratories, and prospects for much higher future earnings and continuing state of the art facilities.

Restoring State Support

Demanding increased government support for universities is bound to meet resistance in a conservative climate of expenditure cutbacks. Ottawa's 1999 plans reduce total federal spending on programs to 12 percent of GDP in 2000–01, the lowest level in 50 years (Graham 1999).

Health, welfare, and social service sectors already compete for scarce resources. When hospital beds are closed, how can we justify spending more money on universities? No reasonable solution to this conundrum is possible if we continue to pit public services against each other. Rather, we must learn to see these sectors as mutually reinforcing components. Government should take an holistic approach integrating all aspects of a healthy population: physical, economic, emotional, and intellectual.

To change dominant views on this issue, we must counter prevailing arguments that government cannot afford to spend more money on services. Government must set higher priorities for social spending, and renew a commitment to public financing of post-secondary education, *without requirements for commercialization*. Government must support rather than constrain free inquiry.

Government can raise far more money through modest tax adjustments. Taxation and spending policies currently favour business and people with high incomes. Corporations receive copious assistance in the form of subsidies, tax breaks, and technical support. Though this money and effort serve business interests, they are not necessary for business success. The money could be used to strengthen those parts of the public sector most in need: health care, social services, and education.

In 1989 Neil Brooks and Linda McQuaig showed how some $13 billion could be raised by eliminating tax expenditures on high incomes and corporations, introducing modest taxes on wealth, and restoring the taxes on corporations and high incomes cut in the early 1980s (Brooks & McQuaig 1989). Moderate tax reform in the 1998 Alternative Federal Budget prepared by Cho!ces and the Canadian Centre for Policy Alternatives yielded $12 billion in federal revenue, enough to increase program spending by more than 10 percent (CCPA and Cho!ces 1998).

Many of these reforms simply use bureaucratic structures and procedures already in place to restore previous income tax rates and eliminate some of the more egregious deductions for corporations and individuals. Obstacles to these changes are political, not technical. Conservative budget-balancing favours the wealthy by giving them the largest tax breaks, and proposals to restore tax rates face opposition chiefly from higher income groups. Making the case for reform requires placing human faces on the increased suffering from unemployment, poor health, and poverty (Loxley 1998).

The language of thrift disguises these class conflicts. In principle, governments are mere caretakers who distribute resources from taxpayers to recipients without any vested interest in the funds they receive. They can afford to spend whatever they decide to raise. Appeals to balance the budget are popular because they hint at the spectre of personal debt and bankruptcy, even though there is no logical basis for drawing an analogy between personal and government finance.

Government rhetoric about balancing expenditures with revenues is a diversion from the more significant impacts of spending reduction. Large-scale cutbacks involve reducing the size of the state and transferring services and benefits to the private sector. Reduced taxes leave the wealthy with more disposable income, and corporations with higher net profits. Privatization transfers assets that generate income and wealth from the non-profit public domain to the profit-seeking private sector.

The greatest irony of budget reductions is that they do not really save money: they simply shift the burden of paying for services from the taxpayer to the consumer. Patients pay a rising portion of the costs of health care services. Students contribute a rapidly rising share of university expenses. Public sector employees subsidize service costs through lower salaries and benefits.

Privatization is commonly defended on grounds that service delivery is more efficient, yet services to the public have not been noticeably improved by privatized railroads, airlines, and telephone companies. Publicly run automobile insurance in Manitoba and Saskatchewan offers greater efficiencies, at lower rates, than in any other province. The public sector is in fact highly productive, especially in education, health, social services, and utilities.

Privatized services may be even more expensive in the long run. Government services are free of such costs as marketing expenses, costs of overlapping administration, and executive salaries that far exceed those in the public sector. Private businesses earn profits to drive up the price of their shares on stock markets and cover shareholder dividends. The cost of profits is passed on to the public through higher prices for goods and services.

Accountability   Canadian public policy is following the global path to a more privatized world. Greater shares of income and wealth are accruing to those at the top end of the scale. Canadian business people maintain that to be competitive they must control more aspects of the economy and form alliances with global corporations. We have already placed major public assets under private control. Universities risk being absorbed in this wave. Yet the costs of transforming universities into businesses far exceed any potential benefits. Instead of operating in the public interest, the university's products would accrue to a small, elite sector of Canadian society.

If current trends continue, public education will become a branch of private industry. Research critical of the status quo will disappear. Basic research and advances in general knowledge will suffer from a steady decline in funding. Universities will produce studies for business and share the profits with corporate donors and partners. Research targeted towards giving investors a return on their money will replace broadly-based scholarship.

Business already exerts too much influence over university governance. Corporate representatives traditionally hold an inside track to universities through seats on governing boards; this presence is becoming more focussed as expert consultants in privatization gain prominence on university boards. Tom O'Neill, president of Price Waterhouse, reputed to be the world's largest privatization consulting firm, became a governor of Queen's University in 1997. KPMG, ranked third among global privatization consultants, has worked on contracting out public education systems and privatizing municipal services; its chair and chief executive officer was a member of the University of Toronto's Governing Council in 1997, while another KPMG executive was chair of the board at the University of Regina. Ernst & Young, a leading consulting firm whose published manuals identify the profit-making opportunities from privatizing publicly-run organizations, had representatives on the boards of McGill, Concordia, and Queen's (Desbarats 1998).

University boards should be more representative of the wider community. People from labour, community organizations, non-profit groups, and health, education, and social service agencies are likely to advocate strengthening the university's capacity to serve community needs and ensure greater accountability to the public.

Universities: Not for Sale

Privatization restricts university access to those who can afford costly tuition, or to those fortunate enough to earn scholarships or venturesome enough to assume considerable debt. High tuition is a particularly ill-conceived way for government to save money. Discouraging a broad base of eligible students from entering university results only in a less-educated and under-productive labour force.

Advanced education greatly improves one's prospects for better jobs and higher lifetime earnings. Lower tuition opens the university's doors to immigrants, foreign students, and domestic students from economically disadvantaged backgrounds; higher tuition narrows the opening. Improved accessibility creates opportunities for people with disabilities. People turned away from the professions and excluded from better paying occupations are far more likely to experience periods of unemployment and dependence on welfare.

Adequately financed public universities contribute a crucial foundation of inquiry, deeper and broader than other institutions. The university is designed to be radical, its investigators expected to explore root causes and explanations. It is the only place we have that purposely fosters creative synergies by bringing together people with radically different views.

If we are to protect and preserve universities' independence and autonomy, Canadian governments must take bold steps to ensure they can operate free of commercial constraints. Commercialization policies must be abandoned in favour of grant programs that consider quality above all. The outcome will affect generations of future students, who have every right to expect and demand the highest quality education possible.

This will appear difficult, perhaps even radical, in the face of overwhelming pressure to commercialize everything. It is nothing of the sort. It makes good sense for the state to support diverse institutions which challenge market behaviour and values. Industry fuels a nation's economic engine, but it must coexist with institutions outside the realm of commerce. This kind of autonomy and free expression make up the heart of democracy. Democratic societies thrive on differences of ideas and ideologies, and universities are a crucial component of this mix. Debate, criticism, and unfettered inquiry are their raison d'être. Ensuring the full expression of these differences allows a society to flourish; hindering them signals a nation's decline. We risk placing too much faith in business and the market, abandoning our noncompetitive institutions.

Professors find themselves in the front line of this struggle. They may be motivated by self-interest over threats to pay, tenure, and academic freedom, but their efforts confront the essential question of the university's future—whether it will remain an independent force that contributes broadly to society, or instead be sold to the highest bidder.

Tables

Table A-1
University Enrolment in Canada
Full-time and Part-time, by sex

YEAR	WOMEN		MEN		TOTAL
	Number	*Percent*	*Number*	*Percent*	
	FULL-TIME				
1970–71	108,759	35.1%	200,710	64.9%	309,469
1972–73	118,856	36.9%	203,548	63.1%	322,404
1974–75	137,585	39.6%	209,771	60.4%	347,356
1976–77	159,160	42.3%	217,346	57.7%	376,506
1978–79	160,549	43.6%	207,724	56.4%	368,273
1980–81	171,673	44.9%	210,944	55.1%	382,617
1982–83	194,975	45.7%	231,414	54.3%	426,389
1984–85	216,797	47.0%	244,227	53.0%	461,024
1986–87	230,243	48.4%	245,174	51.6%	475,417
1988–89	248,922	49.8%	251,067	50.2%	499,989
1990–91	272,866	51.3%	259,266	48.7%	532,132
1992–93	296,456	52.1%	273,024	47.9%	569,480
1994–95	305,643	53.1%	270,061	46.9%	575,704
1996–97	309,731	54.0%	263,904	46.0%	573,635
1997–98	312,663	54.6%	260,436	45.4%	573,099
	PART-TIME				
1970–71	63,735	40.8%	92,481	59.2%	156,216
1972–73	75,297	49.2%	77,684	50.8%	152,981
1974–75	80,828	49.2%	83,421	50.8%	164,249
1976–77	101,237	53.0%	89,720	47.0%	190,957
1978–79	119,910	55.4%	96,430	44.6%	216,340
1980–81	140,468	57.3%	104,660	42.7%	245,128
1982–83	155,365	58.3%	111,021	41.7%	266,386
1984–85	162,965	58.6%	115,029	41.4%	277,994
1986–87	173,684	60.4%	113,813	39.6%	287,497
1988–89	190,126	62.1%	116,111	37.9%	306,237
1990–91	192,560	62.3%	116,638	37.7%	309,198
1992–93	194,878	61.6%	121,287	38.4%	316,165
1994–95	172,951	61.1%	110,301	38.9%	283,252
1996–97	156,248	61.0%	99,885	39.0%	256,133
1997–98	151,695	60.8%	97,978	39.2%	249,673

SOURCE: *Statistics Canada, various years.*

Table A–2
Degrees, Diplomas and Certificates, by Sex and Year
Canada
(*thousands*)

YEAR	MALE	FEMALE	TOTAL
1970	48.0	28.5	76.5
1975	59.5	43.5	103.0
1980	59.0	55.5	114.5
1985	65.0	68.0	133.0
1990	68.5	84.5	153.0
1995	76.0	102.0	178.0
1997	72.1	99.6	171.7

SOURCE: Statistics Canada, 1992, 18. Statistics Canada Website, *statcan.ca/english/Pgdb/People/Education/educ21.htm*, "University degrees granted by field of study, by sex." CANSIM cross-classified table 00580602, 1999.

Table A–3
Research on the Contribution of Education to Economic Growth[1]
Canada

Study	1909–29	1929–57	1950–62	1962–73	1973–81	1981–86
Bertram (1966)	.35	.67				
	12.4	22.9				
Lithwick (1967)		.35				
		11.9				
Walters (1970)			.2			
			4.7			
Kendrick (1981)[2]				.5	.6	
				8.8	20.0	
MacDonald (1985)				.5	.8	
				8.8	26.7	
CLMPC (1990)						.54
						16.2

SOURCE: Canadian Labour Market Productivity Centre (1990), 21–31.

[1]The first line is the estimate of the absolute contribution to output growth. For example Bertram estimated that for the 1909–29 period education increased Gross Domestic Product (GDP) by an average of .35 percent per year. The second line is the relative contribution. Using the same period for Bertram, he estimated that education accounted for 12.4 percent of the growth in GDP over the period.

[2]For Kendrick, the estimate in the 1962–73 column is for 1960–1973. The 1973–81 column is for 1973–79.

Table A–4
Enrolment and Public Expenditure on Higher Education 1970—1983
$Constant

Country	A Expenditure Increase (%)	B Enrolment Increase (%)	A/B (%)	Public Spending on Higher Education as % of GDP, 1983
Australia				1.58
Austria	49.4%	157.8	31.3	0.77
Canada	3.9%	62.2	6.3	2.00
Denmark	-7.0%	45.7	-15.3	0.89
Finland	104.4%	100.7	103.7	
France	-25.0%	47.2	-53.0	0.69ª
Germany	29.9%	179.0	16.7	0.59
Italy	24.2%	49.8	48.6	0.53
Japan	27.6%	31.5	87.6	0.41ª
Luxembourg	46.8%	159.9	29.3	
Netherlands	21.6%	64.6	33.4	1.76ª
New Zealand	-7.7%	35.0	-22.0	.011
Norway	43.0%	64.9	66.3	0.79
Sweden	-29.9%	53.2	-56.2	0.62
United Kingdom	-4.8%	42.8	-11.2	1.09ª
United States	13.6%	46.2	29.4	2.49ᵇ

SOURCES: Science Council of Canada, 1988.; OECD, 1986.
Real public expenditure uses OECD educational expenditure deflators. Public spending on higher education as percent of GDP, from
UNESCO, *Statistical Yearbook* 1986, Paris.
ªData from 1982; ᵇData from 1981

Table A-5
University Operating Income
By Source of Funds
In $million

Year	Government Amount	Government %	Fees Amount	Fees %	Gifts, Donations Non-Govt Grants Amount	%	Other Amount	%	Total
1977-78	1978	83.4	328	13.8	12	0.5	53	2.2	2,371
1978-79	2147	83.8	340	13.3	16	0.6	59	2.3	2,562
1979-80	2302	83.5	358	13.0	20	0.7	77	2.8	2,757
1980-81	2546	83.2	401	13.1	23	0.8	89	2.9	3,059
1981-82	2842	82.4	469	13.6	21	0.6	115	3.3	3,447
1982-83	3194	81.7	568	14.5	28	0.7	120	3.1	3,910
1983-84	3371	81.5	632	15.3	26	0.6	106	2.6	4,135
1984-85	3472	80.8	689	16.0	30	0.7	108	2.5	4,299
1985-86	3658	81.0	730	16.2	31	0.7	99	2.2	4,518
1986-87	3917	81.3	768	15.9	34	0.7	98	2.0	4,817
1987-88	4201	81.4	827	16.0	32	0.6	104	2.0	5,164
1988-89	4488	80.9	912	16.4	31	0.6	116	2.1	5,547
1989-90	4847	79.9	1012	16.7	43	0.7	162	2.7	6,064
1990-91	5,214	78.9	1,178	17.8	45	0.7	174	2.6	6,611
1991-92	5,646	77.2	1,406	19.2	75	1.0	185	2.5	7,312
1992-93	5,665	75.8	1,565	21.0	53	0.7	186	2.5	7,469
1993-94	5,713	74.1	1,727	22.4	75	1.0	199	2.6	7,714
1994-95	5,419	72.2	1,826	24.3	61	0.8	197	2.6	7,503
1995-96	5,333	70.4	1,941	25.6	76	1.0	226	3.0	7,576
1996-97	4,922	66.8	2,118	28.8	70	1.0	255	3.5	7,365
1997-98	4,832	63.4	2,410	31.6	71	0.9	309	4.1	7,622

SOURCE: AUCC 1991, 1999a

Table A-6
Full-time Faculty
By Sex

Year	Male		Female		Total
	Number	Percent	Number	Percent	
1961	5,719	88.7%	726	11.3%	6,445
1966	10,545	87.3%	1,540	12.7%	12,085
1976	24,590	86.1%	3,961	13.9%	28,551
1980	26,565	85.4%	4,534	14.6%	31,099
1984	28,257	84.1%	5,351	15.9%	33,608
1988	28,946	82.0%	6,345	18.0%	35,291
1991	29,281	79.5%	7,563	20.5%	36,844
1992	29,282	78.7%	7,938	21.3%	37,220
1993	28,829	78.1%	8,082	21.9%	36,911
1994	28,094	77.3%	8,267	22.7%	36,361
1995	27,519	76.4%	8,488	23.6%	36,007
1996	25,979	75.7%	8,347	24.3%	34,326
1997	24,750	75.0%	8,250	25.0%	33,000

SOURCES: Statistics Canada 1991, AUCC 1999.

Table A-7
Carnegie Corporation Grants to Canadian Universities 1921–40

	Libraries, Art & Music	Teaching Programs	Research	Endowment & General	Total
Acadia	22,500	16,200	5,000	285,000	328,700
Dalhousie	66,000	62,000	7,714	1,215,000	1,350,714
King's	3,000			797,500	800,500
Memorial	14,325	11,500		267,500	293,325
Mount Allison	12,050	5,000		135,000	152,050
New Brunswick	4,500				4,500
Prince of Wales College	4,500			75,000	79,500
St Francis Xavier	4,500	70,000		10,000	84,500
Bishop's	4,500				4,500
Laval	6,000				6,000
McGill	17,250	179,800		5,000	202,050
Montréal	8,000				8,000
McMaster	8,250	48,500			56,750
Ottawa	4,500				4,500
Queen's	22,550	18,100	32,000		72,650
Toronto	23,150	64,100	100,000		187,250
Western	17,550	22,500			40,050
Manitoba	7,550	60,000			67,550
Saskatchewan	19,000	97,500	5,000		121,500
Alberta	22,500	58,500	13,000	50,000	144,000
St. Joseph's College				100,000	100,000
British Columbia	22,500	40,000	10,000		72,500
Other¹	62,500	48,000	6,250		116,750
Total	377,175	801,700	178,964	2,940,000	4,297,839

SOURCE: Harris, 1976, 345–8.

¹Includes small grants to the following colleges: St. Dunstan's; St. Joseph's; Ecole des Hautes Etudes Commerciales; St. Michael's Trinity; Victoria; Assumption; Brescia; Waterloo; Ontario Agricultural; Campion; Luther; Regina; Mount Royal.

Table A–8
Summary of University Expansion in Canada
1949–1979

TYPE	1949–59	1960–69	1970–79	1949–79
New Universities	3	8	1	12
Colleges converted to universities	3	6	5	14
Total	6	14	6	26

SOURCE: AUCC 1999b.

Table A–9
University Expansion in Canada, 1949–1979

1949	Memorial	Newfoundland	Conversion
1954	Sherbrooke	Québec	New university
1957	Laurentian	Ontario	Conversion
1957	Carleton	Ontario	Conversion
1957	Waterloo	Ontario	New University
1959	York	Ontario	New university
1960	Laurentian	Ontario	Conversion
1963	Victoria	B.C.	Conversion
1963	Trent	Ontario	New university
1963	Moncton	New Brunswick	Conversion
1964	Guelph	Ontario	New university
1964	Brock	Ontario	New university
1965	Simon Fraser	B.C.	New university
1965	Lakehead	Ontario	New university
1965	OISE	Ontario	New university
1966	Mount St. Vincent	Nova Scotia	Conversion
1966	U. of Calgary	Alberta	Conversion
1967	Lethbridge	Alberta	New university
1969	U. du Québec	Québec	New university
1969	U. PEI	P.E.I.	Conversion
1970	Athabasca	Alberta	New university
1971	Ryerson	Ontario	Conversion
1973	Wilfred Laurier	Ontario	Conversion
1974	Regina	Saskatchewan	Conversion
1974	Cape Breton	Nova Scotia	Conversion
1974	Concordia	Québec	Conversion

SOURCE: AUCC 1999b

207

Table A-10
Strikes and Lockouts in Canadian Universities

University	Year	Duration	Main Issues
Laval	1976	107 days	academic freedom, salary scale, sabbaticals, maternity leave, personal files
Québec à Montréal	1976-7	133 days	salaries, part-time staff, hiring, promotion, tenure
T.U. N.S.	1981	1 day	salaries
Windsor	1982	6 days	salaries, past practice, access to information, retirement, sabbaticals.
Laval	1984	23 days	lock-out, benefits.
Dalhousie	1985	1 day	pension, salary, financial exigency
Laurentian	1985	3 days	salaries
York	1985	2 days	salaries, class size, sabbaticals
N.S C.A.D.	1986	23 days	fair procedures, job security, consultation, salary equity
Dalhousie	1988	2 1/2 weeks; strike/lock-out	workload, salaries & benefits, gender equity, replacement of staff who leave
Lakehead	1988	18 days	salaries (catch-up), benefits, maternity leave, pension
Saskatchewan	1988	10 days — legislated back	salaries, benefits.
T.U. N.S.	1988	17 days	Salaries and service awards
Laurentian	1989	22 days	salaries, promotions, working conditions
Mt. St. Vincent	1989	9 days	salaries
Laval	1990	9 days over a 5 week period	tenure positions, pension, salary catch-up
Trent	1991	3 weeks	salaries, benefits, pension, early retirement
Mount Allison	1992	3 weeks	mandatory retirement, salaries, sabbaticals, lay-offs
Sherbrooke	1992	6 days	salaries, hiring and promotion criteria
Manitoba	1995	23 days	financial exigency, redundancy (discontinuance article), academic freedom
Trent	1996	2 weeks	salaries, pensions
York	1997	55 days	salaries, retirement plan, workload, copyright, technological change
Dalhousie	1998	8 days	salaries and faculty complement
Brandon	1998	3 days; strike and lock-out	salaries, benefits, tenure, copyright, privacy, technological change
Mount Allison	1999	26 days	salaries

SOURCE: CAUT, *The Negotiator*, VII, 2 (April 30, 1990), 8, and correspondence with CAUT Staff

Number of strikes: 25 Number of universities: 16 Total days on strike: 566

Table A-11
Post-secondary Education Fiscal Transfers under EPF
As a Percentage of Provincial Operating Grants
To Universities and Colleges

	Transfers as a % of Provincial Operating Grants		Increase in the Federal Share
	1977–78	1984–85	
Newfoundland	83.3%	106.9%	23.6%
PEI	101.5%	106.9%	5.3%
Nova Scotia	0.9%	91.6%	4.1%
New Brunswick	98.1%	101.8%	3.7%
Quebec	56.1%	59.6%	3.5%
Ontario	73.7%	88.7%	15.0%
Manitoba	80.3%	102.9%	22.5%
Saskatchewan	81.6%	90.3%	8.7%
Alberta	63.9%	73.1%	9.2%
British Columbia	78.9%	104.3%	25.4%
Average	68.9%	79.6%	10.7%

SOURCE: Standing Senate Committee on National Finance (1987), *Federal Policy on Post-Secondary Education*, Ottawa.

Table A-12
Cuts to Post-Secondary Education under EPF
In $million

Year	No cuts	6 & 5	Bill C-96	Bill C-69	Budget 91	Total cut	Net
1977–78	1,991	0	0	0	0	0	1,991
1978–79	2,283	0	0	0	0	0	2,283
1979–80	2,609	0	0	0	0	0	2,609
1980–81	2,940	0	0	0	0	0	2,940
1981–82	3,310	0	0	0	0	0	3,310
1982–83	3,704	0	0	0	0	0	3,704
1983–84	4,075	117	0	0	0	117	3,958
1984–85	4,442	253	0	0	0	253	4,189
1985–86	4,781	273	0	0	0	273	4,508
1986–87	5,192	296	91	0	0	387	4,805
1987–88	5,595	319	195	0	0	514	5,081
1988–89	6,030	344	313	0	0	657	5,373
1989–90	6,530	373	448	0	0	821	5,709
1990-91	7,119	406	604	321	0	1,331	5,788
1991-92	7,605	434	769	546	0	1,749	5,856
1992-93[a]	8,022	458	940	625	71	2,094	5,928
1993-94[a]	8,435	481	1,123	705	120	2,429	6,006
1994-95[a]	8,943	510	1,329	795	227	2,861	6,082
Total	93,606	4,264	5,812	2,992	418	13,486	80,120

SOURCE: AUCC 1991 [a]Estimate

References

Abbott, Frank (1984), "Academic Freedom and Social Criticism in the 1930s," *Interchange*, 14/4–15/1(1983-84), 107–23.

Abbott, Frank William Charles (1985), *The Origin and Foundation of the Canadian Association of University Teachers*, Ph.D. Thesis, University of Toronto.

Adell, B.L. (1970), *The Legal Status of Collective Agreements in England, The United States and Canada*, Kingston, Ontario: Industrial Relations Centre, Queen's University.

Adell, B.L. and D.D. Carter (1972), *Collective Bargaining for University Faculty in Canada, A Study Commissioned by the Association of Universities and Colleges of Canada*, Kingston, Ontario: Industrial Relations Centre, Queen's University.

Adell, Bernard (1975), "Establishment of Faculty Collective Bargaining: The Developing Law," *Universities and the Law*, Winnipeg: Legal Research Institute, University of Manitoba, 45–59.

Altbach, Philip G. ed. (1977), *Comparative Perspectives on the Academic Profession*, New York: Praeger.

Alternatives Information (1997) website, *www.alternatives.com* (July 7).

Andrews, Alan (1993), "'Chilly Climate' controversy sparks review at Uvic," *CAUT Bulletin*, October, 7.

Apotex Inc. (1999), *Home Page, www.apotex.com*.

ARA Consulting Group Inc. (1997), *Evaluation of the Networks of Centres of Excellence Program*, prepared for the NCE Program Evaluation Committee, Ottawa: January.

Arvay, Stephen (1984), *The Role of Intra-Capitalist Class Conflict in the Development of Education in Ontario, 1955–1962*, PhD Thesis, Toronto: York University.

AUCC (1965), *Financing Higher Education in Canada*, a report of the Association of Universities and Colleges of Canada, Ottawa: June 30.

———— (1972), "Not a 'Trade Union' Waterloo Faculty Association Discovers," *University Affairs*, 13(March), 4.

———— (1974) "Certification request withdrawn at UBC," *University Affairs*, 15-(December), 16.

———— (1975g), "Faculty Union Signs First Collective Agreement," *University Affairs*, 16(March), 8.

———— (1976a), "AIB Orders Roll-Back in Salary Increases at Carleton," *University Affairs*, 17(July), 13.

———— (1976b), "AIB Rolls Back Salaries At Ottawa U," *University Affairs*, 17(November), 18.

———— (1976c), "UBC opts for collective bargaining outside provincial labor code," *University Affairs*, 17(July), 14.

——— (1979), "Survey Shows Universities Becoming More Concerned with Status of Women," *University Affairs*, 13 (Sept), 15.

——— (1981), "Mandatory Retirement Illegal in Manitoba, Court Rules," *University Affairs*, 22(3), 40.

——— (1989), "7-year terms average for university presidents," *University Affairs*, 30(4), 27.

——— (1990), *Fundraising Campaigns*, Ottawa: Association of Universities and Colleges of Canada, June.

——— (1991), *Trends: The Canadian University in Profile*, Ottawa: Association of Universities and Colleges of Canada.

——— (1996a), "Hiring 'thaw' at Waterloo," *University Affairs*, March, 21.

——— (1996b), "Augustana holds seat sale," *University Affairs*, October.

——— (1996c), "Coke is it at UBC, *University Affairs*, April, 23.

——— (1996d), "Guarding intellectual assets," *University Affairs*, April, 23.

——— (1999a), *Trends: The Canadian University in Profile*, Ottawa: Association of Universities and Colleges of Canada.

——— (1999b), *The Directory of Canadian Universities*, Ottawa: Association of Universities and Colleges.

Avery, Donald H. (1998), *The Science of War: Canadian Scientists and Allied Military Technology During the Second World War*, Toronto: University of Toronto Press.

Axelrod, Paul (1981), "Business Aid to Canadian Universities, 1957–65," *Interchange*, 11(1), 25–38.

Axelrod, Paul (1982), *Scholars and Dollars: Politics, Economics, and the Universities of Ontario, 1945–1980*, Toronto: University of Toronto Press.

——— (1982b), "Historical Writing and Canadian Universities: The State of the Art," *Queen's Quarterly*, 89, 1 (Spring), 137–44.

——— (1984), "Higher Education, Utilitarianism, and the Acquisitive Society: Canada, 1930–1980," in Michael S. Cross and Gregory S. Kealey, eds., *Modern Canada, 1930–1980*, Toronto: McClelland & Stewart.

Axelrod, Paul, and John G. Reid, eds. (1989), *Youth, University and Canadian Society: Essays in the Social History of Higher Education*, Montréal: McGill-Queen's University Press.

Backhouse, Constance, Roma Harris, Gillian Michael and Alison Wylie (1989), "The Chilly Climate for Faculty Women at UWO: Postcript to the Backhouse Report," Unpublished paper, London, University of Western Ontario, November.

Baldridge, Victor (1973), "Research," *Change*, 5, 4 (May).

Balzarini, David (1989), "The Fading Economic Status of the Academic," *CAUT Bulletin*, 36(4), 5.

Barkans, John and Norene Pupo (1974), "The Board of Governors and the Power Elite: A Case Study of Eight Canadian Universities," *Sociological Focus*, Summer.

Barkow, Jerome (1988), "'Professional' management can lead to trouble in universities," *Financial Post*, Dec. 19.

Barnes James G. and G. Ross Peters (1987), *The Teaching Company Scheme: A Study of its Application in Canada*, a Science Council of Canada discussion paper, Ottawa: Minister of Supply and Services.

Bartley, Ted (1979a), "Bargaining Talk," *CAUT Bulletin*, 26, 3(May), 20.

———— (1979b), "Bargaining Talk," *CAUT Bulletin*, 26, 4(September), 8.

———— (1979c), "Bargaining Talk," *CAUT Bulletin*, 26, 6(December), 11.

Barton, Tim (1983), "Sessionals Treated as 'Second-Class Citizens' Studies Show," *CAUT Bulletin*, 30, 1(February), 7.

Baxter, Helen (1978a), "Women Discriminated Against, Says U. of A. Study," *CAUT Bulletin*, 25, 10(September), 11.

Baxter, Helen (1978b), "CAUT Board Votes to Censure Memorial," *CAUT Bulletin*, 25, 11(December), 1, 18.

Baxter, Helen (1979a), "CAUT Censures Memorial and Calgary," *CAUT Bulletin*, 26, 4(September), 3.

———— (1982), "Faculty and Students Join in Country-Wide Protests Against University Underfunding," *CAUT Bulletin*, 29, 3(May), 1, 7.

———— (1988), "Gender Gap Persists in Ontario Universities," *CAUT Bulletin*, 35(6), 10.

Bedford, A.G. (1976), *The University of Winnipeg: A History of the Founding Colleges*, Toronto: University of Toronto Press.

Belanger, Charles H. (1989), "University Entrepreneurship and Competition: The Case of the Small Universities," *Canadian Journal of Higher Education*, 19(2), 13–22.

Bell, Stephen (1990), "Using Matching Grants to Facilitate Corporate-University Research Linkages: A Preliminary Examination of Outcomes From One Initiative," *The Canadian Journal of Higher education*, XX-1, 57–73.

———— and Jan Sadlak (1992), "Technology Transfer in Canada: Research Parks and Centres of Excellence," *Higher Education Management*, 4, 227–44.

Bercuson, David, Robert Bothwell and J.L. Granatstein (1984), *The Great Brain Robbery: Canada's Universities on the Road to Ruin*, Toronto: McClelland and Stewart.

———— (1997), *Petrified Campus: The Crisis in Canada's Universities*, Toronto: Random House of Canada.

Berman, E.M. (1990), "The Economic Impact of Industry-funded University R&D," *Research Policy*, 19.

Bernard, Jessie Shirley (1964), *Academic Women*, University Park, Pa.: Pennsylvania State University Press.

Bertram, G.W. (1966), *The Contribution of Education to Economic Growth*, Ottawa: Economic Council of Canada, June.

Beverley, John (1978), "Higher Education and Capitalist Crisis," *Socialist Review*, 8, 6(Nov-Dec), 67–91.

Bigelow, Charles, Sylvia Gold and Paul Siren, (1987), *Report of the CAUT External Review Committee*, Ottawa: CAUT, March.

Bissell, C.T., ed. (1957), *Canada's Crisis in Higher Education*, Toronto: University of Toronto Press.

Bissell, Claude (1974), *Halfway Up Parnassus: A Personal Account of the University of Toronto, 1932–1971*, Toronto: University of Toronto Press.

Black, Errol (1978), "Affiliation with the CLC—the Logical Culmination of the Unionization of University Faculty," *CAUT Bulletin*, 25(7), 10–11.

——————— (1979), "Social Relations and Collective Bargaining in the University, Brandon: A Case Study," *CAUT Bulletin*, 26, 6(December), 15–18.

Bladen (1965), *Financing Higher Education in Canada*, A Report of the AUCC, Ottawa: AUCC.

Bloom, Michael, ed. (1990), *Reaching for Success: Business and Education Working Together, First National Conference on Business-Education Partnerships*, Ottawa: The Conference Board of Canada.

Blum, Debra (1990), "Ten Years After High Court Limited Faculty Bargaining, Merits of Academic Unionism Still Hotly Debated," *Chronicle of Higher Education*, 36(20), A15.

Bok, Derek (1982), *Beyond the Ivory Towers: Social Responsibilities of the Modern University*. Cambridge, Massachusetts: Harvard University Press.

Bordt, Michael and Cathy Read (1999), *Survey of Intellectual Property Commercialization in the Higher Education Sector, 1998*, Ottawa: Statistics Canada, Science and Technology Redesign Project, February.

Bowles, S. and H. Gintis (1976), *Schooling in Capitalist America*, New York: Basic Books.

Boyd, Monica (1979), *Rank and Salary Differentials in the Seventies: A Comparison of Male and Female Full-Time Teachers in Canadian Universities and Colleges* Ottawa: Association of Universities and Colleges of Canada.

Branswell, Helen (1993), *Tuitions soar 58% in five years*, Winnipeg Free Press, November 17, A2.

Braverman, Harry (1974), *Labor and Monopoly Capital*, New York: Monthly Review Press.

Brewster, Kingman Jr. (1972), "On Tenure," *AAUP Bulletin* (Winter), from Brewster's 1971–72 presidential report at Yale University.

Brody, Bernard (1972), "Professorial Unions and Collective Bargaining: A Few Fundamental Principles," *CAUT Bulletin*, 20(2), 52–59.

Brooks, Neil and Linda McQuaig (1989), "OK Michael Wilson, Here's The Alternative," *This Magazine*, 23, 5(December).

Brunet, Huguette (1982), "Collective Bargaining: Yeshiva Decision Not Applicable Here Says Board," *University Affairs*, 23(10), 19.

Buchbinder, Howard and Janice Newson (1985), "Corporate-University Linkages and the Scientific-Technical Revolution," *Interchange*, 16, 3(Fall).

——————— (1985), "The Academic Work Process, The Professoriate and Unionization," in Higher Education Group.

———————(1990), "Corporate-University Linkages in Canada: Transforming a Public Institution," *Higher Education*, 20, 355–79.

Buckley, K. (1954), "The Declining Status of the University in the Canadian Community," *CAUT Bulletin*.

———————— (1955), "The Economic Status of University Teachers," *NCCU Proceedings*, June, 30–31.

Byleveld, Herbert (1966), *Corporate Aid to Higher Education in Canada, the Search for a New Policy*, Montréal: National Industrial Conference Board.

———————— (1967), "Business Aid to Universities: A Margin of Freedom," *Canadian Business*, January.

Cameron, David (1991), *More Than An Academic Question: Universities, Government, and Public Policy in Canada*, Halifax, Nova Scotia: The Institute for Research on Public Policy.

Campbell, Duncan D. (1982), "Western Canada," in Sheffield, Campbell et. al.

Campbell, R. Lynn (1986), "Academic Status and Judicial Review," *Interchange*, 17, 3(Autumn), 28–41.

Campbell, Teresa D. (1995), *Protecting the Public's Trust: A Search for Balance Among Benefits and Conflicts in University-industry Relations*, Ph.D. dissertation, University of Arizona, Tucson.

Canada, Parliamentary Task Force on Federal-Provincial Fiscal Arrangements (1981), *Fiscal Federalism in Canada*, Ottawa: Minister of Supply and Services.

Canada (1989), *Networks of Centres of Excellence: Report of the International Peer Review Committee and Report of the Minister's Advisory Committee*, Ottawa.

Canada, Senate, Special Committee on Science Policy (1970), *A Science Policy for Canada*, Ottawa: Queen's Printer, vol. 1.

Canada, Senate, Standing Senate Committee on National Finance (1988), *Twenty-Sixth Report*, July 27, 47:16.

Canadian Centre for Policy Alternatives and Cho!ces: A Coalition for Social Justice (1997), *Alternative Federal Budget Papers 1997*, Ottawa: Canadian Centre for Policy Alternatives.

Canadian Federation of University Women (1975), "The Potential Participation of Women in University Affairs," Ottawa: CFUW.

Canadian Institute for Advanced Research (1995), "The Commercialization of University Research in Canada: A Discussion Paper," June, downloaded from Industry Canada's *Trans-forum* Website, October 13, 1998.

Canadian Labour Market Productivity Centre (1990), "The Linkages Between Education and Training and Canada's Economic Performance," *Quarterly Labour Market and Productivity Review*, Winter 1989/1990.

Canadian Press (1989), "Halifax professors strike for more money," *Montreal Gazette*, April 6.

———————— (1989), "Professors stage strike at Laurentian University," *The Globe and Mail*, September 12.

Caplan, Paula J. (1992), *Lifting A Ton of Feathers: A Woman's Guide to Surviving in the Academic World*, Toronto: University of Toronto Press.

Caplow, Theodore and Reece J. McGee (1958), *The Academic Marketplace*, New York: Basic Books.

Carnegie Foundation For the Advancement of Teaching (1982), *The Control of the Campus: A Report on the Governance of Higher Education*, Princeton, N.J.: Princeton University Press.

Carrigan, D. Owen (1977), "Unionization in Canadian Universities," *International Journal of Institutional Management in Higher Education*, 1, 1(May), 17–31.

Carroll, William K., Linda Christiansen-Ruffman, Raymond F. Currie and Deborah Harrison, eds. (1992), *Fragile Truths: Twenty-Five Years of Sociology and Anthropology in Canada*, Ottawa: Carleton University Press.

Carswell, John (1985), *Government and the Universities in Britain: Programme and Performance, 1960-1980*. Cambridge: Cambridge University Press.

Carter, D.D. (1975), "Collective Bargaining for University Faculty: A Legal Perspective," *Canadian Journal of Higher Education*, 5(1), 25–31.

Carter, George E. (1971), *Canadian Conditional Grants Since World War II*, Toronto: Canadian Tax Foundation.

——————— (1977), "Financing Health and Post-Secondary Education: A New and Complex Fiscal Arrangement," *Canadian Tax Journal*, xxv(5).

——————— (1982), *The Federal Impact of Financing Higher Education in Canada*, Canberra: Centre for Research on Federal Financial Relations, The Australian National University.

Cassin, A. Marguerite and J. Graham Morgan (1992), "The Professoriate and the Market-Driven University: Transforming the Control of Work in the Academy," in Carroll et al.

CAUT (1971a), "Survey: Tenure In Institutions of Higher Education In Canada," *CAUT Bulletin*, 19(2), 39–55.

——— (1971b), "CAUT Censure of Administration at Mount Allison University," CAUT Bulletin, 19(2), 30.

——— (1974a), "Large Gaps in Salaries Between Men, Women Faculty at Manitoba," *CAUT Bulletin*, 23, 2(October), 5.

——— (1974b), "Certification Drive Held Up," *CAUT Bulletin*, 23, 3(December), 1.

——— (1974c), "Sabbatical and Other Leaves in Canadian Universities," *CAUT Bulletin*, 23, 2(October), 10–19.

——— (1974d), "Notre Dame Gets Second Contract," *CAUT Bulletin*, 23, 3(December), 32.

——— (1975a), "Guelph Study Shows Inequalities," *CAUT Bulletin*, 24, 2(October), 5.

——— (1975b), "Ottawa seeks voluntary recognition," *CAUT Bulletin*, 23(6), 6.

——— (1975c), "Settlement Near At Victoria," *CAUT Bulletin*, 23, 4(February), 1.

——— (1975d), "UBC Drafts Collective Agreement," *CAUT Bulletin*, 24,2(October), 4.

——— (1975e), "Court Clears Way For Union", *CAUT Bulletin*, 24,1(September), 1.

——— (1975f), "St. Mary's Faculty Sign Collective Agreement," *CAUT Bulletin*, 23,4(February), 1, 2.

——— (1976a), "Tenure Quotas," *CAUT Bulletin*, 24, 7(September), 23.

——— (1976b), "Moncton Under Censure," *CAUT Bulletin*, 24, 7(September), 34.

———— (1976c), "Situation at Université Laval," *CAUT Bulletin*, 24, 8(October), 7.

———— (1977a), "Laval University Strike Ends With Victory for Faculty," *CAUT Bulletin*, 25, 1(January). 1.

———— (1978a) "U. of A. Awards Salary Adjustments to Women," *CAUT Bulletin*, 25, 11(December), 7.

———— (1978b), "Certification at Dalhousie," *CAUT Bulletin*, 25, 8(April), 9.

———— (1978c), "Memorial to Certify-Regents Call Special Plan 'Window-Dressing,'" *CAUT Bulletin*, 25, 9(May), 2.

———— (1978d), "Collective Bargaining Conference a First," *CAUT Bulletin*, 25(11), 13.

———— (1979a), "The Webber Case at Memorial University," *CAUT Bulletin*, 26, 4(September), 15–18.

———— (1979b), "CAUT Censures Memorial and Calgary," *CAUT Bulletin*, 26, 4(September), 1,

———— (1979c), "The Abouna Case at the University of Calgary," *CAUT Bulletin*, 26, 4(September), 18–22.

———— (1979d), "Adell Named Investigator at Acadia," *CAUT Bulletin*, 26, 1(February), 1,5.

———— (1979e), "Women Academics in Canadian Universities: Little Change in Status over Past Decade," *CAUT Bulletin*, 26(6).

———— (1980a), "CAUT Council and Board Censure President and Board of Governors of Nova Scotia Technical College, Escalate Censures at Calgary and Memorial, Adopt Redundancy and Appointment Policies," *CAUT Bulletin*, 27, 4(June), 1.

———— (1980b), "CAUT Imposes Third Stage of Censure on Memorial and Calgary," *CAUT Bulletin*, 27, 4(June), 1,2.

———— (1980c), "CAUT Board Recommends Censure of Nova Scotia Technical College," *CAUT Bulletin*, 27, 3(May), 6.

———— (1980d), "CAUT Censures Nova Scotia Technical College, *CAUT Bulletin*, 27, 4(June), 2.

———— (1980e), "Strike at Windsor Averted," *CAUT Bulletin*, 27, 2(April), 13.

———— (1981), "McIntire Ruling Makes Waves," *CAUT Bulletin*, 28, 1(February), 1.

———— (1981b), "Sexual Harassment Guidelines Adopted by CAUT Board," *CAUT Bulletin*, 28, 3(May), 5.

———— (1983a), "Bargaining Talk," *CAUT Bulletin*, 30, 5(September), 13.

———— (1983b), "Part of Ontario's Restraint Act Ruled Unconstitutional," *CAUT Bulletin*, 30, 7(December), 20.

———— (1985a), "Dal Settlement is Reached After A One-Day Strike," *CAUT Bulletin*, 32, 1(February), 1.

———— (1985b), "Crisis at Dalhousie," *CAUT Bulletin*, 32, 1(February), 12, 43.

———— (1987a), "Gov't Lowers Axe at U of R Forcing Drastic Cuts," *CAUT Bulletin*, 34, 5(May), 1, 5.

———— (1987b), "University/Business Relationships in Research and Development: A Guide for Universities and Researchers," *CAUT Bulletin*, 34, 9(November), 17, 18, 20, 22.

———— (1988a), "Dalhousie on Strike," *CAUT Bulletin,* (December 1988), 1, 12.

———— (1988b), "Lakehead and TUNS on stirke," *CAUT Bulletin*, February.

———— (1992a), "Strike at Mount Allision," *CAUT Bulletin*, 39,5(May), 1, 13.

———— (1996a), "Settlement Averts Strike at Memorial," *CAUT Bulletin*, 43, 3(March), 1, 9.

———— (1997a), "Are Rising Tuition Fees Squeezing our Students?" *CAUT Bulletin*, 44, 9(November).

———— (1998a), "Dalhousie Faculty Give Green Light for Strike," *CAUT Bulletin* March.

———— (1998b), "Week Long Faculty Strike Ends at Dalhousie," *CAUT Bulletin*, April.

———— (1998c), "New Contract for Trent," *CAUT Bulletin*, March.

———— (1998d), "Western Ontario Faculty Vote in Favour of Certification," *CAUT Bulletin*, April.

———— (1999a), "CAUT Deplores Final Expert Panel Report," *CAUT Bulletin*, 46, 6(June).

———— (1999b), "Top Scientist to Lead off Conference," *CAUT Bulletin*, 46, 6(June).

Cave, Martin, Stephen Hanney, Mary Henkel and Maurice Kogan (1996), *The Use of Performance Indicators in Higher Education: The Challenge of the Quality Movement*, London: Jessica Kingsley Publishers.

Canadian Centre for Policy Alternatives and Cho!ces (1998), *The Time is Now: Alternative Federal Budget 1998*, Ottawa: The Canadian Centre for Policy Alternatives and Cho!ces.

———————— (1999), *Vital Measures: Alternative Federal Budget 1999*, Ottawa: The Canadian Centre for Policy Alternatives and Cho!ces.

Chaison, Gary N. (1979), "The Certification Campaign at the University of New Brunswick," *CAUT Bulletin*, 26,5(October), 17–20.

Chilly Climate Collective, eds. (1995), *Breaking Anonymity: The Chilly Climate for Women Faculty*, Waterloo: Wilfred Laurier University Press.

Cho!ces and the Canadian Centre for Policy Alternatives (1998), *Show Us the Money The Politics and Process of Alternative Budgets*, Winnipeg: Arbeiter Ring.

Cinman, Israel (1973a),"CAUT Council Censures U of Ottawa," *CAUT Newsletter*, June, 1.

———————— (1974a), "Boycott Suspended-Censure Remains," *CAUT Bulletin*, 23, 3(December).

———————— (1974b), "University of British Columbia Faculty votes overwhelmingly for certification," *CAUT Newsletter*, April, 6.

———————— (1974c), "University of Manitoba Faculty Association Ruled as Certified Bargaining Agents for U of M Faculty," *CAUT Newsletter*, April, 3.

———————— (1975a), "Ontario Labour Board Defines Faculty Union Composition," *CAUT Bulletin*, 24, 1(September), 1, 2.

———————— (1975b), "Carleton Staff Members Endorse Union," *CAUT Bulletin*, 23(6), 1.

———————— (1977a), "Peer Evaulation Salary Study Results in Adjustments for Women," *CAUT Bulletin*, 25, 3(April), 5.

———————— (1977b), "CAUT Board Suspends Simon Fraser, University of Ottawa and Mount Allison Censures,", *CAUT Bulletin*, 25, 3(April), 1.

———————— (1977c), "Simon Fraser, Mount Allison, Ottawa Censures Lifted," *CAUT Bulletin*, 25, 4(September), 1.

———————— (1977d) "Value of Regional Offices Questioned as Delegates Debate Budget," *CAUT Bulletin*, 25, 4(September), 1.

———————— (1977e), "Bishop's Collective Agreement Good Model to Follow Says Faculty President," *CAUT Bulletin*, 25, 4(September), 5,7.

———————— (1977f), "Government Launches Attack on Basic Faculty Rights," *CAUT Bulletin*, 25, 5(October), 1.

———————— (1977g), "University Research and the Intelligence Community," *CAUT Bulletin*, October, 13,14,17.

———————— (1978a), "CAUT Council 1978: Delegates Approve Lobbying, Change Constitutional Structure," *CAUT Bulletin*, 25,10(September), 1.

Clark, Burton (1987), *The Academic Life: Small Worlds, Different Worlds*, Princeton: The Carnegie Foundation for the Advancement of Teaching.

Clarke, Robert (1984), "Public Constituencies and Commitment: Overcoming Impediments to Relevant Research," in Science Council of Canada, 143–8.

Clement, Wallace (1975) *The Canadian Corporate Elite: An Analysis of Economic Power*, Toronto: McClelland and Stewart.

Cochrane, David (1997), "Cola controversy rocks the Rock," *Manitoban*, 84, 17(January 8), 1.

Cockburn, Cynthia (1983), *Brothers*, London: Pluto Press.

Cohen, Maxwell (1964), "The Highest Academic Body," in Whalley, 101–15.

Cole, R. Taylor (1972), "The Universities and Government Under Canadian Federalism," *Journal of Politics*, 34(May), 524–53.

Cole, Trevor (1998), "Ivy-League Hustle," *Report on Business Magazine*, June , 34–44.

Commission on Post-Secondary Education in Ontario (1972), *The Learning Society: Report of the Commission*, Toronto: Ministry of Government Services.

Commission on the Future Development of the Universities of Ontario (1984), *Ontario Universities: Options and Futures*, Edmund Bovey, chair, Toronto: 1984.

Commission on the Government of the University of Toronto (1970), *Toward Community in University Government*, Toronto: University of Toronto Press.

Committee for University-Industry Cooperation in Continuing Education (1990), *Investing in Learning: The Role of Canadian Universities in Economic Renewal*, Ottawa: Canadian Association for University Continuing Education.

Committee of the Presidents of the Provincially Assisted Universities of Ontario (1963), *Post-Secondary Education in Ontario, 1962-1970*, Toronto.

Cordell, Arthur and James Gilmour (1976), *The Role of Government Laboratories and the Transfer of Technology to the Manufacturing Sector*, Science Council of Canada Background Study No. 35. Ottawa: Supply and Services.

Corner, George W. (1964), *A History of the Rockefeller Institute, 1901–1953*, New York: Rockefeller Institute Press.

Corporate-Higher Education Forum (1987), *From Patrons to Partners, The Report of the Task Force on Funding Higher Education: Corporate Support for Universities*, Montréal: Corporate-Higher Education Forum.

Corry, J.A. (1970), *Farewell the Ivory Tower: Universities in Transition*, Montréal: McGill-Queen's University Press.

Coté, André (1978), "Laval University: One Year After The Strike," *CAUT Bulletin*, 25, 7(February), 15.

Crispo, John (1975), "Collective Bargaining By Professionals: Advisability, Practicability and Feasibility," *CAUT Bulletin*, 23(6), 12.

Crossland, Fred E. (1976), "Will The Academy Survive Unionization?" *Change*, 8(1), 38–42.

Croteau, Michel (1982), "Quebec Tightens Screws On Its Universities," *CAUT Bulletin*, 29,1(February).

Crouch, Martha L. (1998), *How the Terminator terminates: an explanation for the non-scientist of a remarkable patent for killing second generation seeds of crop plants*, Washington: The Edmonds Institute, Website: www.bio.indiana.edu/people/terminator.html.

Currie, Jan and Janice Newson, eds. (1998), *Universities and Globalization: Critical Perspectives*, Thousand Oaks, California: Sage Publications.

Daly, Rita and Theresa Boyle (1998), "Sick Kids cleared in doctor dispute," *Toronto Star*, December 10.

Darknell, Frank A. (1986), "Pilot Study of Consulting by Science and Engineering Faculty at the University of Montréal, the University of Waterloo, and the University of Alberta," Unpublished study.

Davidson, Robert (1985), "A Statistical Profile of the Social Sciences in Canada," in Science Council of Canada.

———————————— (1988), *University-Industry Interaction in the Social Sciences and Humanities: A Threshold of Opportunity*, Ottawa: Science Council of Canada.

Davis, Arthur K. (1978), "Letter to the Editor," *CAUT Bulletin*, 25,10(September), 2, 18.

Day, S. (1973), *A Report on the Status of Women at the University of British Columbia*, January.

De Benedetti, George (1995), "Performance Indicators—A Matter for Collective Bargaining," *CAUT Bulletin*, June.

Decore, Anne Marie and Raj S. Panny (1986), "Educational Financing in Canada 1970–71 to 1983–84: Who Calls the Tune, Who Pays the Piper?" *The Canadian Journal of Higher Education*, XVI–2, 27–49.

Dennison, John D. and Robert Harris (1984), "Governing Boards in Postseconday Education," *Canadian Journal of Higher Education*, 14(2), 13–31.

Department of the Secretary of State of Canada (1990), *Profile of Higher Education in Canada*, Ottawa.

Desbarats, Peter (1998), "Who's on the barricades?" *Globe and Mail*, June 3.

Dickson, David (1981), "MIT Agrees to Accept Whitehead Grant: Faculty Votes Yes, but Strings Remain," *Nature*, 204(November 28).

Dodge, David (1972), *Returns to Investment in University Training: The Case of Canadian Accountants, Engineers and Scientists*, Kingston: Queen's University.

Dong, Betty J., W. Hauck, John G. Gambertoglio, Lauren Gee, John R. White, Jeff L. Bubp, Francis S. Greenspan (1997), "Bioequivalence of Generic and Brand-name Levothyroxine Products in the Treatment of Hypothyroidism," *Journal of the American Medical Association*, 277, 1205-13.

Douglas, Joel M. (1981), "Faculty Collective Bargaining in the Aftermath of Yeshiva," *Change*, 13(2), 36–43.

Doutriaux, Jerome and Margaret Barker (1995), "The University-Industry Relationship in Science and Technology," Occasional Paper Number 11, Science and Technology Review, Industry Canada, August.

Draaisma, Muriel (1986), "UBC's Poor Salaries Cited in Drain of Talents, Grants," *CAUT Bulletin*, 33(7), 17.

Dubinski, R. (1972), "Models for Determination of Salaries and Terms and Conditions of Employment," *CAUT Bulletin*, 20(2), 39–42.

Duff, Sir James and Robert O. Berdahl (1966), *University Government in Canada: Report of A Commission Sponsored by the Canadian Association of University Teachers and the Association of Universities and Colleges of Canada*, Toronto: University of Toronto Press.

Dunlop, Bruce (1971), "Guidelines on Appointment and Tenure: the CAUT's or the AUCC's?" *CAUT Bulletin*, 19(4), 3.

Dzeich, B.W. and L. Weiner (1984), *The Lecherous Professor: Sexual Harassment on Campus*, Boston: Beacon Press.

Economic Council of Canada (1965), *Towards Sustained and Balanced Economic Growth*, Second annual review, Ottawa: Queen's Printer.

Education Research and Promotion Directorate, Education Support Branch (1990), *Profile of Higher Education in Canada, 1990 Edition*, Ottawa: Department of the Secretary of State of Canada.

Edwards, Mark (1998), "Targeting University Technology," *Signals*, an online magazine of analysis for biotechnology executives.

Edwards, Richard (1979), *Contested Terrain: The Transformation of the Workplace in the Twentieth Century*, New York: Basic Books.

Eggleston, Wilfrid (1950), *Scientists at War*, London and Toronto: Oxford University Press.

————————— (1978), *National Research in Canada: The NRC, 1916–1966*, Toronto: Clarke Irwin & Co.

Elliott, James F. (1995), *Provincial Expenditures for Postsecondary Education in Canada, 1977–1991*, Ph.D. Dissertation, University of Arisona, Tucson.

Emberley, Peter C. (1996), *Zero Tolerance: Hot Button Politics in Canada's Universities*, Toronto: Penguin Books.

England, G. and I. McKenna (1977), "Special Plan Collective Agreements," *CAUT Bulletin*, 25, 4(September), 12–13.

Enros, Philip and Michael Farley (1986), *University Offices for Technology Transfer: Toward the Service University*, Ottawa: Science Council of Canada.

Enros, Philip C. (1981), "The University of Toronto and Industrial Research in the Early Twentieth Century," in Jarrell and Roos, 155–66.

———————— (1991), "The Bureau of Scientific and Industrial Research and School of Specific Industries' The Royal Canadian Institute's Attempt at Organizing Industrial Research in Toronto, 1914–1918," in Jarrell and Hull, 210–22.

Entwistle, H. (1978), *Class, Culture and Education*, London: Methuen.

Epp, Ernest (1980), "The Rise and Fall of Notre Dame University," *CAUT Bulletin*, 27, 6(October), 14.

Euruch, Nell P. (1985), *Corporate Classrooms: The Learning Business*, Princeton, N.J.: Carnegie Foundation for the Advancement of Teaching.

Expert Panel on Commercialization of University Research (1999), *Public Investments in University Research: Reaping the Benefits*, Presented to The Prime Minister's Advisory Council on Science and Technology, Ottawa, May 4.

Fairbairn, Brett (1988), "The Prof Motive: Radical Conservatism at the University of Saskatchewan," *NeWest Review*, 14, 1(October/November), 20–23.

Fairweather, James S. (1988), *Entrepreneurship and Higher Education*, Washington, D.C.: Association for the Study of Higher Education.

———————— (1989), "Academic Research and Instruction:The Industrial Connection," *Journal of Higher Education*, 60, 388–407.

Farr, William D. (1979), "Some Comments on York," *Interchange*, 9, 3(1978–79), 87.

Firestone, O.J. (1969), *Industry and Education*, Ottawa: University of Ottawa.

Fisher, Donald (1978), "The Rockefeller Foundation and the Development of Scientific Medicine in Great Britain," *Minerva*, XVI, 1(Spring).

Fitzgerald, Beth (1996), *Not Ready for Roundup: The Dangers of Genetically Engineered Soybeans*, A Greenpeace Report, www.greenpeace.org/~usa/reports/biodiversity/roundup/index.html.

Ford, Anne Rochon (1985), *A Path Not Strewn with Roses: One Hundred Years of Women at the University of Toronto, 1884–1984*, Toronto: University of Toronto Press.

Ford, Christine Tausig (1994), "Universities take aim on performance measures," *University Affairs*, February.

Forster, Donald (1982), "Hopeful Signs in Lean Times," *Guelph University News Bulletin* June 24, 1.

Foss, Krista (1998). "Drug firm, hospital relations anger MDs," *The Globe and Mail*, August 15, A5.

Foulkes, Jim (1979), "Academic Freedom and Tenure: A CAUT Special Report," *CAUT Bulletin*, 26(4), 15–16.

Fowke, V.C. (1964), "Professional Association: A History of the CAUT," in Whalley, 195–215.

Francis, Douglas (1975), "The Threatened Dismissal of Frank H. Underhill From the University of Toronto—1939–1941," *CAUT Bulletin*, 24, 3(December), 16–21.

Fraser, H.J. (1961), *The University and Business, Papers presented to the Royal Society of Canada, Canadian Universities Today*, Toronto: University of Toronto Press.

Freedman, Martin H. Q.C. (1994), *In The Matter of An Arbitration Pursuant to A Collective Agreement Between The University of Manitoba and The University of Manitoba Faculty Association, Grievance of Koenraad Lindner, Award of Arbitrator on Production of Documents*, October 7.

Freundlich, Naomi (1998), "Will increasingly aggressive licensing terms on research tool patents hurt basic research?" *Signals*, an online magazine of analysis for biotechnology executives, June 4.

Frost, Stanley Brice (1980), *McGill University: For the Advancement of Learning, Vol. I, 1801–1895*, Kingston and Montréal: McGill-Queen's University Press.

——————— (1984), *McGill University: For the Advancement of Learning, Volume II, 1895–1971*, Kingston and Montréal: McGill-Queen's University Press.

Galt, Virginia (1996), "Ivory tower tongues wagging over disclosure," *The Globe and Mail*, March 30.

Garbarino, J.W. (1975), *Faculty Bargaining: Change and Conflict*, New York: McGraw-Hill.

Garbarino, Joseph W. (1980), "Faculty Unionization: The Pre-Yeshiva Years, 1966–1979," *Industrial Relations*, 19, 2(Spring), 221–230.

Garson, Barbara (1977), *All the Livelong Day: The Meaning and Demeaning of Routine Work*, New York: Penguin.

Garson, G. David (1996), "The Political Economy of Online Education," unpublished draft.

Gerson, Mark (1987), "9 Professors With Tenure Are Among 12 Laid Off by U of BC," *CAUT Bulletin*, 34, 10(December), 17–18.

Giberson, Mark (1997), "Giving," *University Affairs*, June–July, 8–9.

Gibson, Frederick W. (1983), *Queen's University, Volume II, 1917–1961: To Serve and Yet be Free*, Kingston and Montréal: McGill-Queen's University Press, 204–5.

Gillett, Margaret (1981), *We Walked Very Warily: A History of Women at McGill*, Montréal: Eden Press.

Gingras, Yves (1989), "Financial Support for Post-Graduate Students and the Development of Scientific Research in Canada," in Axelrod and Reid, 301–19.

Glassco Commission (1963), *Royal Commission on Government Organization*, Ottawa: Queen's Printer, January.

Goodspeed, D.J. (1958), *A History of the Defence Research Board of Canada*, Ottawa: E. Cloutier, Queen's Printer.

Gorman, Robert A. (1980), "The Yeshiva Decision," *Academe*, (May), 188–197.

——————— (1998), "Intellectual Property: The rights of Faculty as Creators and Users," *Academe* 3, 14–18,

Graham, Bill (1999), "Zero Increase for University Transfers," *CAUT Bulletin*, 46, 3 (March).

Grant, Jill (1989), "Moving Back From the Brink?" *New Maritimes*, 7, 3 (January/February), 9–10.

Gregor, Alexander, and Keith Wilson, eds. (1979), *Higher Education in Canada: Historical Perspectives*, Monographs in Education 2, Winnipeg: University of Manitoba.

Gregor, Alexander D. (1970), "The University of Manitoba: the Denominational College System," in Gregor and Wilson, 1979.

Grigoroff, Isabella (1996), "Academia Inc.: University Spin-offs Make it Big Time," *University Affairs*, June-July, 11–14.

Gu, Wulong and Lori Whewell (1999), "University Research and the Commercialization of Intellectual Property in Canada," prepared for the Expert Panel on the Commercialization of University Research of the Advisory Council on Science and Technology, Ottawa: March.

Gunderson, M. (1990), *Women and Labour Market Poverty*, Ottawa: Canadian Advisory Council on the Status of Women.

Gunther, Magnus and Richard J. Van Loon (1981), "Federal Contributions to Post-Secondary Education: Trends and Issues," in Nowlan and Bellaire.

Guppy, Neil (1989), "Pay Equity in Canadian Universities, 1972–73 and 1985–86," *Canadian Review of Sociology and Anthropology*, 26(5), 743–758.

Gwynne-Timothy, J.R.W. (1978), *Western's First Century*, London: The University of Western Ontario.

Ham, James (1982), "A Strategic Assessment," *The Graduate*, November-December, 10-13.

Hamilton, Joan O'C. (1997), "Stanford's DNA patent 'enforcer' Grolle closes the $200M book on Cohen-Boyer," *Signals*, an online magazine of analysis for biotechnology executives, November 25.

Hammonds, Keith H. and Susan Jackson, with Gail DeGeorge and Kathleen Morris (1997), "The New University: A tough market is reshaping colleges," *Business Week*, December 22.

Hanly, C., N. Shulman and D.N. Swaan (1971), *Who Pays? University Financing in Ontario*, Toronto: James Lewis and Samuel.

Hardy, Cynthia (1984), "The Management of University Cutbacks: Politics, Planning and Participation," *The Canadian Journal of Higher Education*, XIV–1.

———————— (1996), *The Politics of Collegiality: Retrenchment Strategies in Canadian Universities*, Montréal and Kingston: McGill-Queen's University Press.

Harris, Robin S. (1975), "The Universities of Canada," *Commonwealth Universities Yearbook*, London: Association of Commonwealth Universities, 799–813.

———————— (1976), *A History of Higher Education in Canada, 1663–1960*, Toronto: University of Toronto Press.

Hartnett, Richard (1980), "The ABC's of Faculty Collective Bargaining: Projections of American, British, and Canadian Directions in the 1980s," *Interna-*

tional Journal of Institutional Management in Higher Education, 4, 3 (November), 221–34.

Hayden, Michael (1983), *Seeking a Balance: The University of Saskatchewan, 1907–1982*, Vancouver: University of British Columbia Press.

Hazleton, Ralph (1978), "Final Offer Selection: The Experience at the University of Prince Edward Island," *CAUT Bulletin*, 25, 11 (December), 12–13.

Helwig, David (1992), "Fund Would Push Biomedical Research" *Globe & Mail*, Nov 10.

Hercus, Terry F. (1978), "Unionism And The University Faculty," *Canadian Personnel and Industrial Relations Journal*, (January), 12–18.

Higher Education Group (1985), *The Professoriate-Occupation in Crisis*, Toronto: Ontario Institute for Studies in Education.

Higher Education Group (1987), *Governments and Higher Education—The Legitimacy of Intervention*, Toronto: Ontario Institute for Studies in Education.

Holmes, Jeffrey (1982), "The Atlantic Provinces," in Edward Sheffield et al, 37–63.

Hook, Sydney et al, eds. (1978), *The University and the State*, Buffalo: Prometheus Books.

Horn, Michiel (1979), "Academics and Canadian Social and Economic Policy in the Depression and War Years," *Journal of Canadian Studies*, 13, 4 (Winter 1978-79), 3–10.

———————— (1980), "Professors in the Public Eye: Canadian Universities, Academic Freedom, and the League for Social Reconstruction," *History of Education Quarterly*, (Winter), 425–447.

———————— (1981), "Academic Freedom in Canada: Retrospect and Prospect," *CAUT Bulletin*, 28, 1 (February), 13–14.

———————— (1982a), "The History of Academic Freedom in Canada: A Comment," *CAUT Bulletin*, Special Edition, March, 3–4.

———————— (1982b), "Academic Freedom and the Canadian Professor," *CAUT Bulletin*, 29, 7 (December), 19–22, 26.

———————— (1984), "Government Funding and the Independence of Teaching and Scholarship," in *Interchange* special issue 6–12.

———————— (1999), *Academic Freedom in Canada: A History*, Toronto: University of Toronto Press.

House of Commons, Standing Committee on Industry, Science and Technology, Regional And Northern Development (1993), *Beyond Excellence: The Future of Canada's Networks of Centres of Excellence*, 33rd session, 34th parliament, April 27.

Houwing, J.F. and A.M. Kristjanson (1975), *Composition of Governing Bodies of Canadian Universities and Colleges, 1975*, Ottawa: Association of Universities and Colleges of Canada.

Hurtubise, René, and Donald C. Rowat (1970), *The University, Society and Government: The Report of the Commission on the Relations Between the Universities and Governments*, Ottawa: University of Ottawa Press.

Ikeda, Jane Yoshiko (1971), *The Struggle over Decision-Making Power at Simon Fraser University, 1965–1968*, M.Ed. thesis, University of Calgary.

Independent Study Group (1993), *The Report of the Independent Study Group on University Governance*, Ottawa: CAUT.

Industrial Foundation on Education (1962), *The Case for Corporate Giving to Higher Education*, #14, Ottawa.

Innis, Harold (1946), *Political Economy in the Modern State*, Toronto: Ryerson Press.

Interchange Special Issue (1984), "The Independence of the University and the Funding of the State: Essays on Academic Freedom in Canada," *Interchange*, 14, 4(1983/84).

Irving, Allan (1980), "Social Science Research in the University: An Examination of the Views of Harry Cassidy and Harold Innis," *The Canadian Journal of Higher Education*, X–1, 95–109.

——————— (1986), "Leonard Marsh and the McGill Social Science Research Project," *Journal of Canadian Studies*, 21, 2(summer), 6–25.

Irving, Allan D. (1997), "Faculty of Social Work, University of Toronto, Fundraising and Corporate Links," unpublished list, circulated widely, Toronto, November.

Ivins, Molly (1999), "USA: World Wide Protests Over Monsanto," *Star Telegram*, Austin, Texas, January 4.

Jackson, Susan (1997), "Meanwhile the Ivy League is Rolling in Clover," *Businsss Week*, December 22, Internet edition.

Jarrell, Richard A., and Arnold E. Roos (1981), *Critical Issues in the History of Canadian Science, Technology and Medicine*, Thornhill and Ottawa, Ontario: HSTC Publications.

Jarrell, Richard A., and James P. Hull, eds. (1991), *Science, Technology and Medicine in Canada's Past*, Thornhill, Ontario: The Scientia Press, Ltd.

Jencks, Christopher, and David Riesman (1968), *The Academic Revolution*, Garden City, N.Y.: Doubleday.

Johnson, A.W. (1985), *Giving Greater Point and Purpose to the Federal Financing of Post-Secondary Education and Research in Canada*, A report prepared for the Secretary of State of Canada, February 15.

Johnson, W.G. (1984), "Cutting the pattern to fit the cloth: Access to post-secondary education," *Canadian Public Administration/Administration Publique Du Canada*, 27, 1(Spring), 102–109.

Johnston, C.M. (1976), *McMaster University: vol 1, the Toronto Years*, Toronto: University of Toronto Press.

——————— (1981), "Aspects of Science and Technology at McMaster University with Special Reference to Chemistry and Physics, 1939–1959," in Jarrell and Roos, 3–15.

——————— (1981), *McMaster University: vol. 2, the early years in Hamilton 1930–1957*, Toronto: University of Toronto Press.

Julien, Gilles (1989), "The Funding of University Research in Canada: Current Trends," *Higher Education Management*, 1, 66–72.

Kalfruss, Elisabeth (1990), "Laval professors stage walkout in bid to speed contract talks," *Montréal Gazette*, February 13.

Kaplan, Craig, and Ellen Schrecker, eds. (1983), *Regulating the Intellectuals: Perspectives on Academic Freedom in the 1980s*, New York: Praeger Publishers.

Kemerer, Frank R., R. Frank Mensel and J. Victor Baldridge (1981), "The Twilight of Informal Faculty Personnel Procedures," *Journal of the College and University Personnel Association*, 32, 1(Spring), 17–25.

Kendrick, J.W. (1981), "International Comparisons of Recent Productivity Trends," in W. Fellner, ed., *Essays in Contemporary Economic Problems*, American Enterprise Institute.

Kenney, M. (1986), *Biotechnology: The University-Industrial Complex*, New Haven: Yale University Press.

Kerr, Clark (1963), *The Uses of the University* Cambridge, Mass.: Harvard University Press.

Kiefer, Nancy, and Ruth Roach Pierson (1989), "The War Effort and Women Students at the University of Toronto, 1939–1945," in Axelrod and Reid, 161–83.

King, Ralph T. Jr. (1996), "Bitter Pill: How a Drug Firm Paid for University Study, Then Undermined it," *The Wall Street Journal*, April 25.

Klein, Naomi (1997), "Academics can't give in to corporate agenda," *Toronto Star*, April 28.

Kniffin, Kevin (1997), "Serving Two Masters: University Presidents Moonlighting on Corporate Boards," *Multinational Monitor*, 18,11(November).

Kogan, Maurice (1988), "Government and the Management of Higher Education: An Introductory Review," *International Journal of Institutional Management in Higher Education*, 12(1), 5–15.

——————— (1991), "Changing Patterns of University Government and Management," Unpublished paper.

Kohler, Robert E. (1978), "A Policy for the Advancement of Science: The Rockefeller Foundation, 1924–1929," *Minerva*, XVI, 4(Winter), 480–515.

Krimsky, L.S., P. Stott Rothenberg, and G. Kyle (1996), "Financial Interests of Authors in Scientific Journals: A Pilot Study of 14 Publications," *Science and Engineering Ethics*, 2, 3(October).

Krimsky, Sheldon (1991), *Biotechnics and Society: The Rise of Industrial Genetics*, New York: Praeger.

LaBerge, Ray (1975), "Faculty Members Turn to Collective Bargaining," *Labour Gazette*, August.

Ladd, Everett Carll and Seymour M. Lipset (1973), "Unionizing the Professoriate," *Change*, 5,6(Summer), 38–43.

Laidlaw, Toni and Christine Boyle (1984), "Sexual Harassment: Action at Dalhousie," *CAUT Bulletin*, 31,8(December), 8–9.

Lawless, David J. (1981), "The Canadian University Under the Impact of Academic Trade Unions," *Minerva*, 14, 3(Autumn), 464–79.

Learned, William S. and Kenneth C.M. Sills (1922), *Education in the Maritime Provinces of Canada*, New York: Carnegie Foundation for the Advancement of Teaching, summarized in Reid 1984.

Lee, Barbara A. and James P. Begin (1984), "Criteria for Evaluating the Managerial Status of College Faculty: Applications of Yeshiva University by the NLRB," *Journal of College and University Law*, (10), 515–39.

Lee, Yong S. (1997), "Technology Transfer and the Research University: A Search for the Boundaries of University-industry collaboration," *Research Policy* 25, 843–63.

Lefancois, Roger (1984), "A Challenge for the 1980s: Productivity-Oriented University Management," *Cost and Management*, 58, 1 (Jan–Feb), 55–59.

Léger, Robert (1981a), "The Results of the Arbitration Between the University of British Columbia and the Faculty Association," *CAUT Bulletin*, 28, 7 (December), 9.

Léger, Robert (1985a), "Négocions/Bargaining, *CAUT Bulletin*, 32, 4 (June), 4.

——— (1985b), "Négocions/Bargaining," *CAUT Bulletin*, 32, 7 (November).

——— (1986a), "Négocions/Bargaining," *CAUT Bulletin*, 33, 7 (September), 23.

——— (1986b), "Strike ends at NSCAD, new agreement ratified," *CAUT Bulletin*, 33, 10 (December), 1, 19.

——— (1987a), "Négocions/Bargaining," *CAUT Bulletin*, 34, 2 (February), 11.

Lehrman, Jonas (1975), "Faculty Wanted a United Community of Scholars," *University Affairs*, 16 (July), 19.

Leslie, Larry L. (1995), *Toward Privatization of Public Universities*, Tucson, Arizona: Center for the Study of Higher Education.

Leslie, Peter M. (1980), *Canadian Universities, 1980 and Beyond: Enrolment, Structural Change and Finance*, Ottawa: AUCC.

Levesque, Ronald C. (1983), "A Lobbyist's Notebook," *CAUT Bulletin*, 30, 2 (April), 8.

Levin, Benjamin (1990), "Tuition Fees and University Accessibility," *Canadian Public Policy*, XVI, 1.

Levin, Benjamin and Nancy Sullivan (1988), "Governments and Universities," *The Canadian Journal of Higher Education*, 18(1), 1–5.

Lewington, Jennifer (1994), "Canada Proposes Major Changes in Financing," *Chronicle of Higher Education*, October, 60.

——— (1996), "Universities turning to variable tuition," *The Globe and Mail*, March 27, A5.

Link, A.N., and J. Rees (1990), "Firm size, university-based research and the returns to R&D," *Small Business Economics*, 2, 25–31.

Lithwick, N. (1967), *Economic Growth in Canada: A Quantitative Analysis*, Toronto: University of Toronto Press.

Little, Don (1997), "Financing Universities: Why are students paying more?" Statistics Canada, *Education Quarterly Review*, 4, 2 (Summer), 10–26.

Loney, Bretton (1989), "Mount faculty strike muddies exam picture," *Chronicle-Herald*, April 6.

Lowe, Mick (1985), "Strike by faculty closes Laurentian University," *The Globe and Mail*, September 10.

Lowe, Ron (1977), "NDU Closed; B.C. Government Denies Collective Bargaining Rights to Faculty," *CAUT Bulletin*, 25, 4(September), 6.

———— (1978), "Government Policy vs. Bargaining Rights," *CAUT Bulletin*, 25, 7(February), 11, 17, 21.

Loxley, John (1998), "Introduction", Cho!ces and the Canadian Centre for Policy Alternatives, *Show Us the Money The Politics and Process of Alternative Budgets*, Winnipeg: Arbeiter Ring.

MacAulay, James B., in collaboration with Paul Dufour (1984), *The Machine in the Garden: The Advent of Industrial Research Infrastructure in the Academic Milieu*, A discussion paper for the Science Council of Canada, Ottawa: Minister of Supply and Services.

Macdonald, John B. (1962), *Higher Education in British Columbia as a Plan for the Future*, Vancouver: The University of British Columbia.

Macdonald John B. et al. (1969), *The Role of the Federal Government in Support of Research in Canadian Universities*, Special study No. 7, Ottawa: Science Council of Canada, Queen's Printer.

MacDonald (1985), *Royal Commission on the Economic Union and Development Prospects for Canada*, Vol. 2, Ottawa: Minister of Supply and Services.

MacLennan, Hugh, ed. (1960), *McGill: The Story of a University*, Toronto: Thomas Nelson & Sons.

Macpherson, C.B., J.B. Milner and J.P. Smith (1968), "Report on Simon Fraser University," *CAUT Bulletin*, 17, 2(December).

MacRae, Phyllis (1986), "CAUT Censures Three Universities, Lifts One Censure," *University Affairs*, 21(7), 16.

Mair, Debra Louise (1977), *Unionization and the Middle Class: The Case of University Faculty*, M.A. Thesis, Ottawa: Carleton University.

Malloch, A.E. (1971), "Annual Report of the Committee on Academic Freedom and Tenure," *CAUT Bulletin*, 17(4), 44–50.

———— (1972), "Annual Report," *CAUT Bulletin*, 21(1), 6–8.

———— (1973), "Tenure and Cutbacks," *CAUT Bulletin*, 22,(1), 12–13.

———— (1974), "Report on Behalf of the Academic Freedom and Tenure Committee," *CAUT Bulletin*, 22(6), 30.

———— (1988), "Academic Freedom and its Limits," *CAUT Bulletin*, 35(4), 1.

———— (Chair) and K. Norman (1987), "CAUT Committee of Inquiry University of British Columbia, Final Report, February 1987," *CAUT Bulletin*, 34, 10(December), 17–18.

Mandel, David (1987), *The Academic Corporation*, Montréal: Black Rose Books.

Mandelbaum, Henry (1987), "Alberta Universities 'Must Help Pay' for Deficit," *CAUT Bulletin*, 34, 5(May), 5.

Mansfield, E. (1991), "Academic Research and Industrial Innovation," *Research Policy*, 20, 1–12.

Marchese, Ted (1998), "Not-So-Distant Competitors: How New Providers Are Remaking the Postsecondary Marketplace," *AAHE Bulletin*, May.

Maritime Union Study, (1970), *The Report on Maritime Union Commissioned by the Governments of Nova Scotia, New Brunswick and Prince Edward Island*, October.

Marsden, Lorna (1984), "Changing the Bathwater, Keeping the Baby," in Science Council of Canada, 169–77.

Marsh, Leonard (1975), *Report on Social Security for Canada 1943*, Toronto: University of Toronto Press.

Martin, Sandra (1996), "Sex, race and recriminations at UBC," *The Globe and Mail*, September 28.

Masleck, Carolyn (1975a), "Manitoba Negotiates Collective Agreement," *CAUT Bulletin*, 24, 2(October), 1, 2.

———————— (1975b), "Carleton Ratifies First Collective Agreement," *CAUT Bulletin*, 24, 3(December), 1, 2.

———————— (1976), "Ottawa Ratifies First Collective Agreement," *CAUT Bulletin*, 24(6), 1.

Massey, Vincent (1951), *Report of the Royal Commission on the Arts, Letters and Sciences*, Ottawa: Queen's Printer.

Masters, D.C. (1950), *Bishop's University: The First Hundred Years*, Toronto: Clarke, Irwin & Co.

———————— (1966), *Protestant Church Colleges in Canada: A History*. Toronto: University of Toronto Press.

Matas, Robert (1984), "Teach More to Save Costs, Professors Urged," *The Globe and Mail*, October 17.

———————— (1988), "Salaries of professors below par, firm finds," *The Globe and Mail*, March 15.

Mathews, Robin, and James Steele (1969), *The Struggle for Canadian Universities*, Toronto: New Press.

Mathis, M.S.(1975), *A History of the Financial Administration of the University of Manitoba, 1877–1936*, Winnipeg: MA thesis, University of Manitoba.

Matthews, Jana B. and Rolf Norgaard (1984), *Managing the Partnership Between Higher Education and Industry*, Boulder, Colorado: National Center for Higher Education Management Systems.

Maxwell, Judith and Stephanie Currie (1984), *Partnership for Growth: Corporate-University Cooperation in Canada*, Montréal: Corporate-Higher Education Forum.

May, Stacy (1936), *Notes on Dalhousie Project*, 3 May, RG1.1, Series 427, Box 33, Folder 345, Rockefeller Foundation Archives, summarized in Reid, 1984.

McDonald, Kim (1982), "Universities urged to bar secrecy in pacts with private industry," *Chronicle of Higher Education*, 24(April 7), 1, 12–13.

McInnes, Craig (1995), "UBC spends freely to ensure future," *The Globe and Mail*, December 14.

McKillop, A.B., (1994), *Matters of Mind: The University in Ontario, 1791–1951*, Toronto: University of Toronto Press.

McManus, Patrick and Virginia Byfield (1988), "Professors on the picket line," *Western Report*, 3, 12(April 11), 26–7.

McMurtry, John (1983), "Boom at the Top," *CAUT Bulletin*, 30, 3(May), 9.

McNeill, Murray (1999), "U of M lands crops lab," *Winnipeg Free Press*, March 11, B6, B8.

McQuaig, Linda (1987), *Behind Closed Doors: How the Rich Won Control of Canada's Tax System...*, Toronto: Penguin Books.

——————— (1993), *The Wealthy Banker's Wife: The Assault on Equality in Canada*, Toronto: Penquin Books.

Metzger, Walter P., ed. (1977), *Professors on Guard: The First AAUP Investigations*, New York: Arno Press.

Miller, Henry (1995), "States, Economies and The Changing Labour Process of Academics: Australia, Canada and the United Kingdon," *Academic Work*, 40–49.

Millett, J.D. (1962), *The Academic Community*, New York: McGraw-Hill.

Milner, J.B., chairman, Alwyn Berland and J. Percy Smith (1968), "Report on Simon Fraser University by the Special Investigating Committee of the Canadian Association of University Teachers," 9 February, *CAUT Bulletin*, 14, 4(April), 4–28.

Minister of Finance and Minister of State for Science and Technology, Canada (1987), *Strengthening the Private Sector/University Partnership: The Matching Policy Rules*, Ottawa: Minister of Supply and Services Canada.

Mintzes, Barbara (1998), *Blurring the Boundaries: New Trends in Drug Promotion*, HAI-Europe.

Moffat, L.K. (1980), *Room at the Bottom: Job Mobility Opportunities for Ontario Academics in the Mid-Seventies*, Toronto: Ministry of Colleges and Universities.

Mohrman, Kathryn (1989), "Principals and Agents in Campus Governance," in Schuster and Miller, 59–84.

Monahan, Edward (1970), "Academic Freedom and Tenure and the CAUT—The First Twenty Years," *CAUT Bulletin*, 18(4), 80–91.

——————— (1984), "Tenure and Academic Freedom in Canadian Universities," *Interchange*, 14/4–15/1(1983–84), 94–106.

Monsanto Company (1998), *1997 Annual Report*, www.monsanto.com/monsanto /investor/summary/default.htm.

Monsanto Company (1999), *Financial Summary*, for 1998 and 1997, www.monsanto.com/monsanto/investor/summary/default.htm.

Morgan, M.O., I. Cinman and Gordon P. Jones (1978), "Correspondence," *CAUT Bulletin*, 25, 11(October), 2, 24.

Morissette, Michelle (1983), "Grant of merit increases to UBC faculty boosts morale, but low salaries still contentious issue," *CAUT Bulletin*, 33(9), 11–12.

Morissette, Michelle (1984a), "Headhunters Lure Top Academics Out of B.C.: Bennett Government Squeeze Provoking Hostility, Lowering Morale," *CAUT Bulletin*, 31, 3(May), 1, 7.

——————— (1984b), "Outlook Bleak on B.C. Campuses," *CAUT Bulletin*, 31, 6(September), 8, 9.

———————— (1985a), "1985 A Grim Year for Universities in British Columbia—Prospects for Next Year No Brighter," *CAUT Bulletin*, 32, 5 (September), 5–6.

———————— (1985b), "Pederson Says Impossible to Manage A University in British Columbia Now," *CAUT Bulletin*, 32, 2 (April), 7.

———————— (1986), "Faculty praise UBC president's role in settlement," *CAUT Bulletin*, 33 (3), 5.

———————— (1987a), "Meanwhile...The Scene is a Bit Brighter in B.C.," *CAUT Bulletin*, 34, 5 (May), 5, 22.

Morton, Desmond (1957), *One University: A History of the University of Manitoba 1877–1952*, Toronto: McClelland and Stewart.

Mulcahy, G.A. (1975), "Women Ph.D's Underpaid and Underemployed," *CAUT Bulletin*, 24, 1 (September), 28, 31.

Mullan, David (1975), "The Modern Law of Tenure," in H.N. Janisch, ed., *The University and the Law*, Halifax: Faculty of Law, Dalhousie University.

Multinational Monitor (1989), "Phillip Morris, King of the Cancer Trade," *Multinational Monitor*, (November).

———————— (1994), "The Corporate Smokescreen," *Multinational Monitor*, (April)

———————— (1997), "The Corporatized University," *Multinational Monitor*, (November).

Mulvihill, Imelda (1987), *From Patron to Manager: The Canadian State and Higher Education in the Postwar Period*, Ottawa: M.A. Thesis, Carleton University.

Murray J.G. (1985), *Power and Politics in Academe: Faculty Unionism in Ontario*, Toronto: Doctor of Education Dissertation, University of Toronto.

National Institutes of Health (1998), "Report of the National Institutes of Health Working Group on Research Tools," NIH, June 4.

Neatby, Blair (1985), "The Academic Profession: An Historical Perspective—Communities of Scholars in Ontario," in Higher Education Group.

Neatby, H. Blair (1987), "The Historical Perspective," in Higher Education Group, 19–40.

Nelson, R.W., and D.A. Nock, eds. (1978), *Reading, Writing and Riches: Education and the Socio-Economic Order in North America*, Kitchener: Between the Lines Press.

Networks of Centres of Excellence program (1995), *Policies and Guidelines, Networks of Centres of Excellence Phase II*, NCE, December 15.

New Brunswick Royal Commission on Higher Education (1962), *Report*, Fredericton, 1962.

Newson, Janice (1983), "Overstepped Authority," *CAUT Bulletin*, 30, 6 (October), Letters, 6, 10.

———————— (1992), "The Decline of Faculty Influence: Confronting The Effects of the Corporate Agenda," in Carrol et al.

———————— and Howard Buchbinder (1985), "Corporation/Cooperation/Co-optation?", *CAUT Bulletin*, 32, 2 (April), 10, 11, 14.

——————— and Howard Buchbinder (1988), *The University Means Business: Universities, Corporations and Academic Work*, Toronto: Garamond Press.

Nicholls, R.V.V. (1981), "Canada's Contribution to R.D.X.: Super Explosive of World War II," annual conference, Canadian Society for the History and Philosophy of Science, Halifax, June.

Nielsen, Robert M. (1978), *Corporate Management Invades Academe*, Washington, D.C.: American Federation of Teachers.

Nisbet, Robert (1971), *The Degradation of the Academic Dogma*, New York: Basic Books.

——————— (1973), "The Future of Tenure," *Change*, 5(3), 27–33.

Noble, David F. (1977), *America by Design: Science, Technology, and the Rise of Corporate Capitalism*, New York: Knopf.

——————— (1995), *Progress Without People: New Technology, Unemployment, and the Message of Resistance*, Toronto: Between the Lines.

——————— (1997), "Digital Diploma Mills: The Automation of Higher Education," Toronto: distributed by OCUFA, October.

——————— (1998), "Digital Diploma Mills, Part II: The Coming Battle Over Online Instruction," Toronto: distributed by OCUFA, March.

Norissette, Michelle (1987), "Campus Controversy Leads to Harassment Guidelines," *CAUT Bulletin*, 34, 4(April), 13, 14.

Nova Scotia (1985), *Report of the Royal Commission on Post-Secondary Education*, Halifax Queen's Printer.

Novek, Joel (1985), "University Graduates, Jobs and University-Industry Linkages," *Canadian Public Policy*, 11(2), 180–95.

Nowlan, David M., and Richard Bellaire (1981), *Financing Canadian Universities: For Whom and By Whom?* Toronto: OISE Press.

NSERC (1985), *Completing the Bridge to the 90's: NSERC's Second Five-Year Plan*, Ottawa: Natural Sciences and Engineering Research Council of Canada, June.

——————— (1991), *Research Partnerships: University-Industry Cooperative R&D Activities*, Ottawa: Minister of Supply and Services, Canada.

——————— (1997), *Industry Liaison Offices at Canadian Universities, Teaching Hospitals, Technical Institutes, and Colleges*, Ottawa: NSERC.

——————— and The Conference Board of Canada (1997), *University-Industry Synergy*, Ottawa: Minister of Public Works and Government Services.

OECD (1975), *External Examiners' Report on Educational Policy in Canada*, Paris.

——————— (1984), *Industry and University: New Forms of Cooperation and Communication*, Paris.

——————— (1986), *Costs, Expenditures and Financing: An Analysis of Trends*, Ed(86)10.

Office of Institutional Analysis, University of Manitoba (1997), "Comparison of Research Expenditures from External Sources," *IS Book*, Winnipeg: University of Manitoba.

Office of the Provost, University of Toronto (1974), *Report of the Committee on Employment Conditions of Full-Time Women Faculty*, Toronto: April.

Oliver, Michael (1973), "Factors Reshaping the Financing of Higher Education in the 1970's," *Canadian Journal of Higher Education*, 3(2), 105–11.

————— (1973), *Report of the Task Force on Post-Secondary Education in Manitoba*, Winnipeg: Queen's Printer.

————— (1979), "Post-Secondary Commissions," in Gregor and Wilson.

Olivieri, Nancy F., Gary M. Brittenham, Christine E. McLaren, Douglas M. Templeton, Ross G. Cameron, Robert A. McClelland, Alastair D. Burt, and Kenneth A. Fleming, "Long-Term Safety and Effectiveness of Iron-Chelation Therapy with Deferiprone for Thalassemia Major," *New England Journal of Medicine*, 339, 7(August 13).

Olivieri, Nancy F., Gary M. Brittenham, Doreen Matsui, Matitiahu Berkovitch, Laurence M. Blendis, Ross G. Cameron, Robert A. McClelland, Peter P. Liu, Douglas M. Templeton, and Gideon Koren (1995), "Iron Chelation Therapy with Oral Deferiprone in Patients with Thalassemia Major," *New England Journal of Medicine*, 332, 14(April 6).

Owram, Doug (1986), *The Government Generation: Canadian Intellectuals and the State, 1900–1945*, Toronto: University of Toronto Press.

Peitchinis, Stephen (1971), *Financing Post-Secondary Education in Canada*, Ottawa: Council of Ministers of Education in Canada.

Penner, Roland (1979), "Faculty Collective Bargaining in Canada: Background, Development and Impact," *Interchange*, 9, 3(1978/79), 71–86

Pfaffenberger, William E. (1989), "Our aging Professoriat: What it may mean to our Universities, *CAUT Bulletin*, 36(5), 8.

Philpott, Rodger F. (1994), *Commercializing the University: The Costs and Benefits of the Entrepreneurial Exchange of Knowledge and Skills*, Ph.D. dissertation, University of Arizona, Tucson.

Picot, Garnet, John Myles and Ted Wannell (1990), *Good Jobs/Bad Jobs and the Declining Middle: 1967–1986*, Ottawa: Business and Labour Market Analysis Group, Analytical Studies Branch Statistics Canada.

Picot, W. Garnett and Ted Wannell (1987), *The Changing Labour Market for Post Secondary Graduates*, Ottawa: Ministry of Supply and Services.

Pike, Robert M. (1970), *Who Doesn't Get to University—And Why: A Study on Accessibility to Higher Education in Canada*, Ottawa: Association of Universities and Colleges of Canada.

Pilkington, Gwendoline (1983), *Speaking With One Voice: Universities in Dialogue with Government*, Montréal: History of McGill Project, McGill University.

Polanyi, Margaret (1985), "York professors walk out in dispute over salaries," *The Globe and Mail*, October 8, 1985, M1.

Porter, John (1965), *The Vertical Mosaic: An Analysis of Social Class and Power in Canada*, Toronto: University of Toronto Press.

————— (1970), "The Democratisation of the Canadian Universities and the Need for a National System," *Minerva*, 8, 3(July), 325–60.

Prince Edward Island (1965), *Report of the Royal Commission on Higher Education for Prince Edward Island*. Charlottetown.

Quarter, Jack (1973), *The Student Movement of the 1960's*, Toronto: OISE.

Québec (1964), Royal Commission of Inquiry on Education, *Report*, Part One, *The Structure of the Educational System at the Provincial Level*; Part Two, *The Pedagogical Structures of the Educational System*, Québec: Government Printer.

RAFI (1998), "US Patent on New Genetic Technology Will Prevent Farmers from Saving Seed," *RAFI Communique*, March 11.

Rajagopal, I. and W.D. Farr (1989), "The Political Economy of Part-time Academic Work," *Higher Education*, 18(3), 267–85.

Rajagopal, Indhu and William D. Farr (1991), "Unpacking the notion of 'part-time faculty," *University Affairs*, April, 40.

————————— (1992), "Hidden academics: the part-time faculty in Canada," *Higher Education* 24(3), 317–31.

Readings, Bill (1996), *The University in Ruins*, Cambridge, Mass.: Harvard University Press.

Reid, Gordon (1997), "Pepsi wins exclusive rights to U of M," *Manitoban*, 84, 17(January 8).

Reid, J. Stewart (1964), "Origins and Portents," in Whalley, 3–25.

Reid, John G. (1984), "Health, Education, Economy: Philanthropic Foundations in the Atlantic Region in the 1920s and 1930s," *Acadiensis*, 14, 1(Autumn).

————————— (1984), "Some Recent Histories of Canadian Universities," *American Review of Canadian Studies*, 14, 3(Fall), 369–73.

————————— (1984), *Mount Allison University, vol. I, 1863–1914*, Toronto: University of Toronto Press.

————————— (1984), *Mount Allison University, vol. II, 1914–1963*, Toronto: University of Toronto Press.

————————— (1989), "Beyond the Democratic Intellect: The Scottish Example and University Reform in Canada's Maritime Provinces, 1870–1933," in Axelrod and Reid, eds., 275–300.

Reiter, Ester (1992), "The Price of Legitimacy: Academics and the Labour Movement," in Carroll et al.

Rhoades, Gary (1997), *Managed Professionals: Restructuring Academic Labor in Unionized Institutions*, Albany, N.Y.: State University of New York Press.

————————— and Sheila Slaughter (1991), "Professors, Administrators, and Patents: The Negotiation of Technology Transfer," *Sociology of Education*, 64, 65–77.

Ridgeway, James (1968), *The Closed Corporation: American Universities in Crisis*, New York: Random House.

Riesman, David (1980), *On Higher Education: The Academic Enterprise in an Era of Rising Student Consumerism*, San Francisco: Jossey-Bass.

Rimmington, G.T. (1966), "The Founding of Universities in Nova Scotia," *The Dalhousie Review*, 46, 3(Autumn).

Riseborough, Rosalind (1987), "University Financing Update: Some Gains, Some Losses," *CAUT Bulletin*, 34, 2(February), 12.

Rivett, David (1948), "Soviet Science", *Meanjin: A Literary Magazine*, (Second quarter).

Robson, Reginald A.H. and Mireille Lapointe (1971), *A Comparison of Men's and Women's Salaries and Employment Fringe Benefits in the Academic Professions*, Ottawa: Royal Commission on the Status of Women.

Rochon, P.A., J.H. Gurwitz, R.W. Simms et al. (1994), "A Study of Manufacturer-supported Trials of Nonsteroidal Anti-inflammatory Drugs in the Treatment of Arthritis," *Archives of Internal Medicine*, 154, 157–63.

Rodyhouse, R.H. (1978), "Special Plan Bargaining: Model Best Suited for U.B.C. Faculty," *CAUT Bulletin*, (February).

Rosenbluth, G. and R.A. Holmes, (1967), "The Structure of Academic Salaries in Canada," *CAUT Bulletin*, 15, 4(April), 19–27.

Ross, J.T. (1980), "Being First Not Always the Best: No Precedents Forced Algoma to Improvise in Exigency Process," *CAUT Bulletin*, 27, 6(October), 15.

Ross, Murray G. (1972), "The Dilution of Academic Power in Canada: The University of Toronto Act," *Minerva*, 10, 2(April), 242–58.

Rowat, Donald (1956), "The Government of Canadian Universities," *Culture*, xvii, 268–83.

——————— (1957), "Faculty Participation in Canadian University Government," *AAUP Bulletin*, 43(Autumn).

——————— (1964), "The Business Analogy," in Whalley, 73–85.

Sadlak, Jan (1992), "New Reality in University-Industry Relations: A Search for Foundations and Forms," *Interchange*, 23, (1 & 2), 111–122.

Sanger, David E. (1982), "Corporate Links Want Scholars," *New York Times*, October 17, 4.

Santin, Aldo (1995), "A storm over academe," *Winnipeg Free Press*, January 7.

——————— (1995), "In the business world, universities flunk out," *Winnipeg Free Press*, January 11.

Saunders, Doug (1996), "Fruits of academe are golden for some," *The Globe and Mail*, December 4.

Savage, Donald C. (1974), "Collective Bargaining: The State of the Nation," *CAUT Bulletin*, September, 10–12.

——————— (1980a), "Two Approaches to Cutback Policy," *CAUT Bulletin*, 27, 6(October), 13.

——————— (1981a), "Power Now Shared at TUNS," *CAUT Bulletin*, 28, 7(December), 5–6.

——————— (1983), "The Shame of British Columbia," *CAUT Bulletin*, 30, 7(December), 8.

——————— (1983a), "An Insider's View of Canadian Bargaining," *Academe*, 69(6), 16–20.

——————— (1985a), "UBC Reaches Agreement," *CAUT Bulletin*, 33,1(January), 1, 16.

——————— (1985b), "UBC Faculty Vote No Confidence in Administration, Bd. of Governors," *CAUT Bulletin*, 32, 5(September), 1, 21.

———————— and Christopher Holmes, (1976), "The CAUT, the Crowe Case, and the Development of the Idea of Academic Freedom in Canada," *CAUT Bulletin*, 24, 3(December), 22–27.

Scarfe, Janet and Edward Sheffield (1977), "Notes on the Canadian Professoriate," in Altbach, 92–113.

Schmidt, Sarah (1997), "Networking from the boardroom to the classroom, Universities making links with corporate Canada," *Varsity News*, University of Toronto, November 17.

Schrank, Bernice (1996), "On the Edge: Negotiations at Memorial University of Newfoundland, 1995-6," paper presented at Society for Socialist Studies annual conference, Brock University, June.

Schrank, W. (1977), "Sex Discrimination in Faculty Salaries," *Canadian Journal of Economics*, 10, 411–33.

Schrecker, Ellen W. (1986), *No Ivory Tower: McCarthyism and the Universities*, Oxford: Oxford University Press.

Schuster Jack H., and Lynn H. Miller, eds. (1989), *Governing Tomorrow's Campus: Perspectives and Agendas*, New York: Collier Macmillan.

Science Council of Canada (1969), *Report No. 5: University Research and the Federal Government*, Ottawa: The Queen's Printer.

Science Council of Canada (1984), *Social Science Research in Canada: Stagnation or Regeneration,"* Conference proceedings, Ottawa: Minister of Supply and Services.

———————— (1986), *University Spin-off Firms: Helping the Ivory Tower Get to Market*, Ottawa: Minister of Supply and Services.

———————— (1988), *Winning in a World Economy: University-Industry Interaction and Economic Renewal In Canada*, Report 39, Ottawa: Minister of Supply and Services.

Senate Task Force on the Status of Women (1975), *Report on Academic Women*, University of Alberta.

Shapiro, S. (1991), "Universities and the Capitalist State," *Journal of Higher Education*, 62(3), 341–343.

Sheffield, Edward F. (1955), "Canadian University and College Enrolment projected to 1965," *National Conference of Canadian Universities, Proceedings, 1955*, 39–46.

———————— (1960), *University Costs and Sources of Support*, Ottawa: CUF, 28–9. Industrial Foundation on Education #1.

———————— (1970), "The Post-War Surge in Post-Secondary Education: 1945–1969," in Wilson, Stamp and Audet, 416–43.

———————— (1978), "Most Significant Changes Result of Government Initiative," *University Affairs*, March, 6.

———————— Duncan D. Campbell, Jeffrey Holmes, B.B. Kymlicka, and James H. Whitelaw (1982), *Systems of Higher Education: Canada*, New York: International Council for Educational Development.

Shere, Waris and Ronald Duhamel, eds. (1987), *Academic Futures: Prospects for Post-Secondary Education*, Toronto: The Ontario Institute for Studies in Education.

Shore, Marlene (1987), *The Science of Social Redemption: McGill, the Chicago School and the Origins of Social Research in Canada*, Toronto: University of Toronto Press.

Shore, Valerie (1982), "Cuts cuts cuts restraint restraint..." *University Affairs*, November 23, 6, 14.

Shorten, Sarah (1983), "Why Bill 3 Affects Us All," *CAUT Bulletin*, 30, 7(December), 10.

Shulman, Seth (1999), *Owning the Future*, Boston and New York: Houghton Mifflin Company.

Sibley, W.M. (1976), "Modes of University Government," *Canadian Journal of Higher Education*, 6(1), 19–27.

Sim, Victor (1979), "Dispute at Acadia Comes to a Close," *CAUT Bulletin*, 26, 5(October), 7–8.

————————— (1980), "CAUT Moves to Second Stage of Memorial—Accredited Status of Social Work Program Threatened," *CAUT Bulletin*, 27, 1(February), 19.

Sim, Victor W. (1980b), "Strickler Dismissal Upheld: An Unusual Case Involving Sexual Harassment of a student by a Faculty Member," *CAUT Bulletin*, 27, 7(December), 5–6.

Sirluck, Ernest (1996), *First Generation: An Autobiography*, Toronto: University of Toronto Press.

Skolnik, Michael L. (1982), "Coping With Scarcity in Higher Educaton: The Ontario Experience," *Planning for Higher Education*, 10(3), 5–13.

————————— (1987), "State Control of Degree Granting: The Establishment of a Public Monopoly in Canada," in Higher Education Group, 56–63.

————————— and Geraldine Woodford (1987), "Faculty Unionization and Salary Differentials in Ontario Universities," *Canadian Journal of Higher Education*, 17(2), 9–25.

————————— and Norman S. Rowen (1984), *"Please, sir, I want some more"—Canadian Universities and Financial Restraint*, Toronto: Ontario Institute for Studies in Education.

Slaughter, Sheila and Larry L. Leslie (1997), *Academic Capitalism: Politics, Policies, and the Entrepreneurial University*, Baltimore and London: The Johns Hopkins University Press.

Smallwood, J.R. (1973), *I Chose Canada*. Toronto: Macmillan Press.

Smith, Catherine B. and Vivian S. Hixson (1987), "The Work of University Professors: Evidence of Segmented Labour Markets Inside the Academy," *Current Research on Occupations and Professions*, (4),159–80.

Smith, Jean (1978), "How the Special Agreement Was Reached at the U of T," *University Affairs*, 19(May), 15.

Smith, Jean Edward (1978), "Non-Certified Agreements: The Toronto Approach," *CAUT Bulletin*, 25, 7(February), 16.

Smith, Stuart L. (1991), *Report of the Commission of Inquiry on Canadian University Education*, Ottawa: Association of Universities and Colleges of Canada.

Smith, Sydney (1956), "The Future of Canadian Universities", *University of Toronto Quarterly*, 1955–56.

Smyth, John, ed. (1995), *Academic Work: the Changing Labour Process in Higher Education*, London: Society of Research into Higher Education and Open University Press.

Snow, Howard (1981a),"Bargaining Talk," *CAUT Bulletin*, 28,5(September), 11.

———— (1982a), "Bargaining Talk," *CAUT Bulletin*, 29,7(December 1982), 8.

———— (1982b), "Bargaining Talk," *CAUT Bulletin*, 29,6(October), 10.

———— (1983a), "Bargaining Talk," *CAUT Bulletin*, 30,2(April), 9.

Soley, Lawrence (1997), "Phi Beta Capitalism, Universities in Service to Business," *Covert Action Quarterly*, Spring.

Soley, Lawrence C. (1995), *Leasing the Ivory Tower: The Corporate Takeover of Academia*, Boston: South End Press.

Southern, Lee (1983), *Government-Intermediary-University: The Financial Decision-making Role of the Universities Council of British Columbia*, Unpublished Ed.D. thesis, University of British Columbia, 1983.

SSHRC (1999), *Community-University Research Alliances-A Pilot Program from SSHRC*, Ottawa: Social Sciences and Humanities Research Council of Canada.

Stager, David A.A. (1973), "Federal Government Grants to Canadian Universities, 1951–66," *Canadian Historical Review*, 54, 2(Spring).

Stalker, Jackie (1995), "The chill women feel at Canada's universities," *Globe and Mail*, July 25.

Stankiewicz, Rikard (1986), *Academics and Entrepreneurs: Developing University-Industry Relations*, New York: St. Martin's Press, Inc.

Statistics Canada (1978), *Historical Compendium of Education Statistics from Confederation to 1975*, Ottawa: Statistics Canada.

———— (1989), *Women in Canada: A Statistical Report, Second Edition*, Ottawa: Statistics Canada.

———— (1990), *Teachers in Universities, 1986–1987*, Ottawa: Minister of Supply and Services Canada.

———— (1991), *Teachers in Universities, 1988–89*, Catalogue 81–241, Ottawa: Minister of Supply and Services Canada..

———— (1992), *Universities: Enrolment and Degrees, 1990*, Ottawa: Minister of Industry, Science and Technology, catalogue 81–204.

———— (1998), *Survey of Intellectual Property Commercialization in the Higher Education Sector, 1998*, Preliminary release #2, October 29.

Stewart, E.E. (1970), *The Role of the Provincial Government in the Development of the Universities of Ontario, 1791–1964*, Toronto: Ph.D. thesis, University of Toronto.

Stobbe, Mark (1988), "Underfunding causes strike," *Briarpatch*, 17, 4(May 1988), 2–3.

Strang, Doug (1997), "Intellectual Property Licensing Practice," University of Manitoba. May 23.

Sullivan, Nancy (1976), "UBC Opts for Collective Bargaining Outside Provincial Labor Code," *University Affairs*, 17(July), 14.

———————— (1976b), "Strike of Laval professors is in sixth week," *University Affairs*, 17(November), 2.

———————— (1976c), "Bishop's Faculty Association Applies For Certification," *University Affairs*, 17(January), 8.

———————— (1976d), Carleton Staff Association Signs First Agreement, *University Affairs*, 17(February), 7.

———————— (1977a), "Mediation ends in agreement at Laval," *University Affairs*, 18(February), 4.

———————— (1977b), "Path back to work at UQAM not smooth," *University Affairs*, 18(April), 6.

———————— (1977c), "Aging faculty—a new and complex 'crisis,'" *University Affairs*, 18(March), 4.

———————— (1977c), "Governments legislate against faculty unionization," *University Affairs*, 18(November), 2.

Supreme Court of Canada (1990), *McKinney v. University of Guelph* December 6.

Swan, Kenneth P. (1979), "Professional Obligations, Employment Responsibilities and Collective Bargaining," *Interchange*, 9, 3(1978–79), 99–100.

Sweet, Doug (1997), "Cutbacks change the way universities work," *The Montréal Gazette*, November 22.

Swimmer, Sally (1986a), "Négocions/Bargaining," *CAUT Bulletin*, 33, 4(April), 13.

———————— (1986b), "Négocions/Bargaining," *CAUT Bulletin*, 33, 5(May), 6.

Symons, Thomas H.B. (1976), *To Know Ourselves: the Report of the Commission on Canadian Studies*, Ottawa: AUCC.

Tausig, Christine (1981), "Women's Gains Being Lost," *University Affairs*, 22(1), 40.

Taylor, Paul (1998), "A doctor takes on a drug company," *The Globe and Mail*, August 13, A1.

Thistle, Mel (1966), *The Inner Ring: The Early History of the National Research Council of Canada*, Toronto: University of Toronto Press.

Thompson, Mark (1975), "The Development of Collective Bargaining in Canadian Universities," *Proceedings of the Twenty-Eighth Annual Winter Meeting*, Industrial Relations Research Association, December 29–30, 257–65.

Thomson, W.P. (1970), *The University of Saskatchewan: A Personal History*, Toronto: University of Toronto Press.

Tierney, William G., ed. (1991), *Culture and Ideology in Higher Education: Advancing a Critical Agenda*, New York: Praeger.

Trudeau, G.B. (1997), *Doonesbury*, November 29.

Turk, Jim (1989), "Human Capital Theory: Bad for Education. Bad for the Economy," *Our Schools/Our Selves*, 1, 3(April), 4-8.

Underhill, F.H. (1936), "On Professors in Politics," *Canadian Forum*, XV (March).

UNESCO (1986), *Statistical Yearbook 1986*, Paris.

Unger, Gordon (1978), "Final Offer Selection: An Alberta Experiment in Interest Arbitration," *CAUT Bulletin*, 25, 11(December), 12, 13, 14.

University of Manitoba (1997), "Walls closing in on new Pan Am Gym: opportunties (sic) begin to 'name' spaces," *Bulletin*, University of Manitoba, September 11.

University of Toronto Faculty Association (1999), "Nancy Olivieri and the Scandal at Sick Kids Hospital," *UTFA Newsletter*, February 11.

Vaillancourt, Francois (1986), "The Returns to University Schooling in Canada," *Canadian Public Policy*, XII (3).

Vanderberg, R.D. (1978), "Interest Arbitration at the University of Calgary," *CAUT Bulletin*, 25, 11(December), 15–17.

Vickers, Jill McCalla and June Adam (1977), *But Can You Type? Canadian Universities and the Status of Women*, Toronto: Clarke, Irwin & Company Limited, in association with the Canadian Association of University Teachers.

Vogel, Gretchen (1997), "Long-Suppressed Study Finally Sees Light of Day," *Science*, 276, 5312(April 25), 523–25.

Von Zur-Muehlen, Max (1987), "Myths and Realities: The Fallacy of Faculty Shortages in the Next Decade," *Canadian Journal of Higher Education*, 17(1), 13–25.

Walters, D. (1970), *Canadian Growth Revisited 1950–1967*, Ottawa: Economic Council of Canada.

Warter, F.E. (1970), "Reform of University Government at the University of Toronto," *CAUT Bulletin*, 18(3), 16.

Watson, Cicely, ed. (1985), *The Professoriate: Occupation in Crisis*, Toronto: Ontario Institute for Studies in Education.

Wells, Don O. (1984), "After 10 Years of Collective Bargaining—An Administrative Perspective," *University Affairs*, 25(9), 10.

Whalley, George ed. (1964), *A Place of Liberty: Essays on the Government of Canadian Universities*, Toronto: Clarke Irwin & Company.

Whitelaw, James H. (1982), "PostSecondary Education Systems in Quebec," in Sheffield et al., 65–100.

Whyte, John D. (1975), "Dispute Adjudication in the University," in *Universities and the Law*, Winnipeg, Manitoba: Legal Research Institute, University of Manitoba, 95–105.

Williams, David (1977), "Participatory University Decision-Making: A Myth?" *CAUT Bulletin*, 25, 6(December), 20.

Wilson, J. Donald, Robert M. Stamp and Louis-Philippe Audet, eds. (1970), *Canadian Education: A History*, Scarborough: Prentice-Hall of Canada, Ltd.

Winchester, Ian, ed.(1984), *The Independence of the University and the Funding of the State: Essays on Academic Freedom in Canada*, Toronto: The Ontario Institute for Studies in Education.

Winter, F. E. (1970), "Reform of University Government at the U of T," *CAUT Bulletin*, 18(3), 16.

Woodcock, Lynda (1974), "Manitoba Association Certified As Bargaining Unit," *University Affairs*, 15 (July), 10.

——————— (1975), "Boycott Lifted, Censure Remains," *University Affairs*, 16 (January), 2.

——————— (1977), "CAUT Sets Up Strike Fund," *University Affairs*, 18 (July), 7.

Woodside, H. (1958), *The University Question—Who Should Go? Who Should Pay?*, Toronto: Ryerson Press.

York, Geoffrey (1983), "Universities in debt face loss of control," *The Globe and Mail*, April 27, 4.

York University (1997), *Fact Book*, York University Web Site.

York University Status of Women (1985), *Equity for Women: The First Decade*, Toronto: York University.

Young, Walter (1974), *Report of the University Government Committee*, British Columbia.

Zeidenberg, Jerry (1992), "Robust Industry Defies Sick Economy," *The Globe & Mail*, November 10.

Appendix

Commissions, Organizations,

Inquiries and Reports

The study refers to numerous commissions, organizations, inquiries and reports. This appendix highlights a selection from national, regional and provincial levels. Organizations are listed by the year they were formed.

1906   Royal Commission on the University of Toronto (Flavelle)

The commission's recommendation for a board of governors to control and manage the university, and a senate to handle academic affairs, was adopted at the University of Toronto and copied at most Canadian universities.

1911   National Conference of Canadian Universities (NCCU)

The NCCU represented presidents of Canadian universities.

1916   National Research Council (NRC)

The NRC was formed to promote scientific and industrial research.

1940   Royal Commission on Dominion-Provincial Relations (Rowell-Sirois)

Although it opposed shared-cost or conditional grants, the commission noted that the provinces might welcome small Dominion grants to universities, proportional to population. The commission made no formal recommendation.

1947   Defence Research Board

The Defence Resarch Board was spun off from the NRC.

1951   Royal Commission on the Arts, Letters and Sciences (Massey)

To address severe funding shortages, Massey recommended that Ottawa pay grants directly to universities, based on provincial population and enrolment.

1951   Canadian Association of University Teachers (CAUT)

The CAUT was formed to defend academic freedom, and improve salaries and faculty representation in university governance.

1957	NCCU Opens National Office
1957	Canada Council

The Canada Council is formed to encourage the arts, humanities and social sciences.

1958	CAUT Opens National Office
1958	Committee on University Affairs (Ontario)

The CUA recommended university funding levels to the minister of education. After 1960 it was a clearinghouse for provincial policy on universities.

1960	Medical Research Council (MRC)

The MRC was spun off from the NRC.

1961	Royal Commission of Inquiry on Education (Québec)

The commission laid the basis for a modern, secular university system, with new two-year pre-university institutes (CEGEPs), and new French-language universities .

1961	Royal Commission on Higher Education (New Brunswick)

Commission recommendations led to consolidating a complex network into the University of New Brunswick and the new Université de Moncton, and to creating the New Brunswick Higher Education Commission in 1962 to advise the province on planning.

1962	Macdonald Inquiry into Higher Education in British Columbia

Macdonald called for decentralizing education, establishing a new university (Simon Fraser) and creating two-year colleges.

1963	Report on Post-Secondary Education in Ontario

This first province-wide perspective on the future of higher education, commissioned by the Committee of Presidents of the Provincially Assisted Universities of Ontario, recommended new scholarship programs, expanded libraries, four new liberal arts colleges, and a system of community colleges.

1963	University Grants Committee (Nova Scotia)

The committee advised government on financial support and eliminating duplication.

1964	Association of Atlantic Universities

This was a voluntary membership association for most universities in Nova Scotia, New Brunswick and PEI. Newfoundland's Memorial joined in 1967.

1965	Financing Higher Education in Canada (Bladen Report)

The AUCC-sponsored commission argued for increasing per capita grants and creating a Capital Grants Fund.

1966   Duff-Berdahl Commission

                This CAUT- and AUCC-sponsored national commission argued
                university presidents had too much central power, and advocated
                greater faculty influence through academic bodies.

1966   Alberta Universities Commission

                The commission advised government on funding universities.

1966   Universities Coordinating Council (Alberta)

                Principal officers of each university plus other academics sat on the
                council to advise the Universities Commission on matters affecting
                the universities.

1967   Council of Ministers of Education of Canada

                The provincial ministers of education direct the CMEC to coordi-
                nate, inform, and provide liaison services.

1967   The Federal-Provincial Fiscal Arrangements Act

                The Act transferred to the provinces the greater of $15 per capita or
                50 percent of eligible post-secondary expenditures. A 1972 revision
                limited the annual increase to 15 percent.

1967   Universities Grants Commission (Manitoba)

                The commission advised government on universities' financial needs
                and distributed the annual grant among them. It approved new
                programs and could require universities to eliminate programs.

1968   Universities Act (Saskatchewan)

                The act gave the University of Saskatchewan a board of governors,
                a senate with academic and lay membership, and a general university
                council representing faculty opinion.

1968   Conseil des Universités (Québec)

                The conseil reviewed ministerial proposals for university programs,
                research, operating and capital budgets, and coordination of finance.

1969   The Macdonald Report

                The Science Council and Canada Council commissioned Macdonald
                to report on federal government support of university research.
                Macdonald urged more support for research, more money for
                graduate students, and reorganization of the national research
                councils

1969   Prince Edward Island Commission on Post-Secondary Education

                The commission advised government on financial requirements for
                universities and colleges.

1969 (1970)   Commission on the Government of the University of Toronto

The commission recommended a unicameral system—replacing the board of governors and senate with one governing council.

1970   The Hurtubise-Rowat Commission

Set up by the CAUT, AUCC, Canadian Union of Students and Union Générale des Étudiants du Québec, the commission proposed replacing federal payment to universities with unconditional grants to the provinces, with equalizing features.

1970   Maritime Union Study

The Council of Maritime Premiers was established as a result of the study's recommendations.

1972   The Bonneau-Corry Commission

This AUCC commission argued that universities should more closely manage research to support teaching. "Frontier" research should take place at a small number of specialized institutions.

1972   Commission on Post-Secondary Education (Ontario)

The commission proposed a council to plan and coordinate the university sector.

1973   Task Force on Post-Secondary Education (Manitoba)

The task force stressed accessibility, public participation, institutional accountability, improved planning and coordination, and maintaining low tuition.

1974   Maritime Provinces Higher Education Commission (MPHEC)

The MPHEC replaced commissions in Nova Scotia, New Brunswick and Prince Edward Island, to advise government on higher education needs in the region.

1974   Universities Council of British Columbia

The council advised government on academic planning, new universities, new faculties and degree programs, and allocating annual grants to the universities.

1974   Royal Commission on University Organization (Saskatchewan)

The commission recommended separate universities for the two campuses of the University of Saskatchewan, and establishing an intermediary universities commission.

1974   The Universities Commission (Saskatchewan)

The commission could rationalize institutional budgets, distribute capital and operating funds, and coordinate university programs.

1974   Ontario Council For University Affairs

OCUA advised government on university planning.

1976	The Commission on Canadian Studies (Symons Report)
	Formed by the AUCC in 1972, the commission recommended major expansion of Canadian Studies in all aspects of university and college education.
1976	OECD Report on National Policies for Education—Canada
	The OECD noted that Canada had no coordination of provincial planning for higher education.
1977	Established Programs Financing
	EPF replaced 50 percent cost-sharing under the Federal-Provincial Fiscal Arrangements Act of 1967 with unconditional block grants, and tied annual increases to growth in population and Gross National Expenditure.
1977	Government Organization (Scientific Activities) Act
	The federal government organized support for university research through the Medical Research Council and the new Social Sciences and Humanities Research Council, and Natural Sciences and Engineering Research Council
1980	The Leslie Study
	This AUCC commission recommended replacing unconditional EPF grants with arrangements to support national higher education objectives.
1981	Parliamentary Task Force on Federal-Provincial Fiscal Arrangements (Breau)
	The task force opposed having national standards for post-secondary education, and favoured the provinces receiving separate designated funding for post-secondary education and health under EPF.
1983	Royal Commission on Post-Secondary Education (Nova Scotia)
	The commission proposed a 70-percent tuition increase, to 50 percent of teaching costs, and reciprocal tuition with other provinces, to compensate Nova Scotia's high rate of out-of-province students.
1984	Commission on the Future Development of the Universities of Ontario
	The commission proposed lower enrolment, higher tuition to cover true program costs, and income contingent loan repayments. A new minority liberal government rejected the recommendations.
1985	The Johnson Report
	Johnson recommended different EPF incentives to the Secretary of State of Canada, to induce the provinces to spend their transfers on post-secondary education, increased priority for sponsored research, and developing a select number of world-class centres of excellence.

Ottawa retained the inducements and reduced the annual rate of increase.

1987	Report of the University Committee of the National Advisory Board on Science and Technology to the Prime Minister of Canada (Lortie Report)

Lortie recommended less reliance on federal laboratories for research and more on universities, supported by more money for the three national granting councils.

1991	The Commission of Inquiry on Canadian University Education (Smith Commission)

This AUCC-established independent commission recommended increased university funding, income-contingent loan repayments for students, special efforts to promote women at universities into positions of authority, allowing dismissal of tenured staff for departmental closure or downsizing, and development of performance indicators.

1993	Report of the Independent Study Group on University Governance

The ISGUG, commissioned in 1990 by the CAUT, recommended a system of open governance of autonomous universities along the lines advocated by the 1966 Duff-Berdahl commission.

1999	Report of the Expert Panel on the Commercialization of University Research

This committee of the Prime Minister's Advisory Council on Science and Technology recommended that universities receiving money from the federal government adopt commercialization as a fourth mission.